TENNIS TRAINING
Enhancing On-court Performance

Mark Kovacs, Ph.D.
W. Britt Chandler, MS
T. Jeff Chandler, Ed.D.

Racquet Tech Publishing
An imprint of USRSA
Vista, California, USA

Racquet Tech Publishing
(An imprint of the USRSA)
330 Main Street
Vista, California 92084
760-536-1177
www.racquettech.com

Library of Congress Control Number: 2007933188

Cover design by Kristine Thom

Printed in the United States of America
ISBN-13: 978-0-9722759-7-2
ISBN-10: 0-9722759-7-5

Praise for Tennis Training

"*Tennis Training: Enhancing On-court Performance* is a powerful resource for coaches who are trying to maximize the benefit of physical training and transferring that work to the court. The information is truly tennis-specific and offers the most comprehensive collection of high performance data, structured in a way that is easy to implement for coaches of all levels. Because the sport of tennis is more physical today than ever before and the difference in winning and losing is so minimal, this information is a must-have for developing an elite level tennis player. The book presents a comprehensive and user-friendly guide for on- and off-court conditioning that is ideal for team training. As a college coach, we have utilized Mr. Kovacs's vast knowledge and cutting edge data and it has made a tremendous impact on the success of our team."

—*Billy Pate*
Head Men's Tennis Coach, The University of Alabama

"After winning the national championship in 2006 I realized how important physical conditioning is in relation to our success on the court. It is a constant challenge to develop a strength and conditioning program that will enable us to be the fittest team in the country. *Tennis Training: Enhancing On-court Performance* takes into account every part of the overall conditioning of an athlete and is a marvelous tool for every college tennis player to use to become faster, stronger and leaner. I feel this book really gives you a wonderful practical outline of exactly how to train a tennis player in all these areas. I recommend it highly."

—*Adam Steinberg*
Head Men's Tennis Coach, Pepperdine University
2006 NCAA Division I National Champions

"As Head Boy's Varsity Tennis Coach at one of the top high school tennis programs in Hawaii, it is clear to me how the physical aspects of tennis are vital to success at this level. *Tennis Training: Enhancing On-Court Performance* is a great resource for any high school tennis coach interested in running a top level program and learning the science and physical application of high level tennis training."

—*Rusty Komori*
Tennis Professional and Head Boy's Varsity Tennis Coach, Punahou School
14 consecutive state titles, tying the all-time record in any sport in Hawaii

"*Tennis Training: Enhancing On-Court Performance* has taken the science of tennis training and made it practical and applicable to coaches, parents, and players. The inclusion of drills, exercises, and photographs make this an excellent tool for understanding how to improve on-court performance. I would highly recommend any tennis enthusiast take advantage of this outstanding resource."

—Craig Tiley
Former coach of record-breaking NCAA Championship team at the University of Illinois; current Tournament Director, Australian Open and Director of Player Development, Tennis Australia

"Having worked with women's professional tennis, I feel this book is an absolute ACE! The simplicity with which it presents scientific research will be helpful to all professional athletes looking to gain that extra edge."

—Renuka Pinto, PT, ATC
Sports Physical Therapist, former Coordinator, Sport Sciences & Medicine, Athletic Care for the WTA Tour

"This book will certainly become the Bible of conditioning for tennis. The authors are all experts in the field and knowledgeable about every aspect of strength training. This book further sets itself apart from others in the field by building on a foundation of scientific principles that lay the groundwork for any quality conditioning program. This book should be required reading for anyone involved in tennis conditioning."

—Lee E. Brown, EdD, CSCS*D, FNSCA, FACSM
NSCA President 2006-2009; Professor, California State University, Fullerton

"A must read if you are any coach or tennis player that wants to learn a big part of what it takes to play tennis to your fullest potential. The authors did a fantastic job of covering all the bases when it comes to training to become a better tennis player."

—Paul Pisani
ATP Tour Coach and Trainer

"Kovacs, Chandler, and Chandler have created the most in-depth tennis training manual that I have ever read. *Tennis Training: Enhancing On-court Performance* combines their knowledge of nutrition, flexibility, and strength training into an essential teaching tool for any coach trying to maximize their students' full physical potential."

—John Janes, USPTA
Private coach of 6 nationally ranked juniors

"*Tennis Training: Enhancing On-court Performance* allows its readers to understand how the human body is every player's most important tool. This book allows you to gain the knowledge to enhance every aspect of your game."

—Andrew Colombo
USTA Western Regional Chairman; Head Tennis Professional
Mendon Racquet & Pool Club, Pittsford NY; Former All-American and NCAA
Division I Doubles Champion

"Being in top physical condition is vital to achieve tennis success at the college or professional level. *Tennis Training: Enhancing On-court Performance* provides all the tools to help you achieve your top physical condition."

—Mario Rincon
Head Men's Coach, the University of Miami
Former Top #200 ATP tour

"As expected from such well-respected authors, this is a book which will be valued by sports scientists as an excellent review of current knowledge and by coaches as a source of practical information that they can use to enhance player performance of all ages and abilities. For the objective and accurate nutrition chapter alone, it should have a place on the bookshelf of every Tennis Pro!"

—Dr. Sally Parsonage, Ph.D., R.Nutr, CISSN
Head of Nutrition, IMG Performance Academy; Consultant Nutritionist
Food for Performance LLC

"The definitive tennis training guide for the competitive player! The knowledge, drills and exercises will help every tennis player improve their on-court performance."

—Brian Vahaly
Former Top #100 ATP Tour; 3-time All-American at The University of Virginia

"This is a remarkable book since it blends perfectly practical coaching with sport science research findings. The terminology, principles, methods, exercises and drills presented will be of great help for all those interested in learning more about the latest trends in on-court training programs for high-performance players. Congratulations to the authors for their great job, but also to the many readers who will enjoy this excellent coaching resource."

—Miguel Crespo, Ph.D.
Development Research Officer, Development/Coaching Department
International Tennis Federation

"The great asset of the book *Tennis Training: Enhancing On-court Performance* is that chapters with up-to-date scientific background information on nutrition and hydration, stretching, strengthening and conditioning are immediately followed by very practical chapters with tennis-specific programs, exercises and on-court drills on these same topics. The finishing touch is with two great chapters on physical testing and periodization. The authors have done an outstanding job of making this valuable information easily accessible to coaches and players."

—Dr. Babette Pluim, M.D., Ph.D.
ITF Sport Science & Medicine Commission; Past-President
Society for Tennis Medicine and Science; Team Physician, Dutch Davis Cup Team

"This book represents a comprehensive, evidence-based approach to training for tennis. It is a must read for coaches and sports scientists alike."

—Michael H. Stone, Ph.D.
Laboratory Director, Kinesiology, Leisure and Sport Sciences
East Tennessee State University

"Dr. Chandler brings much experience and expertise to this book from two different disciplines. He has been involved in the physiology of tennis performance with players at all levels for 20 years. In addition, he is one of the leaders in the understanding of the science of sport specific conditioning. This book reflects the integration of both those disciplines. It will be a great resource for players and coaches to both understand why conditioning is important and how to efficiently implement the right type of conditioning."

—W. Ben Kibler MD
Medical Director, Lexington Clinic Sports Medicine Center
Founding President, Society for Tennis Medicine and Science
Member, USTA Sports Science Committee

CONTENTS

CHAPTER 4
NUTRITION & HYDRATION FOR
OPTIMUM TENNIS PERFORMANCE

27

CHAPTER 7
RESISTANCE TRAINING
& TENNIS PERFORMANCE 97

CHAPTER 8
RESISTANCE TRAINING
PROGRAMS FOR TENNIS   115

CHAPTER 9
CARDIORESPIRATORY ENDURANCE & TENNIS PERFORMANCE   137

CHAPTER 10
CARDIORESPIRATORY FITNESS PROGRAMS FOR TENNIS   147

CHAPTER 11
SPEED, QUICKNESS & AGILITY   153

CHAPTER 12
SPEED, QUICKNESS,
& AGILITY DRILLS   169

CHAPTER 13
TRAINING PROGRESSION: LINKING TRAINING TO ON-COURT DRILLS

CHAPTER 14
PHYSICAL TESTING FOR TENNIS PERFORMANCE

CHAPTER 15
PERIODIZATION   217

Chapter 1

Importance of Training

INTRODUCTION

Tennis is a popular sport worldwide played by millions of people from all walks of life, and at many different levels. The physical training required for tennis players to succeed at a high-level has become a major component of an athlete's program. To play tennis at a competitive level certain standards need to be achieved in all the major physical components including strength, power, speed, balance, coordination, and endurance.

Over the past 30 years tennis has developed from a sport based predominantly on strategy, timing and finesse, to a sport dominated by power, speed, and strength. As a result many sports scientists have been researching methods to help train tennis players in the lab and on the court. The major purpose of *Tennis Training: Enhancing On-Court Performance* is to bring over 300 tennis-specific scientific studies to the coaching community to help the coach, strength and conditioning specialist, trainer, physical therapist, medical doctor, and parent develop the tennis athlete's fullest potential.

Training tennis players requires the successful, yet complex, interplay of tactical, technical, physical and psychological components. The physical components are the focus of this book, and the goal is to outline the major physical aspects to successfully train competitive tennis players. Extensive review went into combining well-researched scientific studies with practical coaching know-how to develop a comprehensive guide to tennis training.

This book has been written by three tennis experts who combine years of academic knowledge with real-world practical coaching to truly blend the art and science of tennis performance. Dr. Mark Kovacs combines extensive playing experience, which includes a top 100 ITF junior ranking, winner of a US "gold-ball," competing in many international tournaments including the US and Australian Open before attending Auburn University where he was an All-American and NCAA doubles champion. After playing professionally he pursued his graduate work performing tennis-specific research. He has combined researched scientific evidence in his coaching profession both as a high level tennis coach as well as a strength and conditioning specialist (CSCS) training hundreds of high school, collegiate, and professional athletes. He has previously been the director of a sports performance company as well as the director of education for one of the largest health and fitness certification and education companies.

Britt Chandler has a master's degree in exercise science from Auburn University and played collegiate tennis. He is certified as both a strength and conditioning specialist (CSCS) and certified personal trainer (NSCA-CPT). He also is a certified tennis coach through the USPTA. He currently works as both a tennis coach and strength conditioning specialist with some of the top juniors in the country. Britt is also the editorial assistant for the *Strength and Conditioning Journal* and has contributed book chapters and presentations on tennis specific research and training.

Dr. Jeff Chandler has over 20 years experience as a tennis researcher and sports science consultant, advisor, and author for many tennis organizations including the USTA, USPTA, ITF, STMS and PTR. He has over 100 scientific publications, book chapters, and presentations relating to tennis training and performance. He is currently Department Head of Health, Physical Education & Recreation at Jacksonville State University, Jacksonville, Alabama, and is the editor in chief of the *Strength and Conditioning Journal* published through the National Strength and Conditioning Association. Dr. Chandler is certified with distinction as both a CSCS*D, and NSCA-CPT*D. He is a Fellow in the American College of Sports Medicine (FACSM) and a Fellow in the National Strength and Conditioning Association (FNSCA).

This book has a systematic structure with the introductory chapters providing the basic terminology of training and the principles needed to understand tennis physiology. These introductory chapters lay the foundation for the remainder of the book. The following chapters combine a review of tennis literature on nutrition, strength, speed and agility and flexibility with practical exercises, drills and programs.

Tennis athletes looking to reach their full potential deserve to be trained using the most up-to-date techniques which have been scientifically proven to improve performance. It is the responsibility of the coach or trainer to increase their knowledge and impart this knowledge in a successful evidence-based program to help the athletes achieve their fullest potential.

Chapter 2

Principles of Developing Training Programs

- Adaptation
- Loading
- Specificity
- Intensity
- Volume
- Frequency
- Density
- Individuality
- Recovery
- Variety
- Specialization
- Planning

Introduction

There are numerous "principles of training" that apply to the sport of tennis. Many times, the "principles" overlap or use different terms to mean the same thing. This chapter will cover the essential principles of conditioning that can be used to design conditioning programs for tennis players. Planning conditioning programs for tennis athletes is not an exact science. As more research is done, we must continually re-evaluate our training recommendations. Only then can we make the best decisions on how to condition tennis athletes.

For the sport of tennis, there are a variety of principles that relate to maximizing athletic performance. Some of these principles are soundly backed in the scientific literature, and some are backed by tradition and experience. The goal should be to develop scientific principles of conditioning that are backed by scientific literature. Practical experience, tradition, and the observations of coaches certainly play a role in our decision making. In the end, however, if the observations are correct, the concepts will eventually be supported by scientific research. Where current research is not available, the knowledge gained from research on other sports can have value to the tennis athlete.

Tennis involves many aspects of performance, including but not limited to strength, power, speed, agility, flexibility, and muscular endurance. Training to maximize performance in all these areas simultaneously is a difficult task. These principles of training provide guidelines the player can follow to increase the chances of receiving maximum benefit from training. Avoiding these principles may lead to overtraining, overuse injuries, or simply the failure to reach optimal levels of performance.

Prescribing an exact exercise prescription is important to maximize performance while at the same time minimizing overuse injuries and overtraining. All of the following principles are possible factors in designing an exercise program. In addition, these factors apply to all aspects of athletic preparation, not just the physical conditioning program.

ADAPTATION

Adaptation is the process the body goes through causing improved functioning of a specific system in the body in response to a training load. The principle of adaptation states that the body will adapt and improve with the appropriate application of stress (exercise) to the body. For example, when a tennis player practices serving, the muscles used in the serve are adapting and improving in their ability to perform that specific task. Adaptation is specific to the imposed demand of the activity, which will be further discussed as the principle of specificity.

LOADING

Loading is an important principle of training. The principle of loading also overlaps the principle of specificity, as the training loads should be specific to the sport of tennis. To maximize athletic performance, the body must be "loaded" at a frequency, intensity, or duration higher than the level to which it is accustomed. To build strength, the athlete must be challenged to lift loads heavier than the loads they lift in daily activities. To improve sprint performance, the athlete must be required to run at high speeds.

The "down side" is that if the load is too great, overuse injuries or overtraining may be the result. The goal of training tennis athletes is to maximize performance while minimizing the chance of overtraining or injury. At the highest level of performance (i.e., professional athletes), the goal is to keep the total workload as high as possible without increasing the chances of injury or overtraining. The workload that produces maximum adaptation will likely be very close to the workload that produces overtraining. Obviously, there is a fine line between the two, indicating a need for accurate exercise prescriptions and accurate assessment tools to measure both overtraining and the workloads that produce maximum performance.

SPECIFICITY

The adaptations that occur to the human body due to imposed exercise stress are specific to the nature of the applied stress. In the sport of tennis, specificity may be partially determined by a number of factors including but not limited to the style of play, the level of play, the style of play of the opponent, the surface, and the environment. It is important to realize there are two distinct aspects to specificity—metabolic specificity and mechanical specificity. Metabolic specificity refers to training the primary energy systems as they are used in the sport. Mechanical specificity refers to training specific movement patterns in the way they are used on court.

Metabolic specificity should include the length and intensity of the work intervals as well as the length of the rest intervals. Based on the length of the points, particularly on fast surfaces, it would appear that tennis is primarily an anaerobic sport with the aerobic energy system involved in recovery between points (1). The key is to train each system taking into consideration how it is used in the sport of tennis.

Training should proceed from less specific training in the off-season to becoming progressively more specific as the competitive season approaches. Aerobic training, primarily performed in the off-season, should begin with building an aerobic base with longer distance, slower paced training and progress to an in-season phase where aerobic training consists of repeated bouts of sprints with sport-specific work/rest intervals. Interval training eventually transitions to sprint training with work/rest intervals similar to the actual work/rest intervals in the sport. Although interval training and sprint training is not "traditional" aerobic training, the aerobic energy systems are active during recovery. This nontraditional aerobic training is likely more specific to tennis (2).

In a periodized training plan, specificity should be used as a general guideline in determining the length and intensity of training bouts. If you determine the average duration of a point for a particular player to be 6 seconds, for example, and the average rest interval to be 22 seconds, this does not mean that all work intervals should be exactly 6 seconds and all rest intervals should be exactly 22 seconds. Some training bouts will be longer, and some shorter. Some training bouts will be more intense than a typical point, some will be less intense. By training both over and under the time interval/intensity, the player can improve metabolically to prepare for both shorter and longer points.

Mechanical specificity involves using the muscles specific to they way they are used on the tennis court both in terms of movement patterns and movement speeds. Each stroke involves explosive power from the legs, trunk, and upper extremity. The lower extremity movement prior to the stroke is generally explosive (trying to reach the ball). After the stroke, the movement is generally slower as the player returns to the appropriate position on the court to return the next shot.

Velocity of movement is an important part of mechanical specificity. In order to improve velocity in sport specific movements, training should be intentionally fast. Purposefully slow movement will not provide a stimulus to improve movement velocity. Research has demonstrated that using heavier training loads increases force output, and lighter loads with maximal acceleration increases power output (3). Sports that place high demand on power and strength should perform resistance training exercises at a velocity similar to what is required in their sport. Following a periodized plan for improving tennis performance, strength training with heavier loads should be performed early in the training year. As the competitive season approaches, resistance training should be performed explosively during the concentric phase with light to moderate resistance.

Training specificity has been shown to improve strength and power in athletes from a variety of sports (4). Weightlifters and handball players demonstrated greater strength and power than distance runners and untrained athletes. This suggests that long-term training for sports produces adaptations specific to each particular sport.

Sprint and agility training also causes specific adaptations. One study demonstrated there is very little transfer of performance from speed to agility (5). Athletes who trained using straight line sprinting improved their speed, but there was little improvement in agility or change of direction speed. Likewise, the athletes who trained doing agility drills improved their agility but showed little increase in speed. While speed is important in tennis there are few if any times when a tennis player will reach maximum speed on the court. Points consist of quick changes of direction and rapid acceleration and deceleration. This study suggests that tennis players should focus more on agility and change of direction sprints rather than maximum speed sprinting.

INTENSITY

In the sport of tennis, intensity of training strongly relates to specificity. It is not just the lengths of the points and rest intervals that are important, but the effort or intensity during that time. The purpose of a training program should be to improve performance at the intensities that are specific to the sport of tennis. The intensity of all training sessions is important, whether the athlete is training with a medicine ball, resistance training, or on the court.

Heart rates can be used as a general measure of cardiorespiratory intensity. The specificity principle would state that the heart rate profiles in training should be specific to the heart rate profiles in match play. Because the rating of perceived exertion (RPE) is correlated to heart rate, a rating of perceived exertion can be potentially valuable in determining the intensity of tennis play. No matter what method is used to measure the intensity, tennis points involve relatively high intensity bouts of energy expenditure for a short period of time, followed by an approximate 20-second rest interval. By using sport specific training intensities, we are most likely to produce the greatest increases in sport-specific performance.

VOLUME

Volume is the total training load and should include both on-court and off-court training. Monitoring the volume of training along with the intensity is the best way to monitor the total training workload and help prevent overtraining. The volume of training will be individualized to the extent that specific players have specific weaknesses they should work on. The volume of off-court training will be highest in the preparation phase, and will gradually decrease as the competition phase approaches. The volume of on-court training will begin relatively low in the preparation phase and gradually increase as the competition phase approaches.

FREQUENCY

The frequency of training is the number of training sessions per day or per week. As with volume, the frequency of off-court training should vary with the goals of the individual tennis player. Frequency of training depends on the desired outcomes of the type of training involved. For gains to occur in strength and power, a training frequency of 3-5 days per week is generally recommended. Highly trained athletes may be able to train at higher frequencies. In some instances, athletes during certain phases of training may train several times a day.

It is important to consider the total workload involved in each mode of training. As one mode of training is increased, the frequency of other types of training should be adjusted appropriately. This is important to decrease the possibility of overtraining the athlete and to maximize the specific desired results.

DENSITY

The frequency with which an athlete participates in a series of conditioning exercises per unit of time is considered the density of training. Density describes the relationship between the work and the recovery phases of conditioning expressed per unit of time. Perhaps one of the most overlooked factors in exercise prescription is the length of the rest interval between sets and between exercises. Density then is a description of the compactness of the bouts of exercise per unit of time. The appropriate density for a particular sport like tennis will vary depending on the type of training and the phase of training. The work/rest intervals in a typical tennis match provide some useful information in this regard. Appropriate density promotes maximal sport-specific performance. Appropriate density provides the optimal stimulus for improvement and the appropriate amount of time for recovery while maximizing the potential for improving performance. One method of monitoring the density of training is to monitor the recovery heart rate. In this method, the next work interval begins when the heart rate falls below a specific rate. As the athlete becomes more fit, he can begin the next work interval sooner, thus increasing the density and the total work performed in the training session. This method can be used with tennis players to determine when to start the next drill or the next bout of a conditioning exercise. Ideally, a heart rate monitor would be used for this to be a practical method of monitoring training density.

INDIVIDUALITY

The principle of individuality states that all players have individual differences that must be considered when planning a conditioning program. These differences include specific weaknesses that should be addressed in the training program, the style of play of the individual player, and the differences in physiological capacities, training history, skill level, sex differences, and motivation.

It is important to recognize individual differences when planning a conditioning program. Each player has unique skills and abilities and brings a different level of fitness to the sport. Each player has a different musculoskeletal base and history of previous injuries. Each player will benefit from an individualized training program. The individual style of play is important. If the player is strictly a baseline player, the training program would be modified to utilize more repetitions, longer durations, and lower intensities. Conversely, with a serve and volley player, the exercises would be performed at higher intensities with fewer repetitions and for shorter durations. Often training will be somewhere between these two extremes and may change during the competitive year based on such things as the strengths of the competition and the playing surface.

RECOVERY

The tennis player must allow time for recovery during a training program in order to appropriately adapt to the training stimulus. Without the appropriate recovery time, the player will possibly experience overtraining or overuse injuries. With too much time for recovery, the player will not adapt to an optimal level and therefore will likely not reach maximum performance.

Recovery is important both from one day to the next and also within a workout session. If a player is required to serve for long periods of time without rest, fatigue may cause a decrease in performance, and the player will not receive maximal adaptation to the exercise stimulus. In fact, a player's skill level may decrease from using inappropriate mechanics while serving in a fatigued state. In resistance training, it is important to allow recovery between sets depending on the specific goal of the training session. Recovery within an exercise session can be important to promote maximal adaptation to the exercise stimulus.

VARIETY

The principle of variety of training may appear to conflict with specificity. You should choose a variety of exercises within the limits of specificity to meet the goals of the training activity. Variety is important to prevent boredom and to maximize the potential for improvement in a specific area. Variety within a training session is important to allow recovery within that session, allowing the athlete to participate in a less fatigued state and perhaps decreasing the risk of overuse injuries. Variety from day to day is important to decrease the risk of overtraining and allow for adaptation to occur. By using a variety of exercises or drills, sessions are more enjoyable and players are less likely to become bored. Choose a variety of conditioning exercises within the realm of specificity relative to the goals of training for that particular period of training.

SPECIALIZATION

The age at which an athlete should specialize and focus on a single sport is an important question in terms of maximizing athletic performance in tennis athletes. Specialization at an early age has both positive and negative aspects, both of which should be carefully considered. Specialization leads to specific physiological adaptations to the musculoskeletal system. As a general rule, it is likely better for young athletes to participate in a variety of sporting activities (6). Short-term performance in a specific sport will be enhanced with specialization, and this is often used as a rational for young tennis players to play only tennis. Before encouraging an athlete to specialize at an early age, the following questions should be considered. Do the risks of burnout, overtraining, and negative musculoskeletal adaptations outweigh the benefits? Does specialization at an early age have an effect on long-term performance, say 10 years later? It may be that maximum performance will be more likely to occur if the athlete waits until the middle teens to specialize. It seems logical that young athletes should participate in a variety of sporting activities.

However, it is also possible that a well-rounded conditioning program including speed, agility, and quickness training, plyometric training, resistance training, and aerobic training may be designed in such a manner that it replaces a variety of sporting activities. With an appropriate conditioning plan, a tennis player may be able to specialize sooner assuming they have the emotional maturity to do so.

PLANNING

The concept of planning is essentially a plan for off-court and on-court training over an extended period of time. Periodization, as discussed by Stone and O'Bryant (7), is the form of long-term planning most often used in athletic performance. The purpose is to control the volume and intensity of training to bring about maximum performance at the desired time and to help prevent overtraining.

Variety in loading is an important component of program planning to prevent staleness and lack of progression. An undulating periodization model has been shown (8) to be superior to a more linear model for producing strength and power gains in advanced athletes. The daily variation of volume and intensity may be important to provide the required stress to produce maximum strength and power.

The periodization of both on-court and off-court activity is essential. As an important competition approaches, the volume and intensity of on-court preparation increases. As that occurs, the volume of off-court conditioning should decrease to allow the athlete to recover and decrease the chance of overtraining.

SUMMARY

The application of these principles of training to tennis athletes is both an art and a science. The art is learned with practical experience, getting to know the athletes, and learning as much as possible about the sport of tennis. Science is a dynamic and changing field, and what we accept as fact today may change tomorrow. The principles presented here can serve as guidelines to promote the athletes' best chance of maximal performance while avoiding overtraining and possible overuse injuries. For the coach and/or player to benefit from new information, both must be open to new ideas, must continually evaluate new information, and must be willing to put that information into practice.

REFERENCES

1. Chandler, T.J. Work/rest intervals in world class tennis. Tennis Pro. Vol 3, No. 4, p 4. 1990.

2. Chandler, T.J. Nontraditional Aerobic Training. ADDvantage Magazine. 1989.

3. Jones K., Bishop P., Hunter G., and Fleisig G. The effects of varying resistance training loads on intermediate and high velocity specific adaptations. Journal of Strength and Conditioning Research. Vol. 15, No. 3, 349-356. 2001.

4. Izquierdo M., Hakkinen K., Gonzalez-Badillo J.J., Ibanez J., and Gorostigia E. M., . Effects of long-term training specificity on maximal strength and power of the upper and lower extremities in athletes from different sports. European Journal of Applied Physiology. Vol. 87, No. 3, 264-271. 2002.

5. Young W.B., McDowell M.H., and Scarlett B.J. Specificity of sprint and agility training methods. Journal of Strength and Conditioning Research. Vol. 15, No. 3, 315-319. 2001.

6. Watts, J. Perspectives on sport specialization. JOHPERD. Vol. 73, No. 8, 32-37, 50. 2002.

7. Stone, M. H. and O'Bryant, H. S. Weight training: a scientific approach. Burgess Publishing, Minneapolis. 1984.

8. Rea M. R., Ball S. D., Phillips W. T., Burkett L. N. A comparison of linear and daily undulating periodized programs with equated volume and intensity for strength. Journal of Strength and Conditioning Research. Vol. 16, No. 2, 250-255. 2002.

CHAPTER 3

ENERGY SOURCES FOR TENNIS PROGRAMS

- ENERGY SYSTEMS
  - THE PHOSPHAGEN SYSTEM
  - THE GLYCOLYTIC SYSTEM
  - THE OXIDATIVE SYSTEM
- EFFICIENCY OF THE ENERGY PRODUCING PATHWAYS
- OXYGEN CONSUMPTION
- METABOLIC SPECIFICITY
- ENERGY SYSTEMS & TENNIS
- TENNIS-SPECIFIC ENERGY METABOLISM
- FATIGUE & PERFORMANCE

INTRODUCTION

Providing energy to the body for movement and to maintain life is termed "bioenergetics". This field can be seen as one of the more complex areas of study in training and conditioning athletes for maximal performance. In tennis players, the variation, intensity, and complexity of the energy systems is important to design appropriate training programs. Bioenergetics is directly related to the metabolic specificity of training. Even though most individuals reading this book will not have a background in biology or chemistry, the reader can learn what happens in these biochemical reactions and how they are relevant to both conditioning and performance on the tennis court.

Energy in the food we eat, chemical energy, is stored in the form of bonds between atoms. We measure the amount of energy contained in food as calories.

15

We can store these calories in our body in the forms of glycogen, fat, and protein. We can use that energy, either immediately or at a later time to produce the ultimate source of energy that allows muscles to perform work, adenosine triphosphate (ATP). Chemical reactions can be anabolic or catabolic. Anabolic chemical reactions build up molecules and store energy such as stored fat, protein, and glycogen, and catabolic chemical reactions break molecules down and release energy. Breaking food down to fuel the energy producing metabolic pathways is a catabolic reaction. Storing energy as fat, glycogen, or protein is an anabolic reaction.

"Metabolism" is a series of chemical reactions controlled by enzymes for the purpose of storing or producing energy. Enzymes speed or facilitate certain chemical reactions by lowering the amount of energy required for that chemical reaction to proceed. Enzymes facilitate these chemical reactions without requiring high temperatures inside the body. The enzymes that control these biological energy-producing reactions speed chemical reactions without becoming a part of the product.

ENERGY SYSTEMS

There are three basic ways to form ATP referred to as the three "energy systems" (10). These three systems are 1) the phosphagen system, 2) the glycolytic system, and 3) the oxidative system. It is important to note that all three energy systems are active at a given point in time, but one system will predominate based on the conditions at that time (Table 3.1). The primary determining factor of which energy system is being utilized at any point in time is the intensity of the exercise.

PRIMARY ENERGY SYSTEM	DURATION
Phosphagen system	0-10 seconds
Phosphagen system and glycolytic system	10-30 seconds
Glycolytic system	30 seconds – 2 minutes
Glycolytic system and oxidative system	2 – 3 minutes
Oxidative system	< 3 minutes and rest
NOTE: At submaximal intensity, each system can supply ATP for a longer period of time. At no point is a single energy system supplying all of the ATP as each system overlaps the next. Recovery from all types of energy expenditure is aerobic.	

Table 3.1: The energy systems and their approximate contributions to various durations of exercise at maximal exercise intensity (10).

THE PHOSPHAGEN SYSTEM

In the phosphagen system, also referred to as the ATP-CP system, ATP is broken down to release energy (a catabolic process) with the energy released being used to perform some type of physical work. Table 3.2 lists the primary reactions of the phosphagen system. If ATP is needed for a short period of time, for example when hitting a serve, the phosphagen system is capable of supply-

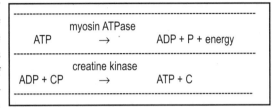

$$ATP \xrightarrow{\text{myosin ATPase}} ADP + P + energy$$

$$ADP + CP \xrightarrow{\text{creatine kinase}} ATP + C$$

Table 3.2: Primary reactions of the phosphagen system.

ing the needed ATP. The phosphagen system will also supply energy in the beginning stages of all types of exercise. High intensity short duration activities such as sprinting and resistance training will be fueled primarily by the phosphagen system. The phosphagen system will last approximately 10 seconds in duration at maximal intensity. Since a tennis point is not "maximal intensity" for 10 seconds, the ATP is generally not depleted in most tennis points.

ATP is produced in the phosphagen system anaerobically (without oxygen present). When we initiate any physical activity, we begin using stored ATP in the muscles. All activities are initiated anaerobically, as it takes time to begin to produce ATP aerobically. The phosphagen system can regenerate ATP anaerobically, allowing anaerobic activity to proceed at an intense level, but only for a short period of time.

In summary, the phosphagen system provides energy through ATP stored in the muscles. The energy is contained in chemical bonds between adenosine and phosphate (Figure 3.1). When ATP is used for energy, energy is released and ADP is formed. When ATP is regenerated, energy is stored.

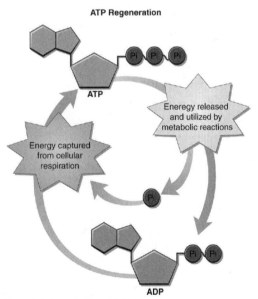

Figure 3.1: Regeneration of ATP (10).

Chapter 3

THE GLYCOLYTIC SYSTEM

The glycolytic system involves the breakdown of carbohydrate anaerobically to produce energy. The carbohydrate (the substrate or the beginning material) comes from either blood glucose or glycogen stored in the liver or muscles.

The lactic acid formed as a result of anaerobic glycolysis is immediately buffered and changed into a salt, lactate. While lactic acid is certainly associated with fatigue, lactate becomes a substrate that can be converted back into pyruvate and used in the Krebs cycle, particularly in the heart and in slow twitch muscle fibers (5, 6, 7, 28). Lactic acid does not cause muscle soreness, it does cause the muscles to burn during intense exercise. The muscle soreness that occurs 24-48 hours after intense exercise is due to microtraumatic damage to muscle fibers.

Control of the glycolytic system is accomplished in part through the enzyme phosphofructokinase (PFK) which essentially controls the amount of glycogen or glucose being broken down to pyruvate. A rate limiting enzyme is the enzyme that catalyzes the slowest step in a series of reactions. Generally, the rate limiting enzyme catalyzes the first step in the series of reactions. To stimulate or inhibit a series of reactions, a substance must affect the rate limiting step (10).

THE OXIDATIVE SYSTEM

If sufficient oxygen is present in the muscle cell, pyruvate is changed into a compound that can enter the Krebs cycle and be completely oxidized to form ATP, carbon dioxide, and water. The oxidative system aerobically oxidizes or "burns" carbohydrates (or other carbon containing structures obtained from fat or protein). The preferred fuels for aerobic metabolism are carbohydrates and fats, but protein can be deaminated and oxidized aerobically. The oxidative system is a complex process that involves two parts; the Krebs cycle and the electron transport system (ETS). The Krebs cycle is a complex series of enzyme controlled metabolic reactions. One molecule of glucose oxidized aerobically produces 32-38 ATP (7, 21, 24).

Fats can also be oxidized aerobically to form ATP. Although it is not a preferred source of energy, protein can be broken down and oxidized aerobically as well. The contribution of proteins to energy production is minimal for anaerobic activities, but may contribute up to 18% of the energy requirements for aerobic exercise (4, 26). The nitrogenous waste, the amino portion of the amino acid, is eliminated from the body as urea or ammonia.

EFFICIENCY OF THE ENERGY PRODUCING PATHWAYS

Efficiency of the energy producing pathways depends on the demands of the activity. At first glance, it may appear the aerobic pathway is the most efficient as it produces many more ATP molecules than the anaerobic pathways. There are, however, different ways to determine efficiency. The anaerobic energy systems are the most efficient at producing ATP immediately because it takes time for the aerobic energy systems to begin producing ATP. The aerobic energy system is the most efficient for producing ATP over a continuous period of time. Anaerobic energy systems provide a majority of the ATP used during a tennis point, and the aerobic system is active during recovery between points.

OXYGEN CONSUMPTION

Oxygen consumption is the ability of the body to take in and use oxygen to produce energy. Since it takes time for the oxidative system to begin to produce adequate ATP to support an aerobic activity, all exercise is supported initially by anaerobic metabolism. The initial portion of energy supplied anaerobically is termed the oxygen deficit. After exercise, this "shortfall" must be

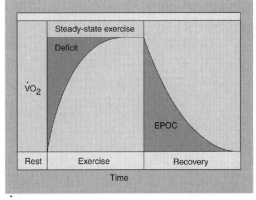

Figure 3.2: Oxygen deficit and recovery for aerobic exercise (10).

replenished aerobically. This replenishment of the anaerobic system occurs during recovery. Recovery oxygen consumption must support 1) an elevated recovery HR, 2) elevated recovery respiration rate, 3) an elevated metabolism for heat dissipation, 4) an elevated metabolism for the breakdown of hormones released during exercise, 5) the resynthesis of ATP

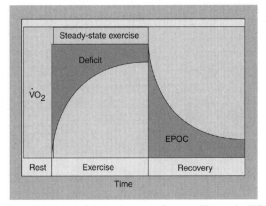

Figure 3.3: Oxygen deficit and recovery for anaerobic exercise (10).

and CP stores, 6) resynthesis of glycogen from lactate, and 7) the resaturation of body tissues (blood and muscle tissue) with oxygen.

Oxygen consumption, oxygen deficit, and recovery are depicted for aerobic work in Figure 3.2 and anaerobic work in Figure 3.3. In aerobic exercise, anaerobic metabolism supplies energy for the first few minutes, creating an oxygen deficit. Although part of this deficit can be paid back during the activity, the deficit must be repaid post-exercise. Again, the energy for this post-exercise metabolic activity comes from aerobic sources. With anaerobic activity, note that the oxygen deficit is much larger because the demand for energy is greater than in the initial stage of aerobic activity. So in the sport of tennis, the athlete is creating relatively large oxygen deficits during a high intensity point. Some of this deficit is paid back during the rest periods between points.

METABOLIC SPECIFICITY

Specificity of training is a key concept in the field of conditioning for athletic performance. If training is to be specific to an actual sport or activity, then the training must focus on the same metabolic energy pathways used in the sport or activity. It is important to note that all energy systems are active to some degree all of the time. Also, the intensity of the activity is also a key determining factor in the energy system utilized.

Training energy systems involves manipulating both the intensity and the duration of the activity. Metabolic specificity does not mean that all training is exactly the same intensity and duration as the activity. Most activities are difficult to classify exactly in terms of intensity and duration. If the average tennis point is 6 seconds, and the average intensity is 60% of maximum, it does not mean that all training should be done for 6 seconds at 60% of maximum intensity. Some points are shorter, and some are longer. Some points are more intense, and some points are less intense. Duration and intensity, then, should be used to determine a reasonable range in which a majority of the training should fall within. Progression, from general training to metabolically specific training, is also a factor that will be discussed in later chapters.

A basic understanding of metabolism and bioenergetics is a key to understanding the field of training and conditioning, and applying that knowledge to improving performance in athletes.

Energy Systems & Tennis
Match Analysis and Work-to-Rest Ratios

Competitive tennis points typically last between 5-20 seconds (15). A majority of the points last less than 10 seconds (16), indicating the utilization of the phosphagen energy system during the point. It should also be considered that aerobic capacity is important to train and compete at a high level as recovery between points utilizes aerobic metabolism (19).

Work-rest intervals during high-level tennis play have been analyzed, and as expected, they show variability depending on level of play, style of play, surface, and other factors (16, 17). A recent review (17) states that most high-level matches consist of a work:rest ratio between 1:2 and 1:5, with points having an average length between three seconds on some of the faster surfaces (grass, carpet and indoor) to close to 15 seconds. The mean duration of points in the studies were 8.00s $\pm$ 2.58s (Figure 3.4).

In a recent study during a high level collegiate tennis tournament, the average point length was recorded as 6.36s $\pm$ 4.69s (18). An athlete's playing style can have a large impact on the length of tennis points (18). When the player in control of the rally was an attacking player, the average duration of the points were found to be 4.8s $\pm$ 0.4s. Rally duration varied between 6s and 11s (mean value equal to 8.2s $\pm$ 1.2s), when the player in control of the rally was a whole-court player. The points lasted on average 15.7s $\pm$ 3.5s when the player in control of the rally was a baseline player. This difference in duration was statistically significant (p < 0.05).

The percentage of the playing time with respect to the total time of the match (on clay courts) has been shown to be approximately 21% $\pm$ 5.5% for the attacking players, 28.6% $\pm$ 4.2% for the whole-court player and 38.5% $\pm$ 4.9% for the baseline player (18). In an earlier study, the percentage of playing time during matches, on hardcourts, were approximately 20% (13). From the research it appears that total playing time is only between 20-30% of total match time (2, 14). Tennis points do not generally last more than 13 seconds and the overwhelming majority of points last less than 10 seconds (15).

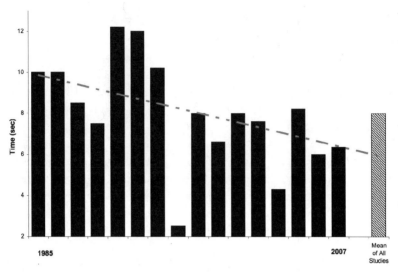

Figure 3.4: Rally time decreases between 1985-2007.

Diet can be a major factor in energy production during athletic competitions. Maintaining carbohydrate stores in the liver and muscles as glycogen is critical to provide fuel for anaerobic exercise. More detailed information is provided in the nutrition chapter of this book (see Chapter 4).

Tennis-Specific Energy Metabolism

Although tennis is characterized by periods of high-intensity exercise, it has been argued that the overall metabolic response resembles prolonged moderate-intensity exercise (15). Coaches and athletes should not infer from this that competitive tennis is a moderate-intensity sport. The average metabolic response does not take into account bursts of high power-output necessary for competitive tennis. In fact, it is the ability to perform during these high-intensity bursts of energy that often determines the outcome of a point. To consistently hit 130 mph serves and equivalent ground strokes, the ability to produce ATP rapidly is very important. As most points in competitive tennis last less than 10 seconds (15) it would be inappropriate to train tennis players in a traditional, aerobic fashion at moderate intensity for long durations.

However, this is still how many coaches and tennis players train for competition. Bergeron and colleagues (1) conclude that because blood plasma lactate does not change during a tennis match (although this result was not supported by other research (9, 27)), conditioning for tennis should generally emphasize exercises at near, but not beyond, anaerobic threshold. However, this method of training might not adequately develop the anaerobic power and explosiveness required to produce effective strokes and movements in tennis players.

Tennis requires multiple bursts of activity requiring anaerobic energy production and focused movement patterns throughout a match or training. Aerobic training will occur during the rest and recovery periods of high-intensity exercise if the work-to-rest ratios are appropriate. As tennis players are athletes that perform high-intensity short-duration sprint activities throughout a match, these athletes should be trained for aerobic development using multiple short-duration sprints (< 1 minute), with adequate rest (1:3 work/rest ratio), to achieve aerobic training benefits (20).

Interval training at high intensities has been shown to improve aerobic fitness to the same extent as traditional aerobic training (26). The duration of recovery, as well as the duration of workloads, is important for the regulation of physiological strain during intermittent exercise. Studies during both sprint and weight training have shown the importance of recovery on subsequent performance (22, 23, 25 26, 27, 28).

FATIGUE & PERFORMANCE

Fatigue may result from inefficiencies related to the athlete's metabolic and physiological levels of performance. As tennis players practice and play matches that last hours, fatigue is a major concern. Power decrements during high-intensity, intermittent exercise, such as tennis, may be related to a continuous degradation of phosphocreatine, thus placing greater demand on the glycolytic energy system to produce ATP, which increases muscle and blood lactate concentrations. Fatigue will be discussed in later chapters of this book.

SUMMARY

In summary, training for tennis should include movement patterns that are individualized to playing style and should include linear, lateral and multi-directional movements of relatively short distances, one to five yards for the most part with no distances greater than 20 yards. Tennis requires short explosive bursts of energy repeated dozens, if not hundreds, of times per match or practice session. By contrast, the length of a tennis match can range from less than one hour to more than five hours in a five-set tennis match. This makes the sport of tennis quite unique in terms of the specific metabolic demands of intense competitive play. One of the biggest challenges facing the tennis coach and tennis conditioning specialist is designing effective training programs to meet these varied metabolic demands. The information discussed in this chapter as well as the in-depth analysis and practical examples provided throughout the remainder of the book should be used as a guide to help structure both on and off-court training programs for tennis players.

Chapter 3

References

1. Bergeron M.F., Maresh C.M., Kraemer W.J. et al. Tennis: a physiological profile during match play. Int J Sports Med 1991;12:474-479.

2. Bergeron M.F., Maresh C.M., Armstrong L.E. et al. Fluid-electrolyte balance associated with tennis match play in a hot environ-ment. Int J Sport Nutr 1995; 5: 180-93

3. Bernardi M., De Vito G, Falvo M.E. et al. Cardiorespiratory adjustment in middle-level tennis players: are long term cardiovascular adjustments possible? In: Lees A, Maynard I, Hughes M, Reilly T, editors. Science and Racket Sports II. London, UK:E & FN Spon; 1998. p. 20-26.2.

4. Brooks, G. A. Amino acid and protein metabolism during exercise and recovery. Med Sci Sp Exerc, 19:S150-S156, 1987.

5. Brooks, G. A. The lactate shuttle during exercise and recovery. Med. Sci. Sp. Exerc., 18, 360-368, 1986.

6. Brooks, G. A., K. E. Brauner, and R. G. Cassens. Glycogen synthesis and metabolism of lactic acid after exercise. Am. J. Physiol., 224: 1162-1186, 1973.

7. Brooks, G. A. and T. D. Fahey. Exercise Physiology: Human Bioenergetics and its applications. New York, Wiley, 1984.

8. Burke, R. E. and Edgerton, V. R. Motor unit properties and selective involvement in movement. J. Wilmore and J. Drough, Eds. Exerc. and Sp. Sci. Rev., 3. 31-81. 1975.

9. Copley B.B. Effects of competitive singles tennis playing on serum electrolyte, blood glucose and blood lactate concentrations. S Afr J Sci 1994; 80: 145

10. Chandler, T. J, and Arnold, E. C. Bioenergetics. In Chandler, TJ, and Brown, LE, Eds. Strength Training and Conditioning for Human Performance. Baltimore, Lippincott, Williams and Wilkins, 2008.

11. Christmass M.A., Richmond S.E. Cable NT, et al. A metabolic characterization of single tennis. In: Reilly T, Hughes M., Lees A., editors. Science and racket sports: London: E&FN Spon, 1995: 3-9

12. Delecluse C., Van Coppenolle H., Willems F. et al. Influence of high-resistance and high velocity training on sprint performance. Med Sci Sports Exerc 1995; 27: 1203-919.

13. Docherty D. A comparison of heart rate responses in racquet games. Br J Sports Med1982;16:96-100.

14. König D., Huonker M., Schmid A. et al. Cardiovascular, metabolic, and hormonal parameters in professional tennis players. Med Sci Sports Exerc 2001;33:654-658.

15. Kovacs, M.S. Tennis physiology: training the competitive athlete. Sports Medicine, 2007. 37(3): p. 1-11.

16. Kovacs, M.S. A comparison of work/rest intervals in men's professional tennis. Medicine and Science in Tennis, 2004. 9(3): p. 10-11.

17. Kovacs, M.S. Applied physiology of tennis performance. British Journal of Sports Medicine, 2006. 40(5): p. 381-386.

18. Kovacs M.S., Strecker E, Chandler WB et al. Time analysis of work/rest intervals in men's collegiate tennis. In: National Strength and Conditioning Conference; 2004; Minneapolis, MN; 2004: e364

19. Kovacs, M.S. et al. Time analysis of work/rest intervals in men's collegiate tennis. in National Strength and Conditioning Conference. 2004. Minneapolis, MN.

20. Kovacs, M. Energy system-specific training for tennis. Strength and Conditioning Journal, 2004. 26(5): p. 10-13.

21. Lehninger, A. L. Bioenergetics. Mejnlo Park, CA. Benjamin, 1973.

22. Linossier M.T., Denis C, Dormois D. et al. Ergometric and metabolic adaptations to a 5s sprint training programme. Eur J Appl Physiol 1993; 68: 408-14

23. Linossier M.T., Dormois D., Geyssant A. et al. Performance and fibre characterisics of human skeletal muscle during short sprint training and detraining on a cycle ergometer. Eur J Appl Physiol 1997; 75: 491-8

24. Powers, S.K., and Howley E.T. Exercise Physiology: Theory and Application to Fitness and Performance. McGraw Hill: New York, 2003

24. Richers T.A. Time-motion analysis of the energy systems in elite and competitive singles tennis. J Hum Mov Stud 1995; 28: 73-86

25. Smith, S.A., S. J. Montain, R. P. Matott, G. P. Zientara, F. A. Jolesz, and R. A. Fielding. Creatine supplementation and age influence muscle metabolism during exercise, J. of Appl. Physiol., 85: 1349-1356, 1998.

26. Tabata I., Nishimura K., Kouzaki M. et al. Effects of moderate-intensity endurance and high-intensity intermittent training on anaerobic capacity and VO_2max. Med Sci Sports Exerc 1996; 28: 1327-30.

27. Therminarias A., Dansou P., Chirpaz-Oddou M.F. et al. Hormonal and metabolic changes during a strenuous tennis match: effect of ageing. Int J Sports Med 1991; 12: 10-6

28. York, J. Oscai, L. B., and Penny, D. G. Alterations in skeletal muscle lactate dehydrogenase isozymes following exercise training. Biochemistry and Biophysics Research Communication, 61: 1387-1393, 1974.

CHAPTER 4

NUTRITION & HYDRATION FOR OPTIMUM TENNIS PERFORMANCE

- ESSENTIAL NUTRIENTS
- PROTEIN
- FATS
- CARBOHYDRATES
- ATHLETE GUIDELINES
- GLYCEMIC INDEX
- ALCOHOL
- VITAMINS & MINERALS
- WHEN & HOW TO EAT
- NUTRITIONAL RECOVERY FROM TENNIS
- HYDRATION
- ERGOGENIC AIDS

INTRODUCTION

The average person will spend about six years of his life eating, which equals approximately 70,000 meals and 60 tons of food (43). Competitive tennis players require a substantially larger amount of nutrients than the typical person. Tennis athletes require the knowledge to help design effective eating programs to aid in performance as well as to speed recovery after training and competition. Optimizing tennis training and competition is a multifaceted process. One of the major influencing factors is an athlete's diet. A competitive athlete's diet should involve careful planning of the type of food and fluid ingested, the timing of the ingestion, and the interplay between different types of nutrients—including supplementation.

Nutrition research and practices have changed substantially in the last 100 years, as a tennis player's diet has gone from being thought as irrelevant to performance to being one of the major factors in an athlete's training routine. Gone are the days when a typical pre-match meal was steak and chips followed by a post-match beer and cigarette. Now terms such as glycemic index, protein half-life, and essential versus non-essential nutrients have become the buzzwords of the 21st century.

Following a productive and effective eating program is difficult for many players to successfully accomplish. It is not uncommon for players to try to maintain appropriate diets during a tournament, but many lack the knowledge about what foods are going to help them perform optimally and recover quickly. Although most players attempt to eat appropriately during tournaments, many eat poorly the rest of the time during training and leading up to tournament play. This type of "crash course" nutrition has been shown to be less effective for optimizing energy stores during competition (38). Competitive tennis athletes have dietary requirements far different from the average person; therefore, the recommendations in this chapter are based on improving tennis performance and helping the athlete recover from the training and competitive stress. The information in this chapter is aimed at a competitive tennis athlete and should not necessarily be taken as general nutritional guidelines.

FOUR MAJOR DIETARY GOALS

1. *Energy balance*—taking in enough calories to sustain and improve performance.
2. *Recovery*—speed of recovery from training and competition.
3. *Body composition*—fat versus fat free mass.
4. *Long term health*—improved well being and prevention of disease.

BASIC NUTRITIONAL BACKGROUND

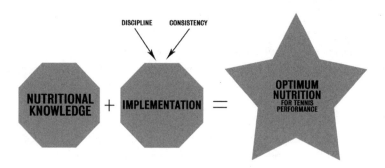

Figure 4.1: Optimum nutrition equation.

ESSENTIAL NUTRIENTS

The human body requires six essential nutrients: proteins, fats, carbohydrates, vitamins, minerals, and water (see Table 4.1). Essential nutrients cannot be created by the body and therefore need to be consumed in food. The energy in foods is expressed in kilocalories. One kilocalorie equals the amount of heat it takes to raise the temperature of 1 liter of water 1°C. However, food labels and typical language uses the word calories to describe kilocalories (1000 calories). Throughout the remainder of the chapter, the word calorie will be used.

From the six essential nutrients only the three macronutrients provide energy (fats, carbohydrates, protein) for exercise, and of these carbohydrates are the primary source of energy. Adequate carbohydrate levels can help prevent premature fatigue.

Nutrient	Calories per Gram	Major Sources	Purpose
Carbohydrates (macronutrient)	4	Breads, pasta, potatoes, fruits, vegetables, grains	Provides energy to cells in brain, nervous system, blood, and muscles
Fats (macronutrient)	9	Animal products, grains, nuts, seeds, fish, vegetables	Provides energy, insulation, cushion organs, is the medium for fat-soluble vitamins
Protein (macronutrient)	4	Meat, poultry, milk products, eggs, fish, legumes, nuts	Parts of enzymes, bone, blood, muscles, some hormones and cell membranes; repair tissue, regulate water and acid-base balance, aids in cell and muscle growth, can supply energy
Water (micronutrient)	0	Vegetables, fruit and fluids 50-70% of body's water weight.	Medium for chemical reactions, transport chemicals reactions, transport chemicals, regulate temperature, remove waste products
Vitamins (micronutrient)	0	All food, but abundant in fruits, vegetables, some grains	Promotes and/or catalyst for chemical reactions within cells
Minerals (micronutrient)	0	Found in most foods	Aids in general body functions; acts as catalysts for the release of energy

Table 4.1: Essential Nutrients.

PROTEIN

Protein has become a major area of scientific research and protein intake and supplementation plays an important role in athletic performance and recovery. *Protein does not provide a major source of fuel for exercising muscles, but it is vital in the diet as it is highly influential in the structure of muscles, enzymes, blood, cell membranes, bones, and some hormones.* In most developed countries where food is plentiful and most athletes are fed on a regular basis, protein provides as little as 5% of energy expended during rest and exercise (41, 89). Proteins are made up of a combination of carbon, hydrogen, oxygen, and nitrogen atoms. Proteins are made from 20 common amino acids found in food. There are 9 essential amino acids needed in the body (histidine, isoleucine, leucine, lysine, methionine, phenylalanine, threonine, tryptophan, valine). These essential amino acids cannot be created by the body and need to be ingested in adequate quantities in the diet. There are 11 amino acids (non-essential) that can be made by the body (see Table 4.2).

Essential Amino Acids	Non-Essential Amino Acids
Histidine	Alanine
Isoleucine	Arginine
Leucine	Asparagine
Lysine	Aspartic acid
Methionine	Cysteine (cystine)
Phenylalanine	Glutamic acid
Threonine	Glutamine
Tryptophan	Glycine
Valine	Proline
	Serine
	Tyrosine

Table 4.2: Essential and non-essential amino acids.

Amino acids are joined to each other by peptide bonds. Dipeptide is two amino acids joined together, whereas polypeptide is several amino acids joined together. Although protein is thought to be the predominant component of muscle, it is only about 20% protein with the rest composed predominantly of water (94).

Complete proteins contain all essential amino acids and supply them in adequate amounts. Incomplete proteins do not provide the required amount of some of the essential amino acids. Meat, poultry, fish, eggs, milk, cheese, and soy provide complete proteins. The incomplete proteins come from plant sources like nuts and legumes and usually contain most of the essential amino acids but are lacking in one or more the 9 essential amino acids.

Major functions of protein in the body
- Building materials for bone, ligaments, tendons, muscles and organs.
- Involved in hormones related to energy metabolism (e.g., insulin, glucagons, epinephrine)
- Enzymes that influence reactions involved in energy production, fuel utilization, and building and repair of tissue—especially muscle.
- Maintenance of fluid and electrolyte balance.
- Acts as a buffer and assists with the maintenance of the acid-base balance.
- Can act as the third energy source (after carbohydrates and fat) during and following exercise if inadequate carbohydrate and fat stores are available. Typically only a small contributor and rarely seen as an important contributor in exercise lasting less than two hours.

Although dietary guidelines are difficult to generalize across an entire population, a good minimum guide should be that tennis players consume protein at a rate of 1.2 g/kg of body weight (0.55 g/lb), as this is the amount that has been shown to maintain nitrogen balance in endurance events (81). However, if the athlete is undertaking an intense strength training program as well as on-court tennis training, the protein intake should be increased to between 1.6-1.7 g/kg (0.73-0.77 g/lb) of body weight per day to allow for the accumulation and maintenance of lean tissue (76, 104). These recommendations are for males, with little research available on female needs at this time.

Protein contains about 16% nitrogen by weight and nitrogen concentration is used as measure of protein usage. When nitrogen intake (dietary protein) equals nitrogen excretion, the athlete is said to be in nitrogen balance. The ability for athletes to maintain nitrogen balance during exercise appears to be dependent on (Figure 4.2) (17, 18, 76):

- Training age of the athlete
- Training state of the athlete
- Quality and quantity of protein consumed
- Total calories consumed
- The body's carbohydrate stores
- Intensity, duration, and type of exercise

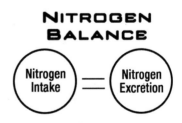

Figure 4.2: Nitrogen balance.

Protein requirements and usage are determined in part by the amount of carbohydrates taken at the same time. The quantity of urea found in sweat (a marker of nitrogen excretion) was 50% less when people were carbohydrate loaded as opposed to carbohydrate depleted (77). This is an important finding for tennis players from both a strength and muscle development perspective as well as for recovery. Adequate carbohydrate consumption is needed before, during, and after tennis play not only for energy, but it aids in the storage and use of protein to help muscle repair.

As there is a limit to the rate at which protein can be used and productively stored (17), consuming excess protein above these values, as is encouraged by many nutritional companies who sell protein powders and bars, will not be beneficial for athletes. In studies looking at protein intake, it has been found that most athletes consume adequate amounts of protein in their normal diets to sustain and aid in optimal body functioning (52).

Concern has been raised about athletes consuming too much dietary protein, especially female athletes and amenorrhea (suppression of normal menstrual flow) (17). Calcium is excreted at much higher rates with high protein diets (57) and amenorrheic athletes already have a lower bone density than those athletes with normal menstrual cycles (40). A high protein diet may increase the problem leading to severe health consequences. Also, excessive doses of some amino acids have potential side effects that are harmful and can cause health concerns.

Protein rich foods—10 g protein is provided by:

2 small eggs
300 ml cow's milk
20 g skim milk powder
30 g cheese
200 g yogurt
35-50 g meat, fish or chicken
4 slices bread
90 g breakfast cereal
2 cups cooked pasta or 3 cups rice
400 ml soy milk
60 g nuts or seeds
120 g tofu or soy meat
150 g legumes or lentils
200 g baked beans
150 ml fruit smoothie or liquid meal supplement

FATS

Fat is the common term to describe lipids. Lipids include triglycerides, such as sterols and phospholipids. The lipids of greatest significance in sports nutrition are triglycerides, fatty acids, phospholipids, and cholesterol. Fat is a major contributor to energy production and utilization during rest and at longer duration exercise. However, as exercise intensity (percent of maximum effort) increases, fat utilization is decreased, in part due to the increase in contribution by carbohydrates (10). The shorter and more explosive the activity, the less energy is produced from fat (Figure 4.3). Due to the nature of tennis, which typically has points requiring high intensity explosive movements lasting less than 10 seconds (71-73) and with total match or practice sessions lasting more than two hours, the fuel usage is split between carbohydrates for the explosive portions of exercise and fat for the long duration of total play.

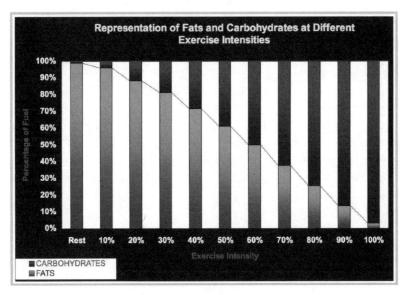

Figure 4.3: Fats and carbohydrates at different exercise intensities.

Fat, unlike carbohydrates and protein, is calorie dense and produces nine calories per gram of fat compared with four calories per gram of carbohydrates or protein. This is great for energy storage and use, but if too much fat is consumed, it can be stored (as adipose tissue) and increase the athletes' fat mass that is typically a hindrance to optimal tennis performance.

The way fat is stored and used in the body is dependent upon the saturation of

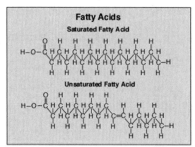

Figure 4.4: Fatty acids chemical structure.

the fatty acids, which refers to the amount of hydrogen it contains. Saturated fatty acids means that every carbon is attached to a hydrogen, whereas unsaturated fatty acids mean that not all carbon bonds are taken up by hydrogen and therefore form double bonds. If there is only one double bond, the fatty acid is called monounsaturated. If there are two or more double bonds, the fatty acid is called polyunsaturated (Figure 4.4). The two essential fatty acids, linoleic acid (omega-6) and alpha-linoleic acids (omega-3), are both polyunsaturated. At least 3 % of all fat consumed should be in the form of omega-6 (linoleic) fatty acids and 1 % from omega-3 (alpha-linoleic) fatty acids (37). Most athletes consume more than the minimum standards of these essential fatty acids in regular diet.

A 200-lb male with 15 % body fat has approximately 15,000 calories of energy stored.

One of the most common fat processing methods is hydrogenation of oils, which makes the fat more saturated. This makes the fat more solid at room temperature. Corn oil and margarine are examples of partially hydrogenated fat. The more solid the form of margarine, the more hydrogenated the product.

Trans fatty acids raise LDL (bad cholesterol) and lower HDL (good cholesterol) similar to saturated fats, whereas polyunsaturated and monounsaturated fats have more positive effects on LDL and HDL levels.

Cholesterol, similar to fat in general, has a negative connotation in the media. However, cholesterol has many essential functions. Cholesterol is vital for healthy cell membrane function and for many hormones, including sex hormones and cortisol. Cholesterol is synthesized in the liver and intestine.

Fat in the general population is a major concern with the increase in adult obesity, but more frightening is the increase in childhood obesity and the onset of type II diabetes in children. This was previously called adult-onset diabetes because it was thought not to occur in children. It is a form of diabetes that is highly correlated with increased body fat. However, obesity is rarely a problem in tennis players due to the physical nature of training and competition, but many tennis athletes do need to monitor their body composition as excess body fat limits speed around the court, and it requires more energy to produce movement that can result in the onset of fatigue sooner. Therefore, the goal of tennis players is to increase lean muscle mass while maintaining or, if necessary, reducing fat mass.

CARBOHYDRATES

Carbohydrates (CHO) have multiple purposes in human function, but from an athletic perspective, the importance lies in aiding in contracting of skeletal muscle, central nervous system function (11), and maintaining appropriate glucose levels for performance (30). Unfortunately, limited study has been performed looking at carbohydrate consumption and metabolism in tennis play, but a large amount of quality research has looked at other sports and activities that are similar to tennis.

Carbohydrate Facts:
- CHO needed for energy and some vital functions
- Simple CHO – Contain only one or two sugar units in each molecule.
  - SUCROSE (table sugar)
  - FRUCTOSE (fruit sugar, honey)
  - MALTOSE (malt sugar)
  - LACTOSE (milk sugar)
- Simple CHO are typically low in vitamins, minerals and fiber (unless fortified)
- Complex CHO– Contains chains of many sugar molecules, starches and most types of fiber
- Starches: wheat, rye, rice, oats etc, legumes, potatoes
- Fiber: fruits, vegetables and grains

Compared to protein and fat stores, carbohydrate stores are severely limited. The total amount of glycogen (stored glucose) ranges from 800-2000 calories. However, stored forms are dependent on multiple factors, such as size, fitness level, time of day, and an athlete's typical carbohydrate consumption (80). The average male stores about 525 grams of glycogen in the muscle and about 25 grams of glucose in the blood. The liver stores about 100 additional grams of glycogen which can be broken down to glucose and released into the blood to maintain blood glucose

> - 55%-58% of energy from carbohydrate
> - 12%-15% of energy from protein
> - 25%-30% of energy from fat

as it is being used by the tissues of the body. The total amount of carbohydrates that the body can store is about 2,600 calories (only 80%, 2000 calories are usable for exercise). This is only enough for about 2 hours of moderate-to-high exercise.

An increase in exercise intensity will increase the use of carbohydrates as the predominant fuel source (13). As exercise length increases, the source of carbohydrates can shift from muscle glycogen to the circulating blood glucose, but in all circumstances, if blood glucose cannot be maintained, the intensity of exercise will be decreased (32).

Five to six hundred grams of carbohydrates, or 7 to 8 g/kg for a 70 kg athlete (150 lbs) is sufficient to maintain muscle glycogen stores on a day to day basis (23, 31). For an athlete who consumes between 4000-5000 calories, this would amount to between 50-60% of daily calories that are within range of the normal general dietary guidelines.

ATHLETE GUIDELINES

The big question from both a practical and scientific standpoint is whether the needs of tennis athletes are substantially different from those of the general population. In a joint position stand from the American College of Sports Medicine, American Dietetic Association, and Dietitians of Canada, it was concluded that there wasn't enough research yet available to suggest that athletes require substantially different diets from the general recommendations (1). These general recommendations suggest the following:

These specific ranges are somewhat difficult for athletes to follow without measuring exact calories in each meal. Listed below is a good general range where tennis athletes should aim to maintain their nutrient breakdown.

- Protein:10-30% of total daily calories (higher part of range for athletes on a rigorous strength training program)
- Fat: 20-35% of total daily calories
- Carbohydrate: 45-65% of total daily calories

GLYCEMIC INDEX

Glycemic index (GI) simply represents how quickly food will raise blood glucose levels after consumption. The GI number is not the actual amount of glucose in the blood. Instead it shows the relative percentage of the effect of food on blood sugar compared to the effect of pure sugar (pure glucose). Pure sugar is given a GI of 100. For example, if a piece of bread has a GI of 70, it would cause an increase (in 120 minutes) of blood glucose of 70% of what would pure sugar (Table 4.2).

High glycemic foods produce a rapid rise in blood glucose and corresponding insulin levels. High glycemic foods also increase muscle glycogen more than foods with a low glycemic index (Figure 4.5).

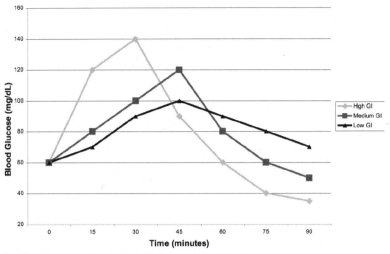

Figure 4.5: Blood Glucose vs Time for High, Medium, and Low GI Foods.

Low Glycemic Foods (GI <60)

Barley	Rice bran	Dried peas	Cherries
Pasta (regular)	Lentils	Milk (whole/skim)	Plums
Beans (most types)	Tomato soup	Pears (not canned)	Yogurt (most types)
Peanuts	Wheat kernels	Apricots (dried)	Apples
Fructose (fruit sugar)	Peaches (fresh)	Grapefruit	

Medium Glycemic Foods (GI 60-85)

Oat bran bread	Oat-bran cereal	Banana	Pita bread (white)
Bran Chex cereal	Kiwi fruit	Pastry (unsweet)	All-bran cereal
Grapes	Rye kernel bread	Popcorn	Grapefruit juice
White rice (long)	Buckwheat	Orange (whole/juice)	Sweet potatoes
Ice-cream (low-fat)	Mango	Basmati rice	Durum pasta
Multi-grain bread	Sweet corn	Wild rice	Cracked barley

High Glycemic Foods (GI >85)

Cheerios	Muffins	Watermelon	Corn bran cereal
Croissant	Carrots	Crispix cereal	Doughnut
Potatoes	Muesli (most)	Bagel (white)	Couscous
Rice Krispies	Whole wheat bread	Sport drinks	Shredded wheat
Rye flour bread	Honey	Total (cereal)	Melba toast
Sugar syrups	Cornmeal	Pizza (normal)	Waffles
Glucose	Brown rice	Soft drinks	Maltose
Hard candy	Corn chips	Sucrose	Rice cakes
Raisins			

Table 4.2: Glycemic index of common foods.

ALCOHOL

Alcohol is the most widely used drug by the athletic population. Alcohol provides approximately seven calories per gram; however, the energy derived from alcohol does not have the same energy capabilities of carbohydrates, fats, or even protein. Regular alcohol consumption influences normal metabolic function and it needs to be considered a toxic substance. A regular size serving of alcohol (12 ounces of beer, four ounce glass of wine or one ounce of liquor) contains approximately half an ounce of alcohol. Half an ounce of alcohol is 14 grams. One standard drink provides approximately 98 calories, but this has the potential to negatively affect the use of this energy as well as the energy from other sources. Alcohol consumption has a negative effect on athletic performance in general and tennis specifically. In fact, alcohol consumption has been shown to reduce tennis specific skills such as reaction time, endurance, coordination and strength (87).

Alcohol is a diuretic, which means that even though the athlete might be consuming large amounts of fluid, it does not adequately hydrate a tennis athlete post-exercise. Yet it is not uncommon for some athletes to have a few drinks after practice or competition, and this is a time when athletes are typically still somewhat dehydrated form the exercise session. It is important to make sure the athletes are hydrated fully after practice to limit any negative consequences form alcohol consumption.

Another negative result of alcohol consumption is the increase in injury rate. It appears that regular drinkers have up to a 50% higher incidence of injury. Researchers have speculated that it may be due to the "hangover effect" which has been shown to reduce athletic performance by about 11% (86, 87). In an analysis of tennis players, it was found that athletes who drink alcohol sustained injuries at a higher rate (83% in drinkers, 33% in nondrinkers) (87).

VITAMINS AND MINERALS

The last decade has seen a rapid rise in the interest, discussion, and debate in vitamin and mineral supplementation. What is good? What is bad? What is helpful and what is just a waste of money? The one area of vitamin and mineral supplementation that people overlook is that if the athlete is taking in enough vitamins and minerals in the food that he/she consumes, any added supplementation via pills, potions, or injections will not improve performance, and if they are fat soluble (vitamin A, D, E, K), they could actually be toxic and harmful.

Vitamins

Vitamins are substances needed by cells to encourage specific chemical reactions that take place in the cell. Some vitamins (particularly B vitamins) are involved in energy reactions that enable cells to derive energy from carbohydrate, protein, and fat.

WHEN & HOW TO EAT
PRE-PRACTICE/COMPETITION NUTRITION

The physical nature of tennis training requires a vast amount of calories on a daily basis. It is not uncommon for tennis players to require more than 4,000 calories to maintain adequate energy production for the exercising muscles. Timing and composition of pre-training meals can have an important affect on tennis performance. The pre-exercise meals typically take two forms—a larger, higher calorie meal about 3-4 hours before practice or competition, or a lighter snack that is typically consumed within two hours of play. In an extensive review looking at CHO needs in athletes, some general daily CHO guidelines have been recommended (16). When athletes are participating in general training when intensity is moderate to high, it is recommended that the athletes consume between $5\text{-}7$ $g \cdot kg^{-1}$ of CHOs on a daily basis (approximately 480 grams, for an 80 kg tennis player) (16). If training is increased or during tournament weeks, it has been advised that athletes should increase CHO intake to between $7\text{-}10$ $g \cdot kg^{-1}$ (approximately 680 grams) daily to maintain sufficient energy stores for performance and to aid in recovery (16, 27).

A high (140 g-300 g) CHO focused meal about 3-4 hours before practice or competition increases muscle glycogen stores (33) and allows for adequate stored glycogen for future use during exercise, which has been shown to improve performance (100). This meal should still contain about 15% protein and 20% fat.

45 MINUTES PRE-TRAINING & COMPETITION

The ingestion of CHO-rich solid or liquid foods within 45 minutes before competition causes a temporary rise, followed by a sharp decline in blood glucose levels in both pre-competition research as well as looking at results between matches (46, 49, 58, 101, 107). Although a consistent drop in blood glucose is seen, this physiological change has not always shown a decrease in tennis performance as measured by stroke accuracy or physical ability (58). This rebound-effect, also known as reactive hypoglycemia, describes how blood glucose quickly rises immediately after caloric consumption, whether it be as solid food or liquid calories, such as a sports drink, but then sharply drops causing the athlete to go into a state of moderate hypoglycemia as a result of excessive insulin secretion (28, 101, 106). As there could be a detrimental effect to the athlete, it may be appropriate for tennis players to limit the consumption of CHO-rich food within 45 minutes of competition or practice. If matches or practice sessions have only short rest periods between sessions (< 45 minutes), or time constraints do not allow for greater than 45 minutes between CHO ingestion and exercise, the consumed nutrients should be in the form of easily digestible food in small amounts (< 10 grams of CHO per 10 minutes) during the first portion of the practice or match session, rather than within the 45 minutes before the match.

DURING PRACTICE/COMPETITION

Two position stands by the leaders in sports science and athletic training—the American College of Sports Medicine and the National Athletic Trainers Association — have recommended that athletes, in general, and not specifically tennis players, should consume between 30-60 g·h^{-1} of CHO during exercise (19, 25). The CHO can be in the form of glucose, sucrose, maltodextrins, or some high glycemic starches. Fructose, as the source of carbohydrates should be limited due to the possibility of gastrointestinal discomfort (19, 25). Ensuring the sufficient rate of CHO ingestion can be accomplished by drinking 600-1200 ml·h^{-1} of solution containing 4-8% CHOs (4-8g·100 ml^{-1}) (19, 25).

Not maintaining appropriate carbohydrate stores during play leads to fatigue in prolonged activity (32, 34). The reason that carbohydrates are encouraged during long duration physical activity is that there is an increase in CHO oxidation which increases the risk of athletes becoming hypoglycemic (low blood sugar) as duration of activity increases without any external consumption of carbohydrates. This risk of hypoglycemia increases when playing tennis in hot and humid conditions (50).

Most athletes prefer to drink fluids during play rather than to consume solid food. Most commercially available sports drinks provide between 60-80 g of CHOs per liter; thus, consuming between 500 -1000 ml per hour would provide adequate CHO replenishment for play lasting greater than 90 minutes. Whether the athlete consumes solid or liquid calories has been shown to have the same effect on glucose and glycogen levels (24). However, fluid ingestion, especially during hot and humid conditions can have a secondary important benefit of aiding in fluid balance. This improved fluid balance can reduce the negative effects of dehydration and possible health concerns associated with less than optimal fluid status.

Apart from the multitude of negative consequences of less than optimal hydration levels, tennis athletes need to avoid becoming dehydrated (> 2%) as this can also have a detrimental effect on carbohydrate levels. Dehydration increases muscle glycogen use during exercise, possibly as a result of increased core temperature, reduced oxygen delivery and/or catecholamines (55). Therefore, the body may require larger amounts of fuel than would ordinarily be necessary which would lead to a reduction in tennis performance.

How Much Is too Much?

Can ingestion of large amounts of carbohydrates above the amounts previously mentioned improve performance even more? Ingesting of higher concentrations of CHOs (> 60 g · h⁻¹) does not increase oxidation rates and performance, but can lead to gastrointestinal discomfort (stomach problems) (109).

Is there a preferred type of CHO that should be consumed during exercise? All simple sugars are absorbed rapidly, and although the different forms do metabolize at slightly different rates, using different mechanisms, they seem to be equally effective in maintaining blood glucose levels during exercise (84). However, fructose can lead to gastrointestinal discomfort and should be avoided, or limited during play (19, 25).

Timing of Carbohydrates during Play

The timing of CHO ingestion during practice or competition should aim to create a regular flow of CHOs from the gut into the bloodstream. This can be achieved by consuming small amounts on a regular schedule throughout play. As CHO feeding can be counterproductive when ingested in large amounts (> 60-90 g · h⁻¹) or sports drink concentrations > 7-8 % of total volume (44, 51), it is advisable to ingest small amounts on a regular basis (i.e., each changeover) instead of consuming a larger amount of CHOs in a single changeover. It is inadvisable to provide a large amount of CHOs early in the practice or match and then refrain from providing more CHOs. This may prime the body for glucose metabolism, and reduce fat oxidation, which may deprive the body of fuel it has been primed to metabolize (29). This eating strategy might actually reduce performance instead of the intended positive effect.

Most commercially available sports drinks contain carbohydrate sources combined with electrolytes. An added benefit to consuming a CHO-electrolyte beverage during prolonged exercise is that it delays the onset of exercise induced *muscle cramps* (69). Although, CHO-electrolyte supplementation during exercise may delay muscle cramps, it has not been shown to prevent exercise-induced muscle cramps (69). Exercise induced muscle cramping is an area of continual study, but very little definitive knowledge is available as to the cause or mechanisms of muscle cramping. It is a multifaceted problem that involves genetic factors, psychological stress, hydration status, electrolyte balance, prior fitness, muscle contraction kinetics, and a host of other possible areas that have not been fully explored.

Although the research is still limited, tournament play seems to have different requirements and fuel utilization compared to practice. Tournament play has been shown to generate higher levels of blood glucose concentration compared to practice (46). The increased glucose level under tournament (increased stress) conditions can be explained by an increase in sympathetic activity with heightened adrenaline (epinephrine) release. This large increase in epinephrine levels has not been seen during practice (45).

NUTRITIONAL RECOVERY FROM TENNIS

Proper post-exercise nutrition is a major component to a competitive tennis player's success. It is not only important for tournament situations where multiple matches may be played on multiple days, but it is also important during training periods to allow for full recovery for a second session of practice on the same day or practice on following days (Figure 4.6).

STAGE OF DAILY ACTIVITY

STAGES	TIME	GOALS
PRE-EXERCISE		*Saturate muscle glycogen
		*Provide enough available
	>45 minutes pre-exercise	glucose/glycogen for performance
WORKOUT		*Limit muscle glycogen loss
		*Limit loss of muscle and cell fluid loss
	During exercise period	*Limit immune system suppression
		*Maintain blood glucose levels
POST-EXERCISE		*Change from catabolic state to
		anabolic (growth) state
		*Speed the elimination of metabolic wastes
		by increasing muscle blood flow
		* Initiate tissue repair and set the stage
	<45 minutes after exercise	for muscle growth
		*Reduce muscle damage and strengthen
		the immune system
<2 HOUR POST-EXERCISE		*Maintain insulin sensitivity
		*Maintain anabolic environment
	1-2 hours post exercise	*Fully restore muscle glycogen
.2 HOUR POST EXERCISE		*Maintain muscle glycogen stores
		*Maintain positive nitrogen balance
	>2 hour post exercise	for recovery and growth
	until next pre-exercise meal	*Promote muscular development

Figure 4.6: Nutritional stages of daily activity.

Since the amount of glycogen that can be resynthesized within a given time period is limited, a major goal of post-tennis CHO feeding is to provide adequate CHOs to replace that which was lost during the previous exercise period. Glycogen synthesis rates are the highest immediately after exercise (12). If CHOs are withheld for two hours post-exercise, it reduces the rate of glycogen synthesis by 47% (64). This accelerated rate of glycogen resynthesis is likely due to the insulin-like effect of exercise on skeletal muscle (91). The specific type of CHO ingested has been shown to be important. Ingestion of high glycemic-index CHOs resulted in a 48% greater rate of muscle glycogen resynthesis than the ingestion of low-glycemic index CHOs (15). It is recommended that players consume 1.5 g·kg[-1] of CHO during the first hour post-exercise, but no greater benefit has been seen on muscle glycogen resynthesis when > 1.5 g·kg[-1] of CHO was ingested (65). For example, a 75kg tennis player should consume approximately 113 g of CHO within the first hour post-exercise. Adding protein to the CHO post-exercise fuel consumption has resulted in a 27% greater rate of muscle glycogen accumulation over 4 hours than the same fuel source without 28 g of protein (80 g CHO and 6 g fat) (63). However, this notion that protein aids in muscle glycogen resynthesis has not been shown consistently (108).

The 45-minute time period immediately post-workout is vital for appropriate nutrition. It is the time when the initial onset of when the muscle proteins that were damaged during exercise begin to be repaired and the need for muscle glycogen stores to be replenished. This 45-minute period is when metabolism of the muscles is the most sensitive to insulin. Nutrients consumed during this time are more effective than those consumed later. Therefore, athletes get a greater return on their nutritional investment if it is consumed within 45 minutes after practice or competition (Figure 4.7).

It has been shown that a high glycemic carbohydrate and protein supplement can dramatically enhance protein synthesis (112). This increased protein synthesis is not only beneficial for muscle growth and repair, but it also aids in recovery and

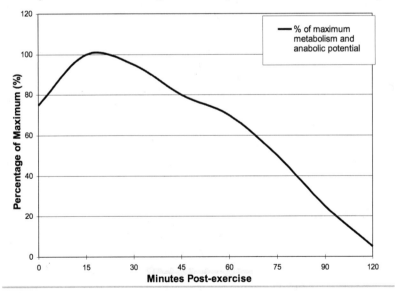

Figure 4.7: Proper nutrition during the first 45 minutes after exercise is crucial to muscle recovery.

can help improve immune system function which will help protect the athlete from sickness associated with hard physical training.

Approximately 45 minutes post-exercise until the next exercise session is when the body is in a combination of recovery and growth. This is the time when the muscle enzymes are aiding in the increase of contractile proteins and the size of muscle fibers. This is also the time when muscle glycogen is attempting to be fully replenished before the next training or competition period.

The most beneficial post-exercise form of protein is whey protein. It contains all nine "essential" amino acids; and it is highly digestible, with higher concentrations of branch-chained amino acids (BCAA) than other protein sources, such as casein or soy. Another benefit of whey protein is it relatively inexpensive compared to other protein sources. Whey protein does typically contain lactose, so for athletes who are lactose intolerant other forms of protein would be more beneficial.

Post-exercise CHO should be a high glycemic food which includes sucrose, maltodextrin, and dextrose. Fructose and galactose should be avoided during the post-exercise supplement as they are weaker stimulators of insulin.

The carbohydrate and protein ratio for a post-exercise supplement should be between 3:1–4:1, three or four grams of carbohydrate for each gram of protein. It would also be beneficial to consume a post-exercise supplement which contains glutamine and leucine (both amino acids) as they can speed the muscle recovery process (66).

Listed below is an example of a post-exercise snack suggested to help aid in recovery, from anaerobic focused activities (66):

200-350 calories in 12-16 oz of water (lower end of the scale for lighter people)
- Whey protein: 10-20 grams
- High glycemic carbohydrates (glucose, sucrose & maltodextrin): 40-70 grams
- Leucine: 1-4 grams
- Glutamine: 1-4 grams
- Vitamin C: 60-180mg
- Vitamin E: 80-600 IU

HYDRATION

Exercise-related hypohydration (less than optimal hydration) and the typically associated increased body temperature have been shown to limit exercise performance (28, 70, 96).

Maintaining appropriate hydration status is essential for good human function and high levels of tennis performance. Most tennis players sweat between 1-2.5 L·h⁻¹.

It is not uncommon for some players to sweat more than 3 L·h⁻¹ (6-8). Tennis athletes can lose 1-3 kg (4-7 pounds) per hour, and it may be possible to lose between 15-20 pounds of fluid over the course of a long match or training session if no fluids are replaced. Most people have a hard time drinking more than 1.2-1.5 L·h⁻¹ because of the gastric emptying rate for beverages (1, 2, 35) . Therefore, it is difficult for tennis athletes to consume enough fluids to keep pace with a sweat rate of greater than1.5 L·h⁻¹. Also, players who do ingest more than 1.25 L·h⁻¹ may feel gastrointestinal discomfort while competing (35, 36, 85). A study in collegiate male tennis players in the early 1990s showed the athletes self-selected drinking pattern resulted in a rate of approximately 1 L·h⁻¹ (8).

Exercise performance may be reduced when an individual is hypohydrated by as little as 2 % of body mass, and a loss of 5 % can decrease work capacity by up to 30 % (3, 96). During exercise, as the magnitude of hypohydration increases, there is an accompanying increase in core body temperature — between 0.10°C and 0.40°C — for each percent decrease in body weight (Figures 4.8 and 4.9)(2, 3, 14 97).

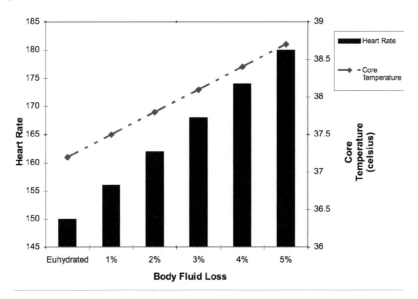

Figure 4.8: Relationship between heart rate, core temperature and body fluid loss.

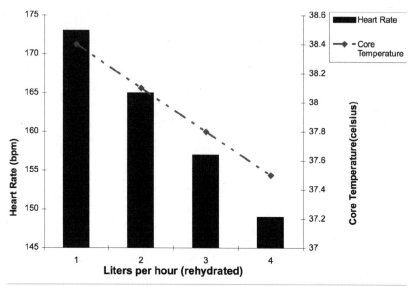

Figure 4.9: Relationship between heart rate, core temperature, and rehydration rates.

DON'T RELY ON THIRST AS A MEASURE OF HYDRATION

Thirst is not a good indicator of body water status or a sufficient stimulus to prevent body water loss during tennis play in a hot environment (7, 59, 74, 110). Voluntary drinking typically leads to involuntary dehydration. One reason for involuntary dehydration is that most people lose about 1.5 liters of body water before thirst is perceived (3, 54, 110). By this time, impaired exercise thermoregulation has already begun (54), resulting in a subtle increase in core temperature which requires the body to work at a higher intensity to accomplish the same amount of work. A tennis player's environment and sweat rate are both vital factors in contributing to hypohydration; however, a player's on-court fluid intake pattern is equally important.

A possible reason why athletic performance is reduced when players are hypohydrated is due to the inability or unwillingness of the athletes to maintain sufficient central nervous system drive to the working muscles (82). It appears that athletes can physiologically perform at a high level, but when hypohydrated they are unwilling to mentally push themselves as hard.

The vast majority of points (>85%) in competitive tennis last less than 10 seconds and have rest periods lasting no more than 25 seconds (9, 20-22, 39, 42, 47, 60, 70, 73, 75, 83, 88, 95, 98, 103, 105, 111). This work/rest ratio can cause large changes in body temperature, but it does allow for ample periods for fluid replacement during games, but especially during the 90 second period after every second game (change of ends). This allows for a structured fluid program to be implemented.

SWEATING, ELECTROLYTE BALANCE, & MUSCLE CRAMPING

Apart from the negative consequences of reduced body water, as a result of sweating and to a less significant degree water loss in respiration, a major concern is the amount of electrolytes that the body loses in sweat. Maintaining electrolyte balance is important to help reduce the likelihood of dehydration, fatigue, and possible muscle cramping (Figure 4.9).

An area that is sometimes misinterpreted by coaches is the percentage loss of different electrolytes. Under normal physiologic conditions for acclimated athletes, potassium (K^+) and magnesium (Mg^{2+}) concentrations will not be high in sweat (7). This is contrary to the belief of many coaches and athletes that K^+ depletion is major cause in heat related muscle cramps. In fact, the evidence supports the relationship between heat-related muscle cramps and extracellular Na^+ depletion—not K^+ depletion (7). The total amount of K^+ lost, via sweat during play, should be rather small, relative to whole-body K^+ stores, and of little physiologic or performance consequence (90). It would be appropriate, therefore, for tennis players to supplement with Na^+ to help prevent electrolyte imbalances (Figure 4.10).

INFLUENCE OF SODIUM ON FLUID CONSUMPTION

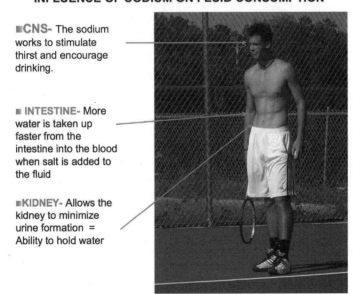

■CNS- The sodium works to stimulate thirst and encourage drinking.

■ INTESTINE- More water is taken up faster from the intestine into the blood when salt is added to the fluid

■KIDNEY- Allows the kidney to minimize urine formation = Ability to hold water

Figure 4.10: Importance of proper electrolyte balance.

Tournament play adds a confounding variable to the hydration puzzle. The cumulative effect of repeated high Na^+ losses in sweat over several days of a tournament in hot and humid conditions may result in a low extracellular Na^+ concentration, especially if daily Na^+ ingestion (through diet and/or supplementation) is low. This may be a reason why players are more likely to cramp in the second or third match on a particular day or in the latter rounds of a tournament. However, exercise induced muscle cramping has multiple factors, and it has been shown that dehydration and electrolyte loss are not the sole reasons for muscle cramping (69). These other reasons have still not fully been determined, but psychological stress in competitive situations is a plausible contributor to the onset of muscle cramping during play.

HYPONATREMIA

Although not common in competitive tennis, the combined effect of large Na^+ losses in a players sweat, combined with the ingestion of large volumes of hypotonic fluid (e.g., unsalted water), could lead to significantly diluted plasma Na^+ (hyponatremia) (6, 8). Hyponatremia is a dangerous situation for any athlete to be in and has severe health consequences. Avoiding hypomatremia is relatively easy by consuming fluid or solids which include an appropriate amount of Na^+. An added benefit of adding Na^+ during play is it maintains the athletes drive to drink. Drinking only plain water can lead to blood which is diluted of appropriate electrolytes and enhanced urine production, which would result in a reduced drive to drink and therefore in increase in hypohydration (78).

Male tennis players appear to be more susceptible to poor hydration and the resultant negative performance and health effects. Males typically sweat at a faster rate than females (4, 8, 56), but they consume a similar amount of fluid during tennis play (8). This creates a negative fluid balance situation which is one possible reason why many more male tennis athletes suffer from on-court muscle cramps than females.

STRUCTURED HYDRATION PROGRAM

As voluntary drinking often leads to unintentional dehydration (54), it is important to have all competitive tennis players on a structured hydration program during practice and match situations. This is easily accomplished in match situations because of the frequent 90 second breaks after every second game. Hydration schedules can be developed by the trainer, coach, and/or athlete by measuring fluid loss—practically. The easiest method is to weigh (kg) the athlete before a practice (match) session and then subtract the athlete's post-exercise weight (kg) and amount of fluid ingested (L) during play (Equation 4.1). This will determine the athlete's fluid volume loss for that particular session. This value can be divided by time (hourly, 15 minutes, etc.) to determine the athlete's approximate fluid loss (sweat rate) per unit of time. From this value an individualized practical hydration routine can be established (74).

$$\text{Total Fluid Loss} = BW_{(pre\text{-}exercise\ kg)} - [BW_{(post\text{-}exercise\ kg)} - \text{Fluid ingested (L)}] \quad (4.1)$$

The following example outlines how this formula can be implemented into a player's program. A tennis player who has a pre-exercise weight of 80 kg and who plays for two hours while ingesting 2 L of fluid with a measured post-exercise weight of 77 kg will have an approximate fluid loss of 5 L in two hours or 2.5 $L \cdot h^{-1}$. This equation does not account for fluid lost due to urination. If the athlete must urinate, it needs to be accounted for in the equation.

ERGOGENIC AIDS

Substances that improve an athlete's performance are referred to as ergogenic aids. An ergolytic agent is a substance that has a detrimental effect on performance. Many tennis players experiment with different substances in the hope of improving performance. The problem is that most athletes and a lot of coaches do not understand how or why certain substances might or might not work and the potential harmful side effects that some might have.

Numerous pharmacological agents have been suggested as having ergogenic properties. The International Olympic Committee (IOC), ATP, WTA, ITF, and National Collegiate Athletic Association all conform to drug testing policies and publish lists of banned substances.

CAFFEINE

Caffeine is a common supplement taken by millions of people to help with energy levels and arousal (Table 4.3). The effects of caffeine on performance have been an area of speculation in many different sporting environments. Not many studies have been conducted on caffeine supplementation in tennis players. The few that have been performed have shown minimal, if any, performance benefit (46, 48, 49). Caffeine has been suggested as a hyperglycemic agent by stimulating glycogenolysis (92), but the measure of hyperglycaemia, blood glucose, has been shown to remain stable whether the tennis player consumed a calorie-free beverage with or without caffeine (130 mg/L) (48, 49). Caffeine has previously been shown in laboratory experiments to increase fat utilization following caffeine ingestion (62); however, in a tennis specific study using doses similar to those found in caffeinated beverages, no change on fat utilization was shown (49). The difference may be explained by the lower dosage of caffeine. A conclusion from the researchers was that caffeine (in the doses typically seen in commercially available soft drinks) was unlikely to induce metabolic effects in tennis competition if ingested during tennis change-overs (49).

In a different study which showed no performance benefits in tennis players when a dose of 364 mg (men) and 260 mg (women) of caffeine was ingested, the authors did suggest that caffeine may have some effect on the regulation of blood glucose at the start of play (48). This may benefit players who frequently experience symptoms related to hypoglycemia, and ingestion of caffeine prior to the second or

CAFFEINE CONTENT IN DIFFERENT DRINKS AND FOOD	
Double espresso (2oz)	45-100 mg
Brewed coffee (8 oz)	60-120 mg
Instant coffee (8 oz)	70 mg
Decaf coffee (8 oz)	1-5 mg
Tea - black (8 oz)	45 mg
Tea - green (8 oz)	20 mg
Coca Cola® (12 oz can)	34 mg
Pepsi® (12 oz can)	38 mg
Barq's® root beer (12 oz can)	22 mg
7-up® (12 oz)	0 mg
Chocolate milk (8 oz)	4 mg
Dark chocolate (1 oz)	20 mg
Milk chocolate (1 oz)	6 mg
Ben & Jerry's® coffee fudge frozen yogurt (8 oz)	85 mg
Red Bull® energy drink (8 oz)	80 mg
Jolt® Cola (8 oz)	75 mg
Lipton® Ice Tea (10 oz)	25 mg
Lucozade® (12 oz)	44 mg
Hershey's® chocolate bar	9 mg
No-Doz® (1 regular pill)	100 mg
Dexatrim® (1 pill)	200 mg
Kit Kat® candy bar	6 mg

Table 4.3: Caffeine content in different drinks and food.

third match during a tournament day may help avoid reactive hypoglycemia. Reactive hypoglycemia is the low blood sugar experienced if exercise is commenced within 45 minutes of carbohydrate rich meal. The typical symptoms are slow and sluggish movement, headache, and even light-headedness. These tennis-specific "field" studies contradict some of the caffeine producing performance benefits (improved power output) seen in later stages of endurance exercise under laboratory conditions (26, 61). These differences may be partly explained by the amount of caffeine ingested as well as that the laboratory studies focused on continuous endurance exercise as opposed to the intermittent exercise in the tennis studies.

CREATINE

"Should I take creatine?"

"What is creatine?"

These two questions are typically asked (sometimes in this order) by most competitive tennis players.

Creatine phosphate as mentioned in Chapter 2 is the fuel source to aid in the production of energy for short duration high intensity movements seen during tennis points. Creatine monohydrate is the supplement form taken by athletes in the hope of improving performance. Depletion of muscle creatine stores is thought to be a primary contributor to muscle fatigue during intense muscle contractions (53). Therefore, added creatine would theoretically be beneficial in repeated performance of explosive movements by delaying the depletion of phosphocreatine and by increasing phosphocreatine resynthesis during recovery (53). Research has shown that creatine supplementation has resulted in increased muscle phosphocreatine levels between 12-18% (68).

The large majority of research on creatine supplementation in explosive power movements such as short sprints and jumping movements have shown positive results (5). Creatine studies have shown the following results:

- Improved recovery from intermittent high intensity exercise bouts (5).
- Similar results in both males and females (5).
- Rapid weight gain due to water retention (67).

What creatine does not do:

- Creatine supplementation has not been shown to reduce the symptoms of associated with eccentric exercise such as DOMS (93).
- Does not improve aerobic performance (5).

Potential Negative Effects of Creatine

Well controlled, long-term studies in humans are lacking in the scientific literature and it is still unknown the long term consequences of creatine use. However, the typical complaints associated with creatine supplementation include gastrointestinal related problems (stomach cramping, nausea, diarrhea, and vomiting) (5). To limit the occurrences of these annoying and potentially performance reducing effects, it is highly encouraged that athletes who take creatine supplementation also make sure hydration level is increased.

Creatine supplementation may be appropriate for certain well-trained athletes, but more research is still needed to determine the long-term benefits and side-effects.

ANTIOXIDANTS

An antioxidant can detoxify free radicals (unstable and produce cellular damage) back into water and oxygen. The most popular antioxidants are Vitamin C (ascorbic acid), Vitamin E, Coenzyme Q10, and ß-carotene (a precursor to Vitamin A). The basis behind antioxidants as possible performance enhancers is that exercise increases oxygen uptake by the body tissues resulting in oxidative stress, which leads to enhanced production of free radicals (1). Limiting the free radicals are important for health and well being, but antioxidants have not been shown to improve athletic performance (67).

EPHEDRA

Ephedra and pseudoephedrine are stimulants. Many athletes use these in hope of increasing energy, delaying fatigue, and as an appetite suppressant to aid in fat loss. Ephedra is classified as an herb and is banned in many countries. Pseudoephedrine is classified as a drug, and is the most common nasal decongestant sold (OTC) without a doctor's prescription. Although some studies have shown positive performance effects (67), the dangers associated with ephedrine and pseudoephedrine have been magnified by high-profile deaths which have been linked to their use. It appears that the dangers of continual ephedra use in tennis athletes may outweigh the possible performance benefits.

ERYTHROPOIETIN (EPO)

EPO is produced naturally in the kidneys and regulates red blood cell production, but in recent years synthetic EPO has been created and athletes, especially endurance athletes (cyclists, runners), have abused this substance. EPO definitely enhances performance in aerobic activities by improving the oxygen carrying capacity of blood. The major adverse consequence of EPO use is the thickening of the blood and the possibility of thrombosis. The performance enhancements of EPO are clear, but so is the chance of severe health consequences including death.

HMB

ß-hydroxy-ß-methylbutyrate (HMB) is a metabolite of the essential amino acid leucine. It is touted as a supplement for strength and lean body mass development due to the anti-catabolic (preventing muscle breakdown) effects. Although a lot of media has promoted HMB, little scientific research supports the benefits (102). Like most recent supplements, no long-term studies have been performed in humans to monitor adverse effects. It appears that HMB is not beneficial to muscle development in trained athletes (67) and is not recommended for tennis players.

ANABOLIC STEROIDS

Anabolic steroids describe a class of drugs which are synthetic derivatives of testosterone. Anabolic steroids can come in oral, injectable, and topical form. Popular steroids such as Winstrol, Dianabol, Nandrolone, and Stanozolol have positive effects on certain performance variables, but at a hefty price (99). Apart from the expensive monetary cost of a cycle of steroids, which can cost over $1000 a month, the health consequences can be very dangerous. Anabolic steroids do increase muscle mass by increasing muscle protein synthesis, but all major tennis governing bodies ban anabolic steroid use, and it is typically tested by measuring the ratio of testosterone to its metabolite, epitestosterone (T:E ratio), which is 1 in most men. The cut-off of 6:1 is generous and is one reason why some athletes might try to beat the system. Many professional tennis players have been caught for taking anabolic steroids and masking agents in the last 10 years, but the tennis governing bodies have really tightened up the punishments for steroid use.

Apart from the benefits of steroid use, the health consequences have also received a major focus. The adverse health consequences include increased virilization in women, menstrual irregularities, premature closure of growth plates, acne, aggressive behavior, liver dysfunction, and increased risk of cardiovascular problems (67). It is clear that anabolic steroids do improve performance, but the health consequences can be highly detrimental. Apart from the fact that anabolic steroids are illegal and banned by all the major tennis governing bodies, the benefits of their use are far outweighed by the negatives.

NICOTINE

Although few tennis players smoke cigarettes on a regular basis, it is not uncommon for tennis athletes to use the smokeless form–chewing tobacco (chew), snuff (dip) and compressed tobacco (plug). Nicotine has been found to be detrimental to athletic performance (110). VO_2max values are typically lower in smokers than non-smokers and nicotine increases heart rate, blood pressure, autonomic reactivity, vasoconstriction, and peripheral circulation (110).

GLUTAMINE

Glutamine is the most abundant amino acid in the body. Skeletal muscle is considered to be the most important glutamine producer in the body. Once released from the skeletal muscle, glutamine acts as an inter-organ nitrogen transporter. Glutamine is used in a high rate by the cells of the immune system and low levels of glutamine have been associated with reduced immune function and respiratory infections, especially during heavy physical training. Evidence is available which supports the use of glutamine to help athletes during times of stress. Therefore, supplementation with glutamine during the overload periods of training or after extremely tough matches or practice sessions may be beneficial.

References

1.   ACSM, ADA, and D. O. Canada. Joint position statement: nutrition and athletic performance. Med Sci Sport Exercise. 32:2130-2145, 2000.

2.   Armstrong, L. E., D. L. Costill, and W. J. Fink. Influence of diuretic-induced dehydration on competitive running performance. Med Sci Sport Exercise. 17:456-461, 1985.

3.   Armstrong, L. E., R. W. Hubbard, P. C. Szlyk, W. T. Mathew, and I. V. Sils. Voluntary dehydration and electrolyte losses during prolonged exercise in the heat. Aviat Space Environ Med. 56:765-770, 1985.

4.   Avellini, B. A., E. Kamon, and J. T. Krajewski. Physiological responses of physically fit men and women to acclimation to humid heat. Journal of Applied Physiology. 49:254-261, 1980.

5.   Bemben, M. G. and H. S. Lamont. Creatine supplementation and exercise performance. Sport Med. 35:107-125, 2005.

6.   Bergeron, M. F. Heat cramps: fluid and electrolyte challenges during tennis in the heat. J Sci Med Sport. 6:19-27, 2003.

7.   Bergeron, M. F., L. E. Armstrong, and C. M. Maresh. Fluid and electrolyte losses during tennis in the heat. Clin Sports Med. 14:23-32, 1995.

8.   Bergeron, M. F., C. M. Maresh, L. E. Armstrong, J. F. Signorile, J. W. Castellani, R. W. Kenefick, K. E. LaGasse, and D. A. Riebe. Fluid-electrolyte balance associated with tennis match play in a hot environment. Int J Sport Nutr. 5:180-193, 1995.

9.   Bergeron, M. F., C. M. Maresh, W. J. Kraemer, A. Abraham, B. Conroy, and C. Gabaree. Tennis: a physiological profile during match play. Int J Sports Med. 12:474-479, 1991.

10.   Bergman, B. C., G. E. Butterfield, E. E. Wolfel, G. A. Casazza, G. D. Lopaschuk, and G. A. Brooks. Evaluation of exercise and training on muscle lipid metabolism. Am J Physiol. 276:E106-E117, 1999.

11.   Bergstrom, J., L. Hermansen, E. Hultman, and B. Saltin. Diet, muscle glycogen and physical performance. Acta Physiol Scand. 71:140-150, 1967.

12.   Bonen, A., G. W. Ness, A. N. Belcastro, and R. L. Kirby. Mild exercise impedes glycogen repletion in muscle. J Appl Physiol. 58:1622-1629, 1985.

13.   Brooks, G. A. and J. Mercer. Balance of carbohydrate and lipid utilization during exercise. The cross over concept. J Appl Physiol. 76:2253-2261, 1994.

14.   Buono, M. J. and A. J. Wall. Effect of hypohydration on core temperature during exercise in temperate and hot environments. European Journal of Physiology. 440:476-480, 2000.

15.   Burke, L. M., G. R. Collier, and M. Hargreaves. Muscle glycogen storage after prolonged exercise: effect of glycemic index of carbohydrate feedings. J Appl Physiol. 75:1019-1023, 1993.

16.   Burke, L. M., G. R. Cox, and N. K. Culmmings. Guidelines for daily carbohydrate intake: do athletes achieve them? Sport Med. 31:267-299, 2001.

17.   Butterfield, G. E. Whole-body protein utilization in humans. Med Sci Sport Exercise. 19 (suppl):S157-S165, 1987.

18.   Butterfield, G. E. and D. H. Calloway. Physical activity improves protein utilization in young men. Br J Nutr. 51:171-184, 1984.

19.   Casa, D. J., L. E. Armstrong, S. K. Hillman, S. J. Montain, R. V. Reiff, B. S. E. Rich, W. O. Roberts, and J. A. Stone. National athletic trainer's association position statement: fluid replacement for athletes. Journal of Athletic Training. 35:212-224, 2000.

20.   Chandler, T. J. Work/rest intervals in world class tennis. Tennis Pro. 3:4, 1991.

21.   Christmass, M. A., S. E. Richmond, N. T. Cable, P. G. Arthur, and P. E. Hartmann. Exercise intensity and metabolic response in singles tennis. Journal of Sports Sciences. 16:739-747, 1998.

22.   Christmass, M. A., S. E. Richmond, N. T. Cable, and P. E. Hartmann. A metabolic characterization of single tennis. In: Science and Racket Sports. T. Reilly, M. Hughes, and A. Lees (Eds.): E&FN Spon, 1994, pp. 3-9.

23.   Coggan, A. R. and E. F. Coyle. Carbohydrate ingestion during prolonged exercise: Effects on metabolism and performance. In: Exerc Sport Sci Rev. J. O. Holloszy (Ed.) Philadelphia, PA: Williams & Wilkins, 1991, pp. 1-40.

24.   Coleman, E. Update on carbohydrate: solid versus liquid. International Journal of Sports Nutrition. 4:80-88, 1994.

25.   Convertino, V., L. E. Armstrong, E. F. Coyle, G. Mack, M. N. Sawka, L. Senay, and W. M. Sherman. American College of Sports Medicine position stand: exercise and fluid replacement. Med Sci Sport Exercise. 28:i-vii, 1996.

26.   Costill, D. L., G. Dalsky, and W. J. Fink. Effects of caffeine ingestion on metabolism and exercise performance. Med Sci Sports. 10:155-158, 1978.

27.   Costill, D. L. and M. Hargreaves. Carbohydrate nutrition and fatigue. Sport Med. 13:86-92, 1992.

28.   Costill, D. L. and J. M. Miller. Nutrition for endurance sport: Carbohydrate and fluid balance. Int J Sports Med. 1:2-14, 1980.

29.   Coyle, E. F. Fluid and fuel intake during exercise. J Sport Sci. 22:39-55, 2004.

30.   Coyle, E. F. Physiological determinants of endurance exercise performance. J Sci Med Sport. 2:181-189, 1999.

31.   Coyle, E. F. Substrate utilization during exercise in active people. Am J Clin Nutr. 61 (suppl):968S-979S, 1995.

32.   Coyle, E. F., A. R. Coggan, M. K. Hemmert, and J. L. Ivy. Muscle glycogen utilization during prolonged strenuous exercise when fed carbohydrates. J Appl Physiol. 61:165-172, 1986.

33.   Coyle, E. F., A. R. Coggan, M. K. Hemmert, R. C. Lowe, and T. J. Walters. Substrate usage during prolonged exercise following a preexercise meal. J Appl Physiol. 59:429-433, 1985.

34.   Coyle, E. F., J. M. Hagberg, B. F. Hurley, W. H. Martin, A. A. Ehsani, and J. O. Holloszy. Carbohydrate feeding during prolonged strenuous exercise can delay fatigue. J Appl Physiol. 55:230-235, 1983.

35.   Coyle, E. F. and S. J. Montain. Benefits of fluid replacement with carbohydrate during exercise. Med Sci Sports Exerc. 24:S324-S330, 1992.

36.   Coyle, E. F. and S. J. Montain. Carbohydrate and fluid ingestion during exercise: Are there trade-offs? Med Sci Sports Exerc. 24:671-678, 1992.

37.   Davis, B. Essential fatty acids in vegetarian nutrition. Vegetarian Diet. 7:5-7, 1998.

38.   Davis, S. N., P. Galasetti, D. H. Wasserman, and D. Tate. Effects of antecedent of hypoglycemia on subsequent counterregulatory responses to exercise. Diabetes. 49:73-81, 2000.

39.   Dawson, B., B. Elliott, F. Pyke, and R. Rogers. Physiological and performance responses to playing tennis in a cool environment and similar intervalized treadmill running in a hot climate. Journal of Human Movement Studies. 11:21-34, 1985.

40.   Drinkwater, B. L., K. Nilson, C. H. I. Chesnut, W. J. Bremner, S. Shainholtz, and M. B. Southworth. Bone mineral content of amenorrheic and eumenorrheic athletes. N Engl J Med. 311:277-281, 1984.

41.   El-Khoury, A. E., A. Forslund, R. Olsson, S. Branth, A. Sjodin, A. Andersson, A. Atkinson, A. Selvaraj, L. Hambraeus, and V. R. Young. Moderate exercise at energy balance does not affect 24-h leucine oxidation or nitrogen retention in healthy men. Am J Physiol. 273:E394-E407, 1997.

42.   Elliott, B., B. Dawson, and F. Pyke. The energetics of singles tennis. Journal of Human Movement Studies. 11:11-20, 1985.

43.   Fahey, T. D., P. M. Insel, and W. T. Roth. Fit and Well: Core Concepts and Labs in Physical Fitness and Wellness. sixth edition ed. New York, NY: McGraw-Hill Companies, 2005

44.   Febbraio, M. A., P. Murton, S. Selig, S. Clark, D. Lambert, D. Angus, and M. Carey. Effect of CHO ingestion on exercise metabolism and performance in different ambient temperatures. Med Sci Sport Exercise. 28:1380-1387, 1996.

45.   Ferrauti, A., K. Neumann, K. Weber, and J. Keul. Urine catecholamine concentrations and psychophysical stress in elite tennis under practice and tournament conditions. J Sports Med Phys Fitness. 41:269-274, 2001.

46.   Ferrauti, A., B. M. Pluim, T. Busch, and K. Weber. Blood glucose responses and incidence of hypoglycemia in elite tennis under practice and tournament conditions. J Sci Med Sport. 6:28-39, 2003.

47.   Ferrauti, A., B. M. Pluim, and K. Weber. The effect of recovery duration on running speed and stroke quality during intermittent training drills in elite tennis players. Journal of Sports Sciences. 19:235-242, 2001.

48.   Ferrauti, A. and K. Weber. Metabolic responses and performance after caffeine ingestion. In: Science and Racket Sports II. A. Lees, I. Maynard, M. Hughes, and T. Reilly (Eds.) London, UK: E&FN Spon, 1998.

49.   Ferrauti, A., K. Weber, and H. K. Struder. Metabolic and ergogenic effects of carbohydrate and caffeine beverages in tennis. J Sports Med Phys Fitness. 37:258-266, 1997.

50.   Fink, W. J., D. L. Costill, and P. J. Van Handel. Leg muscle metabolism during exercise in the heat and cold. Eur J Appl Physiol. 34:183-190, 1975.

51.   Galloway, S. and R. Maughan. The effects of substrate and fluid provision on thermoregulatory and metabolic responses to prolonged exercise in a hot environment. J Sport Sci. 18:339-351, 2000.

52.   Grandjean, A. C. Diets of elite athletes: Has the discipline of sports nutrition made an impact. J Nutr. 127 (suppl):874S-877S, 1987.

53.   Greenhaff, P. L. The nutritional biochemistry of creatine. J Nutr Biochem. 8:610-618, 1995.

54.   Greenleaf, J. E. Problem: Thirst, drinking behavior, and involuntary dehydration. Med Sci Sports Exerc. 24:645-656, 1992.

55.   Hargreaves, M., P. Dillo, D. Angus, and M. Febbraio. Effect of fluid ingestion on muscle metabolism during prolonged exercise. J Appl Physiol. 80:363-366, 1996.

56.   Haymes, E. M. Physiological responses of female athletes to heat stress: A review. Physician Sportsmed. 12:45-55, 1984.

57.   Hegsted, M., S. A. Schuette, M. B. Zemel, and H. M. Linkswiler. Urinary calcium balance in young men as affected by level of protein and phosphorus intake. J Nutr. 111:553-562, 1981.

58.   Horowitz, J. P. and E. F. Coyle. Metabolic responses to preexercise meals containing various carbohydrates and fat. Am J Clin Nutr. 58:235-241, 1993.

59.   Hubbard, R. W., B. L. Sandick, W. T. Mathew, R. P. Francesconi, J. B. Sampson, M. J. Durkot, O. Maller, and D. B. Engell. Voluntary dehydration and alliesthesia for water. J Appl Physiol. 57:868-873, 1984.

60. Hughes, M. D. and S. Clark. Surface effect on elite tennis strategy. In: Science and Racket Sports. T. Reilly, M. Hughes, and A. Lees (Eds.) London: E & FN Spon., 1995, pp. 272-278.

61. Ivy, J. L., D. L. Costill, W. J. Fink, and R. W. Lower. Influence of caffeine and carbohydrate feedings on endurance performance. Med Sci Sports. 11:6-11, 1979.

63. Ivy, J. L., H. W. Goforth Jr, B. M. Damon, T. R. McCauley, E. C. Parsons, and T. B. Price. Early postexercise muscle glycogen recovery is enhanced with a carbohydrate-protein supplement. J Appl Physiol. 93:1337-1344, 2002.

64. Ivy, J. L., A. L. Katz, C. L. Cutler, W. M. Sherman, and E. F. Coyle. Muscle glycogen synthesis after exercise: effect of time of carbohydrate ingestion. J Appl Physiol. 64:1480-1485, 1988.

65. Ivy, J. L., M. C. Lee, J. T. Brozinick, and M. J. Reed. Muscle glycogen storage after different mounts of carbohydrate ingestion. Am J Physiol. 65:2018-2023, 1988.

66. Ivy, J. L. and R. Portman. Nutrient Timing: the future of sports nutrition. North Bergen, NJ: Basic Health Publications, Inc., 2004

67. Juhn, M. S. Popular sports supplements and ergogenic aids. Sport Med. 33:921-939, 2003.

68. Juhn, M. S. and M. A. Tarnopolsky. Oral creatine supplementation and athletic performance: a critical review. Clin J Sport Med. 8:286-297, 1998.

69. Jung, A. P., P. A. Bishop, A. Al-Nawwas, and R. B. Dale. Influence of hydration and electrolyte supplementation on incidence and time to onset of exercise-associated muscle cramps. Journal of Athletic Training. 40:71-75, 2005.

70. König, D., M. Huonker, A. Schmid, M. Halle, A. Berg, and J. Keul. Cardiovascular, metabolic, and hormonal parameters in professional tennis players. Medicine & Science in Sports & Exercise. 33:654-658, 2001.

71. Kovacs, M. Energy system-specific training for tennis. Strength and Conditioning Journal. 26:10-13, 2004.

72. Kovacs, M. S. Applied physiology of tennis performance. Br J Sports Med. 40:381-386, 2006.

73. Kovacs, M. S. A comparison of work/rest intervals in men's professional tennis. Medicine and Science in Tennis. 9:10-11, 2004.

74. Kovacs, M. S. Hydration and temperature in tennis - a practical review. J Sports Sci Med. 5:1-9, 2006.

75. Kovacs, M. S., E. Strecker, W. B. Chandler, J. W. Smith, and D. D. Pascoe. Time analysis of work/rest intervals in men's collegiate tennis. In National Strength and Conditioning Conference. Minneapolis, MN, p. e364, 2004.

76. Lemon, P. W. R. Effects of exercise on dietary protein requirements. International Journal of Sports Nutrition. 8:426-447, 1998.

77. Lemon, P. W. R. and J. P. Mullin. effect of initial muscle glycogen levels on protein catabolism during exercise. J Appl Physiol. 48:624-629, 1980.

78. MacLaren, D. P. M. Nutrition for racket sports. In: Science and racket sports II. A. Lees, I. Maynard, M. Hughes, and T. Reilly (Eds.) London: E & FN Spon, 1998, pp. 43-51.

79. Magal, M., M. J. Webster, L. E. Sistrunk, M. T. Whitehead, R. K. Evans, and J. C. Boyd. Comparison of glycerol and water hydration regimens on tennis-related performance. Med Sci Sports Exerc. 35:150-156, 2003.

80. Manore, M. and J. Thompson. Sport nutrition for health and performance. Champaign, IL: human Kinetics, 2000

81. Meredith, C. N., M. J. Zackin, W. R. Frontera, and W. J. Evans. Dietary protein requirements and body protein metabolism in endurance-trained men. J Appl Physiol. 66:2850-2856, 1989.

82. Montain, S. J., S. A. Smith, R. P. Mattot, G. P. Zientara, F. A. Jolesz, and M. N. Sawka. Hypohydration effects on skeletal muscle performance and metabolism: a 31P-MRS study. J Appl Physiol. 84:1889-1894, 1998.

83. Morgan, L. F., D. L. Jordan, D. A. Baeyens, and J. A. Franciosa. Heart rate responses during singles and doubles tennis competition. Physician Sports Medicine. 15:67-74, 1987.

84. Murray, R., G. L. Paul, J. G. Seifert, D. E. Eddy, and G. A. Halaby. The effects of glucose, fructose, and sucrose ingestion during exercise. Med Sci Sport Exercise. 21:275-282, 1989.

85. Neufer, P. D., A. J. Young, and M. N. Sawka. Gastric emptying during exercise: effects of heat stress and hypohydration. European Journal of Applied Physiology. 58:433-439, 1989.

86. O'Brien, C. P. Alcohol and sport: impact of social drinking on recreational and sport performance. Sport Med. 15:71-77, 1993.

87. O'Brien, C. P. and F. Lyons. Alcohol and the athlete. Sport Med. 29:295-300, 2000.

88. O'Donoghue, P. and B. Ingram. A notational analysis of elite tennis strategy. J Sports Sci. 19:107-115, 2001.

89. Phillips, S. M., S. A. Atkinson, M. A. Tarnopolsky, and J. D. MacDougall. Gender differences in leucine kinetics and nitrogen balance in endurance athletes. J Appl Physiol. 75:2134-2141, 1993.

90. Pivarnik, J. M. and R. A. Palmer. Water and electrolyte balance during rest and exercise. In: Nutrition in Exercise and Sport. I. Wolinsky and J. F. Hickson (Eds.) Boca Raton: CRC, 1994, pp. 245-262.

91. Ploug, T., H. Galbo, J. Vinten, M. Jorgensen, and E. A. Richter. Kinetics of glucose transport in rat muscle: effects of insulin and contractions. Am J Physiol Endocrinol Metab. 253:E12-E20, 1987.

92. Powers, S. K. and S. Dodd. Caffeine and endurance performance. Sports Medicine. 2:165-174, 1985.

93. Rawson, E. S., B. Gunn, and P. M. Clarkson. The effects of creatine supplementation on exercise-induced muscle damage. J Strength Cond Res. 15:178-184, 2001.

94. Reimers, K. and J. Ruud. Nutritional factors in health and performance. In: Essentials of Strength Training and Conditioning. T. R. Baechle and R. W. Earle (Eds.) Champaign, IL: Human Kinetics, 2000.

95. Richers, T. A. Time-motion analysis of the energy systems in elite and competitive singles tennis. Journal of Human Movement Studies. 28:73-86, 1995.

96. Saltin, B. and D. L. Costill. Fluid and electrolyte balance during prolonged exercise. In: Exercise, Nutrition and Metabolism. E. S. Horton and R. L. Terjung (Eds.) New York: MacMillan, 1988, pp. 150-158.

97. Sawka, M. N. Physiological consequences of hypohydration: exercise performance and thermoregulation. Med Sci Sports Exerc. 24:657-670, 1992.

98. Seliger, V., M. Ejem, M. Pauer, and V. Safarik. Energy metabolism in tennis. Int. Z. angew. Physiol. 31:333-340, 1973.

99. Shahidi, N. T. A review of the chemistry, biological action, and clinical application of anabolic-androgenic steroid use among adolescents. Sport Med. 29:397-405, 2001.

100. Sherman, W. M., G. Brodowicz, D. A. Wright, W. K. Allen, J. Simonsen, and A. Dernbach. Effects of 4h preexercise carbohydrate feedings on cycling performance. Med Sci Sport Exercise. 21:598-604, 1989.

101. Short, K. R., M. Sheffield-Moore, and D. L. Costill. Glycemic insulinemic responses to multiple preexercise carbohydrate feedings. Int J Sports Nutrition. 7:128-137, 1997.

102. Slater, G. J. and D. Jenkins. Beta-hydroxy-beta-methylbutyrate (HMB) supplementation and the promotion of muscle growth and strength. Sport Med. 30:105-116, 2000.

103. Smekal, G., S. P. Von Duvillard, C. N. Rihacek, R. Pokan, P. Hofman, R. Baron, H. Tschan, and N. Bachl. A physiological profile of tennis matchplay. Medicine and Science in Sports and Exercise. 33:999-1005, 2001.

104. Tarnopolsky, M. A., S. A. Atkinson, J. D. MacDougall, A. Chesley, S. M. Phillips, and H. Schwarcz. Evaluation of protein requirements for trained strength athletes. J Appl Physiol. 73:1986-1995, 1992.

105. Therminarias, A., P. Dansou, M. F. Chirpaz-Oddou, C. Gharib, and A. Quirion. Hormonal and metabolic changes during a strenuous tennis match: effect of ageing. Int J Sports Med. 12:10-16, 1991.

106. Thomas, D. E., J. R. Brotherhood, and J. C. Brand. Carbohydrate feeding before exercise. Int J Sports Med. 12:180-186, 1991.

107. Thomas, D. E., J. R. Brotherhood, and J. C. Brand. Carbohydrate feeding before exercise: effect of glycemic index. Int J Sports Med. 12:180-186, 1991.

108. van Loon, L. J., W. H. Saris, M. Kruijshoop, and A. J. Wagenmakers. Maximizing postexercise muscle glycogen synthesis: carbohydrate supplementation and the application of amino acid or protein hydrolysate mixtures. Am J Clin Nutr. 72:106-111, 2000.

109. Wagenmakers, A. J., F. Brouns, W. H. Saris, and D. Halliday. Oxidation rates of orally ingested carbohydrates during prolonged exercise in men. J Appl Physiol. 75:2774-2780, 1993.

110. Wilmore, J. H. and D. L. Costill. Physiology of Sport and Exercise. 3rd ed. Champaign, IL: Human Kinetics, 2004

111. Yoneyama, F., H. Watanabe, and Y. Oda. Game analysis of in-play-time and out-of-play-time in the Davis Cup. In 5th IOC World Congress on Sport Sciences. Sydney, Australia, 1999.

112. Zawadzki, K. M., B. B. I. Yaspelkis, and J. L. Ivy. Carbohydrate-protein complex increases the rate of muscle glycogen storage after exercise. J Appl Physiol. 72:1854-1859, 1992.

Chapter 5

Flexibility Training & Tennis Performance

- **Definitions & Background**
- **Timing**
- **Warm-up**
- **Static Stretching & Injury Prevention**
- **Post-Play**
- **Shoulder & Upper Body Demands of Tennis**
- **Dynamic Stabilizers**
- **Shoulder Performance**
- **Shoulder Injury**
- **Lower Back/Core/Hips**
- **Practical Application**

Introduction

The word flexibility is derived from the Latin flectere or flexibilis "to bend," and a practical sports definition is the range of motion (ROM) available in muscle, tendons, and connective tissue around a joint or group of joints. It is generally accepted that a minimum level of flexibility is required for competitive athletes, specifically tennis players, to improve performance and aid in the reduction in injuries. However, what this minimal level is and how best to obtain it, is still up for scientific as well as practical debate.

In the last 15 years hundreds of studies have investigated the how, what, when, and why of flexibility training and the impact on physical performance and injury prevention. Some very interesting and sometimes misinterpreted results have led to better, more effective methods of training athletes. This chapter on flexibility will provide many research studies to help coaches and trainers develop appropriate flexibility and stretching guidelines to help improve the performance of tennis athletes and reduce the likelihood of injury.

DEFINITIONS & BACKGROUND

Many terms have been used and misused to describe different stretching and flexibility movement patterns.

Stretching—the manual increase in ROM.

Active Stretching—the athlete is the person providing the force to stretch the muscle.

Figure 5.1: Active stretching.

Passive Stretching—a partner or machine is used to provide the force to stretch the muscle.

Figure 5.2: Passive stretching.

Static Stretching—
The muscle is stretched and held at a certain length with no movement. This can be accomplished either actively or passively.

Figure 5.3: Static stretching.

Ballistic Stretching—When the muscle is stretched via bouncing, bobbing, and/or rebounding and the muscle is not held at the end-point. There is continual movement. The theory behind ballistic stretching is that momentum is used to help the athlete stretch further than would be possible under a controlled movement.

Dynamic Stretching—Is when the muscle is stretched under a controlled movement pattern. It differs from ballistic as the muscle is elongated under a controlled lengthening and shortening process as opposed to quick jerky movements typical of ballistic stretching.

Figure 5.4: Dynamic stretching.

PNF (Proprioceptive Neuromuscular Facilitation)—PNF refers to any of several stretching techniques in which a muscle group is passively stretched, then contracts isometrically against resistance while in the stretched position, and then is passively stretched again through the resulting increased range of motion. PNF stretching usually employs the use of a partner to provide resistance against the isometric contraction and then later to passively take the joint through its increased range of motion. It may be performed, however, without a partner, although it is usually more effective with a partner's assistance.

AIS (Active Isolated Stretching)—AIS is theorized to work via two major mechanisms. The first is called reciprocal inhibition, which means that if you want to lift your arm, your nervous system has to shut off the muscles that bring your arm down. This means that AIS involves your nervous system in the stretch, making it easier for the muscles to elongate. The second principle is to avoid the stretch reflex. This is achieved by holding the stretch for 1.5 to 2 seconds, and no longer. Holding a stretch for longer than 2.5 to 3 seconds will cause the body to engage a protective reflex known as the stretch reflex. This stretch reflex will cause a muscle contraction in the muscle trying to be stretched. The stretch is repeated 8 to 10 times in a set. By repeating the stretch multiple times, blood flow is increased to the area ROM is gently increased.

TIMING

All forms of flexibility exercises may be appropriate for the tennis athlete, but important research has been undertaken to determine which forms should be applied during warm-up and which forms are more appropriate immediately post-exercise and during recovery sessions. The timing of different stretching exercises is also important from a performance enhancement perspective. Although stretching has been construed as a typically positive exercise for tennis players, certain types of stretching before playing tennis can actually reduce tennis-related performance.

WARM-UP

The warm-up for practice and competition is an important period not only for preparing the mind for the emotional and mental battle about to be undertaken, but it is also an important period to help prepare the body physically to improve performance and potentially reduce the likelihood of injury. Although most coaches and trainers want to help their athletes improve and perform better, the traditional warm-up, which included a period of static stretching, has actually been shown to reduce strength, speed, and power movements in subsequent exercise (2, 12, 13, 15, 20, 21, 34, 36, 40-42, 61, 62). Therefore, a large majority of well-meaning coaches and trainers are reducing their athletes' performance instead of the opposite intended positive effect. Although the reductions in performance have varied across different studies, the reduction in performance has ranged from 5%-30% (2, 12, 13, 15, 20, 21, 34, 40-42, 61, 62). How many athletes would you keep if you told them that after working with you they would be 30% worse?

The deficit in performance following static stretching has been shown to last approximately 60 minutes after the stretching routine (21) and may be due to changes in reflex sensitivity, muscle/tendon stiffness, and/or neuromuscular activation (13, 19, 21, 58). The actual causes and mechanisms for why there is a reduction in athletic performance are still being investigated.

A tennis-specific study looking at static stretching and the subsequent performance on service speed showed no difference in performance of serve speed (positive or negative) (33). The static stretching routine had no effect on either speed or accuracy (performance) of an explosive tennis serve (33). A suggested reason for why static stretching prior to the tennis serve did not reduce performance as observed in other studies was that the pre-activity stretching may not decrease performance in high-speed and/or accuracy-related movements (33). This theory has not typically been supported, as was seen in a recent study looking at sprint speed times (which involves high speed explosive movements) in highly trained athletes over short distance (<20 meters) (40). It was found that static stretching reduced performance by a significant increase in 20 meter sprint speed time (slower time) compared to no stretching (40). This result is of interest to tennis trainers, coaches, and athletes as it uses a population (well trained sprinters) and is measured over distances similar to that encountered during tennis play. The vast majority of studies support the notion that static stretching before activity reduces performance (2, 12, 13, 15, 20, 21, 34, 36, 40-42, 61, 62). From the available research it is clear that static stretching before exercise is not beneficial to performance and in most cases produces negative results on subsequent performance.

STATIC STRETCHING & INJURY PREVENTION

If static stretching does not improve performance if used during the warm-up, does it reduce the chance of injury? The widely-held belief that pre-activity static stretching may reduce injury is linked to the theory that a "tight" muscle-tendon unit is less flexible, meaning that it cannot be stretched to as great a degree (23, 27). This assumption has resulted in the long-held belief that stretching may prevent muscle and tendon related injuries (23). Current research, however, does not support this assumption, supporting instead the opposing view that static stretching before activity does not reduce the occurrence of sport induced injury (11, 23, 24, 26, 27, 38, 44, 45, 51-54, 60).

At the time of this edition, little tennis-specific research is available on this topic, but multiple studies have looked at sport movement patterns which are seen during tennis play. A study looking at the prevention of lower-limb injuries in 1,538 male army recruits found that pre-exercise static stretching had no effect on injury rates after a 12-week stretching protocol (45). In 2001, an extensive review of stretching studies on running injuries found that there was no strong evidence to suggest static stretching exercises are effective in preventing lower limb injuries (60). This finding has been supported in previous reviews looking at stretching and overall injury rates (24, 26, 36, 53, 60).

To provide a fair and balanced review of the scientific literature, it must be mentioned that a small number of studies have shown a tentative link between reduced injury rates and pre-activity stretching (5, 14, 17); however, the large majority of studies and review articles have found no link between pre-activity stretching and a reduction in injury rates (1, 23, 24, 26, 27, 38, 51-54, 60). The evidence is heavily slanted to support the conclusion that static stretching before tennis play will not improve performance, and typically even reduces performance. It will also have no clear benefit on reducing the likelihood of injury.

When designing programs, static stretching should not be included in the pre-activity warm-up. However, limited or poor muscle and joint range of motion can reduce performance and increase the risk of injury (55). Therefore, increasing ROM to an appropriate length is required and static stretching can be used to accomplish this—just not before exercise. Static stretching is a great tool that is easy for the athletes to perform and is the safest method of stretching. A good time to perform static stretching routines are immediately post-practice/competition and during the evening.

MORE POSITIVE WARM-UP ROUTINES

Other forms of warm-up, including general muscle warming exercise (i.e., jump rope or jogging) and/or dynamic (active) range of motion exercises, may be the most beneficial in improving physical performance (4, 7, 20, 50). Although more research is needed to make definitive conclusions about pre-tennis warm-ups, some positive results have shown significantly faster 20-meter sprints times following dynamic warm-ups compared to static stretching during the warm-up period (20). Although limited peer reviewed scientific studies are available (to date) on dynamic ROM training, it has been used by athletes and coaches for many years with great anecdotal results. The major benefit with this dynamic ROM training, if performed correctly, is that it can also correct muscle imbalances in both strength and flexibility and can actually help the athlete improve functional strength in the muscles and movements required to play tennis at a competitive level. Dynamic warm-up exercises can be used to help muscle imbalances, strength weaknesses, and balance-related problems. The benefits of these types of exercises can be far greater than just improving ROM.

Static   Dynamic

Figure 5.5: Comparison of a static Hamstring/Lower back stretch versus dynamic flexibility exercise: Left photo is a static stretch and hold. Middle and right photos show hamstring stretch by dynamic walking out on hands.

POST-PLAY

Post-tennis practice and competition is an important time to implement a structured flexibility program. Many competitive tennis players do not perform adequate post exercise stretching routines. The benefits of performing flexibility training post-exercise are numerous. Static stretching after training/competition and before bed has resulted in 50% fewer injuries according to a 1998 study in the *American Journal of Sports Medicine* (25). The muscle temperature is already warm from the training/competition period, allowing for the muscle and tendon units to be stretched comfortably and to a greater range than when the muscle is cooler. As a result of the increased muscle temperature, greater improvements in muscle and joint ROM can be made. Another possible benefit of performing post-exercise or evening stretching exercise may be the reduction in delayed onset of muscle soreness (DOMS) (26). DOMS is the pain or soreness athletes feel during the days following a hard exercise session. DOMS typically peaks between 48-72 hours post-exercise and the cause is multi-faceted. One of the major causes of DOMS is unaccustomed eccentric exercise. Movements requiring a lot of stop-start and change of direction are typical on-court causes of DOMS, whereas the eccentric (negative) portion of strength training movements are a major off-court cause. However, using stretching to reduce the symptoms of DOMS is still being debated, with both positive and negative studies concerning the effect of stretching on reducing DOMS (26, 56).

How long each static stretch should be held varies depending on the athlete, level of player, training and genetic flexibility capabilities. In a study to determine whether 15, 30, 45 or 60 seconds produces the greatest increase in flexibility, researchers had participants stretch five days a week over a six week period. The groups that stretched 30 or 60 seconds produced the most increases in ROM. The authors concluded that the 30 second hold of the static stretch produces the most time-effective results (3).

SHOULDER & UPPERBODY DEMANDS OF TENNIS

Tennis imposes large demands on the shoulder area in terms of ROM, loads, and velocities. The time of contact between the ball and racquet is very short, only between 0.003-0.006 seconds (47), and the racquet and ball must be in optimal orientation to execute the desired stroke. Epidemiologic data indicates that shoulder injuries are prevalent in many tennis players (32, 59) and the shoulder is the most often injured joint in competitive tennis (32, 46, 59).

The sport of tennis imposes adaptive strength changes in the dominant arm. Primarily, these changes occur by increasing the strength of the internal rotator muscle groups without subsequent strengthening of the external rotator muscle groups. Selective ROM patterns appear to occur from repetitive tennis play, that results in musculoskeletal adaptations that may predispose tennis players to injury if left undetected (18, 31).

The shoulder and elbow of the player's dominant arm is of interest because of the excessive ranges of motion, repetitive high speed movements, and resultant high loads and forces that these joints experience hundreds of times daily. Shoulder movements are the result of a complex interplay between structural bony anatomy and biomechanics and between static ligament and tendon restraints and dynamic muscle forces. Injury to one or more of these components can lead the entire shoulder region to be at an increased risk of overuse acute shoulder injuries.

The interaction between static and dynamic stabilizers and the favorable joint structure allow the shoulder the greatest ROM of any joint in the body. This large ROM makes maintaining stabilization in the shoulder joint a major concern to the tennis player. The difficulty in maintaining this stabilization is a result of the rapid velocity of the tennis strokes. Peak velocity of a tennis racquet in the serve has been reported at 62 to 72 miles per hour (30), which corresponds to ball velocities between 83 to 125 miles per hour (8). These velocities are likely to be higher in today's high level junior, collegiate and professional tennis players as this research was performed in early 1990s, before the advent of the new racquet and string technology.

Maintaining stability in the joints is achieved in two ways: static and dynamic stabilization. Static stability of the shoulder is achieved via the capsuloligamentous structures, including the glenoid labrum, glenohumeral joint capsule, glenohumeral ligaments, and intra-articular pressure providing static joint stability (39). Dynamic stability of the shoulder is achieved by the rotator cuff (supraspinatus, infraspinatus, teres minor, subscapularis), deltoid, bicep brachii, teres major, latissimus dorsi and pectoralis major (39).

The interaction between the static and dynamic components of functional stability is mediated by the sensorimotor system. This sensorimotor system includes the sensory, motor and central integration and processing components of the central nervous system (CNS) involved in maintaining functional joint stability (57). Sensory information (proprioception) travels through afferent pathways to the CNS where it is integrated with input from other levels of the nervous system, causing efferent motor responses (neuromuscular control) vital to coordinated movement patterns and functional stability of the shoulder region.

DYNAMIC STABILIZERS
ROTATOR CUFF MUSCLES

The rotator cuff is a group of muscles consisting of the supraspinatus, infraspinatus, teres minor, and subscapularis that acts as a steering mechanism for the humeral head. The humeral head is the top of the bone that connects into the shoulder joint. Three dimensional movements or rotations of the humeral head are the result of the rotator cuff muscles and static stabilizers. Rotator cuff activation results in humeral head rotation and depression in positions of abduction. Given this anatomical location, the rotator cuff is well situated to provide stability to a dynamic fulcrum during glenohumeral abduction—which is the typical position during most tennis strokes.

The rotator cuff functions to dynamically rotate the humerus, depress the humeral head, and provide joint stability both during tennis strokes and at rest between points. For the rotator cuff to be able to perform its functions, the scapula must provide a stable base at the origin of the cuff muscles. Therefore, the muscles that stabilize the scapula play a large role in dynamic internal and external rotation of the shoulder (9). The rotator cuff functions to provide both acceleration of the humerus during the tennis serve and forehand as well as eccentric deceleration during follow-through (48).

SHOULDER PERFORMANCE

The research on tennis shoulder function and improved performance has produced some information that can be helpful for coaches, clinicians, and players. The unilateral nature of tennis causes asymmetries between the dominant and nondominant shoulder. More torque is produced in internal rotation at 60 and 300 deg/sec in the dominant arm compared to the nondominant arm in tennis players (9). This is a result of the adaptation of training—specifically the service motion. However, tennis players have a decreased internal shoulder range of motion (ROM), that has been explained as an adaptation of the posterior shoulder musculature and capsular structures to the tennis stroke (10). The muscles of the posterior shoulder in the serving arm must decelerate the shoulder via eccentric muscle contractions during the follow-through. The faster the serve, the more strength is required to decelerate the arm. As the game of tennis has evolved with technological and training advancements, the speed of the serve has increased substantially in the last 15 years and will likely continue.

SHOULDER INJURY

The physical demands of tennis cause musculoskeletal adaptations, sometimes positive, like increases in strength, while sometimes negative — decreased joint ROM. These repeated demands to produce force by muscle shortening can cause a cycle of microtrauma to the tight muscle, followed by scar formation, followed by more microtrauma with continued use (22, 32). These adaptations become maladaptations, reducing joint range of motion, changing biomechanical patterns, and decreasing the efficiency of force production, increasing the chance of injury to the muscle (10). Shoulder injuries are typically due to inflammation and/or impingement of the rotator cuff muscles and tendon. Inflammation is usually caused by the repetitive microtrauma received from the stresses imposed by hitting groundstrokes and overhead serving, while impingement is the direct compression of soft tissue between the harder (bony) parts of the joint. Both are usually associated with instability of the glenohumeral joint (6).

Although there could be multiple causes for rotator cuff injuries in tennis players, a large number of injuries are a result of a player's poor technique and strength imbalances between external and internal shoulder rotators. At the time of maximum external rotation where the arm is ready to execute the contact of the ball, the shoulder's internal rotator muscles contract eccentrically, generating a high force. The resultant forward movement produces high accelerations that must be decelerated at the end of the range of movement. Shoulder muscles are susceptible to injury at these two extreme positions in the movement (37).

To further explore the internal/external shoulder ratio, a study looking at the consequence of repetitive elite level tennis was undertaken on the juniors of the United States Tennis Association's National Team and also on touring professionals. The results identified increases in dominant-arm internal rotation deficiencies relative to the nondominant arm as related to increases in both player age and number of years of competitive tennis (49). They found decreases in dominant arm internal ROM and recommended corrective training to enhance performance and prevent injury.

As junior competitive tennis players age, there seems to be an increase in shoulder problems. A study looking at this scenario found a significant increase in internal ROM between ages 14 and 15 that remain stable at age 16, but decreases slightly at age 17 (49). It was also found that the total dominant and nondominant ROM of the players across the four age groups (14-17) revealed a strong significant main effect of age for the nondominant ROM's but not for the dominant ROM's. This study showed that dominant arm internal ROM decreased compared to nondominant internal ROM. External rotation ROM did not significantly change in nationally ranked junior tennis players tested between the ages of 14 and 17 years. This would suggest that junior competitive tennis player's need to include an internal shoulder range of motion program to prevent the onset of flexibility imbalances that are common in players as they age.

Examination of force-velocity relationships (Figure 5.6) shows that muscle tension at the same velocity is always greater in eccentric work, and this difference becomes greater as a function of increases in contraction velocity (35). Eccentric muscular contractions play a role in normal functional activities, but in the tennis shoulder (rotator cuff), the infraspinatus and teres minor are of major importance during the follow through of both the groundstrokes, but more specifically the service motion. These two muscles undergo high decelerative eccentric muscle contractions to preserve healthy joint function (16). The role of the rotator cuff is essential in preventing overhead overuse injuries.

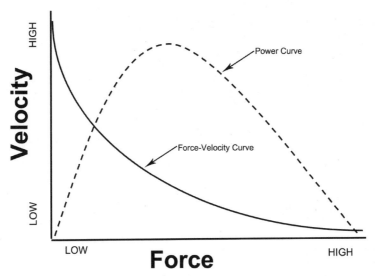

Figure 5.6: Force-velocity curve.

THE ELBOW & THE TENNIS SHOULDER

Many problems with the elbow can originate as a result of shoulder related issues. Lateral epicondylitis (tennis elbow) and medial epicondylitis in the elbow region can be caused by poor mechanics and muscle imbalance in the shoulder region (29).

The structures indicated in tennis elbow are primarily the tendon of the extensor carpi radialis brevis and secondarily the tendon of the extensor carpi radialis longus and extensor digitorum. While both an inflammation response and degeneration can occur in the tendon, the latter appears to be the more accepted mechanism causing "tennis elbow" (43). Shoulder inflexibility, which may alter a player's technical form, can also be a factor in elbow injuries (10).

Today's extreme grips and open stance groundstrokes to increase topspin place a great deal of stress on the shoulder, elbow, forearm, and wrist. These movements are mimicked by younger players who may not have adequate strength and/or coordination to perform them without risk of injury.

LOWER BACK/CORE/HIPS

The back, core, and hips are of vital importance in tennis. They act as a center of rotation and are vital to transmit forces generated in the lower body up through the upper body and into the tennis stroke. Weakness or limitations in this area can reduce force and power transfer. In a six year study of US competitive junior tennis players competing in the boys' national championships between 1986-1992, it was found that lower back injuries were the most common injury (28). Playing on hard court surfaces, which are highly prevalent in competitive junior and professional tennis, is likely to increase the occurrence of lower back injuries. This is due to the higher ground reaction forces on hardcourts as compared to softer surfaces such as grass or clay. For this reason, it is important that appropriate flexibility and strength training is prescribed for athletes, especially if the tennis player trains or competes on hard courts.

The three major lower back/core muscles involved during tennis play are (1) the posterior midline paraspinal musculature which are highly involved during the service motion (2), the quadratus lumborum or oblique muscles which are highly involved in the ground strokes and quick movements during the service motion, and (3) the rectus abdominus which is highly involved in the service motion and hitting overheads.

SUMMARY & PRACTICAL APPLICATION

High level tennis competition requires the fine interplay of performance and injury prevention. Continual tennis play, without an appropriate physical conditioning program, results in reduced range of motion in the glenohumeral joint, and this can cause impingement and other injury and pain symptoms. As junior tennis players age, their internal shoulder ROM is decreased. Total ROM (combined ROM of internal and external rotation) typically increases in the nondominant arm of tennis players, but decreases or does not improve in the dominant arm. As a result all tennis players should have a daily flexibility program for the shoulder area focused on improving ROM.

The greater an athlete's internal shoulder rotational strength the greater the speed of the serve and forehand. Weak external shoulder rotational strength, which is the major contributor to deceleration, will lead to greater injury risk. So developing internal rotational strength without external rotational strength will only increase the imbalance between the internal and external rotation strength, leading to a greater chance of injury. All competitive tennis players should be on a resistance program focused on developing external rotational strength to reduce the muscle asymmetry in shoulder rotation strength.

Tennis training alone does not develop the appropriate shoulder strength or satisfactory ROM. Therefore, supplemental resistive shoulder exercises must be added to any competitive tennis player's program. Exercises for tennis players to strengthen the shoulder in external rotation, including the posterior cuff muscles and the scapular stabilizers, will help maintain a favorable external/internal rotation strength balance and may prevent or lessen the severity of repetitive overload injuries. For a performance conditioning program, either preventative or rehabilitative, to address the needs of the individual tennis player, an appropriate evaluation of the athlete in terms of fitness and injury history must be obtained. From the initial screening a program designed to improve performance and prevent injury should be implemented.

REFERENCES

1.   Andersen, J. C. Stretching before and after exercise: Effect on muscle soreness and injury risk. Journal of Athletic Training. 40:218-220, 2005.

2.   Avela, J., H. Kyröläinen, and P. V. Komi. Altered reflex sensitivity after repeated and prolonged passive muscle stretching. J Appl Physiol. 86:1283-1291, 1999.

3.   Bandy, W. D. and J. M. Irion. The effect of time on static stretch on the flexibility of the hamstring muscles. Phys Ther. 74:845-850, 1994.

4.   Bergh, U. and B. Ekblom. Physical performance and peak aerobic power at different body temperatures. Journal of Applied Physiology. 46:885-889, 1979.

5.   Bixler, B. and R. L. Jones. High school football injuries: effects of a post-halftime warm-up and stretching routine. Fam Pract Res J. 12:131-139, 1992.

6.   Blevins, F. T. Rotator cuff pathology in athletes. Sports Medicine. 24:205-220, 1997.

7.   Blomstrand, E. V., B. Bergh, B. Essen-Gustavsson, and B. Ekblom. The influence of muscle temperature on muscle metabolism and during intense dynamic exercise. Acta Physiologica Scandinavica. 120:229-236, 1984.

8.   Chandler, T. J. Exercise training for tennis. Clinics in Sports Medicine. 14:33-46, 1995.

9.   Chandler, T. J., W. B. Kibler, E. C. Stracener, A. K. Ziegler, and B. Pace. Shoulder strength, power, and endurance in college tennis players. American Journal of Sports Medicine. 20:455-458, 1992.

10.   Chandler, T. J., W. B. Kibler, T. L. Uhl, B. Wooten, A. Kiser, and E. Stone. Flexibility comparisons of junior elite tennis players to other athletes. American Journal of Sports Medicine. 18:134-136, 1990.

11.   Comeau, M. J. Stretch or no stretch? Cons. Strength and conditioning Journal. 24:20-21, 2002.

12.   Cornwell, A., A. G. Nelson, G. D. Heise, and B. Sidaway. The acute effects of passive muscle stretching on vertical jump performance. J Hum Mov Stud. 40:307-324, 2001.

13.   Cornwell, A., A. G. Nelson, and B. Sidaway. Acute effects of stretching on the neuromechanical properties of the triceps surae muscle complex. Eur J Appl Physiol. 86:428-434, 2002.

14.   Cross, K. M. and T. W. Worrell. Effects of static stretching program on the incidence of lower extremity musculotendinous strains. Journal of Athletic Training. 34:11-14, 1999.

15.   DeVries, H. A. The "looseness" factor in speed and O2 consumption of an anaerobic 100-yard dash. Res Q. 34:305-313, 1963.

16.   Duda, M. Prevention and treatment of throwing arm injuries. Physician Sports Medicine. 13:181-185, 1985.

17.   Ekstrand, J. and J. Gillquist. The avoidability of soccer injuries. Int J Sport Med. 4:124-128, 1983.

18.   Ellenbecker, T. S., E. P. Roetert, P. A. Piorkowski, and D. A. Schultz. Glenohumeral joint internal and external rotation range of motion in elite junior tennis players. J. Orthop. Sports Phys. Ther. 24:336-341, 1997.

19.   Evetovich, T. K., N. J. Nauman, D. S. Conley, and J. B. Todd. Effect of static stretching of the bicep brachii on torque, electromyography, and mechanomyography during concentric isokinetic muscle action. Journal of Strength and Conditioning Research. 17:484-488, 2003.

20.   Fletcher, I. M. and B. Jones. The effect of different warm-up stretch protocols on 20-m sprint performance in trained rugby union players. J Strength Cond Res. 18:885-888, 2004.

21.   Fowles, J. R., D. G. Sale, and J. D. MacDougall. Reduced strength after passive stretch of the human plantar flexors. J Appl Physiol. 89:1179-1188, 2000.

22.   Garrett, W. E. Basic science of musculotendinous injuries. In: The lower extremity and spine in sports medicine. E. B. Hershman (Ed.) St.Louis: CV Mosby, 1986, pp. 42-58.

23.   Garrett, W. E. Muscle flexibility and function under stretch. In: Sports and exercise in midlife. S. L. Gordon, X. Gonzalez-Mestre, and W. E. Garrett (Eds.) Rosemont, IL: American Academy of Orthopaedic Surgeons, 1993, pp. 105-116.

24.   Gleim, G. W. and M. P. McHugh. Flexibility and its effects on sports injury and performance. Sports Medicine. 24:289-299, 1997.

25.   Hartig, D. E. and J. M. Henderson. Increasing hamstring flexibility decreases lower extremity overuse injuries in military basic trainees. Am J Sports Med. 27:173-176, 1999.

26.   Herbert, R. D. and M. Gabriel. Effects of stretching before and after exercising on muscle soreness and risk of injury: Systematic review. Br Med J. 325:468-470, 2002.

27.   Hunter, D. G. and J. Spriggs. Investigation into the relationship between the passive flexibility and active stiffness of the ankle plantar-flexor muscles. Clinical Biomechanics. 15:600-606, 2000.

28.   Hutchinson, M. R., R. F. Laprade, Q. M. Burnett, R. Moss, and J. Terpstra. Injury surveillance at the USTA boys' tennis championships: A 6-yr study. Med Sci Sport Exercise. 27:826-830, 1995.

29.   Kibler, W. B. Clinical biomechanics of the elbow in tennis: implications for evaluation and diagnosis. Med Sci Sports Exerc. 26:1203-1206, 1994.

30. Kibler, W. B. and T. J. Chandler. Racquet Sports. In: Sports Injuries, Mechanisms, Prevention, Treatment. F. H. Fu and D. A. Stone (Eds.) Baltimore, MD: Williams & Wilkins, 1994.

31. Kibler, W. B., T. J. Chandler, B. P. Livingston, and E. P. Roetert. Shoulder range of motion in elite tennis players. American Journal of Sports Medicine. 24:279-285, 1996.

32. Kibler, W. B., C. McQueen, and T. Uhl. Fitness evaluations and fitness findings in competitive junior tennis players. Clin Sports Medicine. 7:403-416, 1988.

33. Knudson, D. V., G. J. Noffal, R. E. Bahamonde, J. A. Bauer, and J. R. Blackwell. Stretching has no effect on tennis serve performance. J Strength Cond Res. 18:654-656, 2004.

34. Kokkonen, J., A. G. Nelson, and A. Cornwell. Acute muscle stretching inhibits maximal strength performance. Res Q Exerc Sport. 69:411-415, 1998.

35. Komi, P. V. and H. Rusko. Quantitative evaluation of mechanical and electrical changes during fatigue loading of eccentric and concentric work. Scand J Rehab Med. 3:21-26, 1974.

36. Kovacs, M. S. The argument against static stretching before sport and physical activity. Athletic Therapy Today. 11:24-25, 2006.

37. Lees, A. Science and the major racket sports: a review. Journal of Sports Sciences. 21:707-732, 2003.

38. Levine, U., J. Lombardo, J. McNeeley, and T. Anderson. An analysis of individual stretching programs of intercollegiate athletes. Physician Sports Medicine. 15:130-136, 1987.

39. Myers, J. B. and S. M. Lephart. The role of the sensorimotor system in the athletic shoulder. J Athl Train. 35:351-363, 2000.

40. Nelson, A. G., N. M. Driscoll, M. A. Young, and I. C. Schexnayder. Acute effects of passive muscle stretching on sprint performance. J Sport Sci. 23:449-454, 2005.

41. Nelson, A. G., I. K. Guillory, A. Cornwell, and J. Kokkonen. Inhibition of maximal voluntary isokinetic torque production following stretching is velocity specific. J Strength Cond Res. 15:241-246, 2001.

42. Nelson, A. G. and J. Kokkonen. Acute ballistic muscle stretching inhibits maximal strength performance. Res Q Exerc Sport. 72:415-419, 2001.

43. Pluim, B. M. Rackets, strings and balls in relation to tennis elbow. In: Tennis Science and Technology. S. Haake and A. O. Coe (Eds.) Oxford: Blackwell, 2000.

44. Pope, R. P., R. D. Herbert, and J. D. Kirwan. Effects of flexibility and stretching on injury risk in army recruits. Australian Journal of Physiotherapy. 44:165-172, 1998.

45. Pope, R. P., R. D. Herbert, J. D. Kirwan, and B. J. Graham. A randomized trial of pre exercise stretching for prevention of lower-limb injury. Med Sci Sports Exerc. 32:271-277, 2000.

46. Priest, J. D., V. Braden, and S. G. Gerberich. The elbow and tennis, part 1. Physician Sportsmed. 8:81-91, 1980.

47. Renstrom, P. A. F. H. (Ed.). Tennis. Malden, MA: Blackwell, 2002.

48. Rhu, K. N., F. W. McCormick, F. W. Jobe, D. R. Moynes, and D. J. Antonell. An electromyographic analysis of shoulder function in tennis players. American Journal of Sports Medicine. 16:481-485, 1988.

49. Roetert, E. P., T. S. Ellenbecker, and S. W. Brown. Shoulder internal and external rotation range of motion in nationally ranked junior tennis players: A longitudinal analysis. Journal of Strength and Conditioning Research. 14:140-143, 2000.

50. Shellock, F. G. and W. E. Prentice. Warming up and stretching for improved physical performance and prevention of sports related injuries. Sport Med. 2:267-268, 1985.

51. Shrier, I. Does stretching improve performance?: a systematic and critical review of the literature. Clin J Sport Med. 14:267-273, 2004.

52. Shrier, I. Flexibility versus stretching. Br J Sports Med. 35:364, 2001.

53. Shrier, I. Stretching before exercise does not reduce the risk of local muscle injury. A critical review of the clinical and basic science literature. Clin. J. Sports Med. 9:221-227, 1999.

54. Shrier, I. and K. Gossal. Myths and truths of stretching. The Physician and Sports Medicine. 28:57-63, 2000.

55. Thacker, S. B., J. Gilchrist, and D. F. Stroup. The impact of stretching on sports injury risk: a systematic review of the literature. Med Sci Sport Exercise. 36:371-378, 2004.

56. Wessel, J. and A. Wan. effect of stretching on the intensity of delayed-onset muscle soreness. Clinical Journal of Sport Medicine. 4:83-87, 1994.

57. Wilmore, J. H. and D. L. Costill. Physiology of Sport and Exercise. 3rd ed. Champaign, IL: Human Kinetics, 2004

58. Wilson, G. J., A. J. Murphy, and J. F. Pryor. Musculotendinous stiffness: its relationship to eccentric, isometric, and concentric performance. J Appl Physiol. 76:2714-2719, 1994.

59. Winge, S., U. Jorgensen, and A. L. Nielsen. Epidemiology of injuries in Danish championship tennis. Int J Sports Med. 10:368-371, 1989.

60. Yeung, E. W. and S. S. Yeung. A systematic review of interventions to prevent lower limb soft tissue running injuries. Br J Sports Med. 35:383-389, 2001.

61.   Young, W. and S. Elliott. Acute effects of static stretching, proprioceptive neuromuscular facilitation stretching, and maximum voluntary contractions on explosive force production and jumping performance. Res Q Exerc Sport. 72:273-279, 2001.

62.   Young, W. B. and D. G. Behm. Effects of running, static stretching and practice jumps on explosive force production and jumping performance. J Sports Med Phys Fitness. 43:21-27, 2003.

CHAPTER 6

FLEXIBILITY, WARM-UP, & COOL-DOWN PROGRAMS FOR TENNIS

- DYNAMIC FLEXIBILITY WARM-UP EXERCISES
- NATIONAL/JUNIOR DYNAMIC WARM-UP
- FLEXIBILITY EXERCISES
- TIME SUGGESTIONS FOR FLEXIBILITY IN DAILY PROGRAMS
- HURDLE MOBILITY EXERCISES

INTRODUCTION

This chapter provides information to help coaches plan and implement flexibility programs for their athletes. The goal of the following information is to provide an extensive list of exercises and methodologies so that coaches and trainers can apply appropriate exercises and program designs depending on the level and specific goals of the athletes with whom the coach works. Remember to take into account the science behind flexibility training as outlined in the previous chapter when designing and implementing your programs.

Dynamic Flexibility Warm-up Exercises

DYNAMIC FLEXIBILITY (LINEAR & LATERAL)

Toe Walk

Heel Walk

Heel to Toe Walk

Heel to Toe Skip

Knee to chest walk

Hamstring Hand Walk

Straight Leg Walk (Russian Walk)

Straight Leg Skip (Russian Skip)

1-leg Walking Opposite (1-leg RDL)

Walking Quad Stretch

Butt Kicks

Walking Lunge

Walking Rotational Lunge

Walking Knee to Armpits

Skipping Knee to Armpits

Backward Run

Hip Handwalk

Walking Lunge + Elbow into Knee Pushout

Exaggerated Low Lunge (Gambetta Lunge)

High Knees

Knee-up toe-up Walk

Knee-up toe-up Skip

Lateral (push & reach) walk

Lateral Lunge

Carioca

High Knee Carioca

Quick Rotation Carioca

1/2 Carioca + Ballet kick

Walking Plie Squat

Lateral Walking Knee to Armpits

Lateral Skipping Knee to Armpits

Lateral Straight Leg Bound

Table 6.1: Dynamic flexibility (linear & lateral).

JUNIOR DYNAMIC WARM-UP

Daily Dynamic Warm-Up for Junior Player	Distance	Coaching Cues
Heel and Toe Walks w/arm rotations	Doubles line to doubles line	Each step try and increase height
Knee-to-Chest Walk	Doubles line to doubles line	Pull knee to chest while standing on the toes of opposite leg opposite
Walking Quad Stretch	Doubles line to doubles line	Grab opposite toe with opposite hand and while pushing up on opposite toes and hold 2 seconds. Focus on upper body position
Hamstring Handwalk	Doubles line to doubles line	Start in extended push-up position and walk feet towards hands
Straight Leg Walk	Doubles line to doubles line	Focus on tall body position, with transverse abdominous activation, shoulder back and strong core position
Walking Lung w/arm hug	Doubles line to doubles line	Focus on stable foot plant with solid upper body position focusing on increasing stretch of the hip flexors
Hip Handwalk (crawl)	Doubles line to doubles line	Walk feet out and then follow with hands focusing on keeping body position low
Lateral Lunge	Doubles line to doubles line	Lateral lunge aiming to maintain straight line from patella through the same hip/glute
High Knee Skip	Doubles line to doubles line	Doubles line to doubles line Focus on height and explosion on each skip
60%, 70%, 80% 90% sprint	Doubles line to doubles line	Doubles line to doubles line Focus on increasing speed on each of the four repetition

Table 6.2: Junior dynamic warm-up.

NATIONAL/COLLEGIATE JUNIOR WARM-UP

Daily Dynamic Warm-Up for National/International Junior or Collegiate Player	Distance	Coaching Cues
Heel and Toe Walks w/arm rotations	Doubles line to doubles line and back	Each step try and increase height
Side Ankle Walk w/arm Circles	Doubles line to doubles line and back	Take each step on lateral edge of each step
Knee-to-Chest Walk	Doubles line to doubles line and back	Pull knee to chest while standing on the toes of opposite leg opposite
Walking Quad Stretch	Doubles line to doubles line and back	Grab opposite toe with opposite hand and while pushing up on opposite toes and hold 2 seconds. Focus on upper body position
Hamstring Handwalk	Doubles line to doubles line and back	Start in extended push-up position and walk feet towards hand
1-Leg Walking Opposite	Doubles line to doubles line and back	Focus on maintaining strong upper body posture while bending at the waist. Focus on keeping back straight
Straight Leg Walk	Doubles line to doubles line and back	Focus on tall body position, with TA activation, shoulder back and strong core position
Straight Leg Skip	Doubles line to doubles line and back	Same posture as straight leg walk at faster tempo focus on short ground contact time
Walking Lunge w/Arm Hug	Doubles line to doubles line and back	Focus on stable foot plant with solid upper body position focusing on increasing stretch of the hip flexors

Daily Dynamic Warm-Up for National/International Junior or Collegiate Player (Continued)	Distance	Coaching Cues
Backward Lunge w/rotation	Doubles line to doubles line and back	Step backward into a lunge position, maintaining solid upper body position. As dropping into lunge rotate at the waist increasing ROM on each step
Hip Handwalk (Crawl)	Doubles line to doubles line and back	Walk feet out and then follow with hands focusing on keeping body position low
Lateral Lunge	Doubles line to doubles line and back	Lateral lunge aiming to maintain straight line from patella through the same hip/glute
45° Lunge	Doubles line to doubles line and back	Similar to the regular lunge but performed on a 45°angle trying to mimic low volley position
High Knee Skip	Doubles line to doubles line and back	Focus on height and explosion on each skip
Alley Hops w/Hold	Doubles line to doubles line and back	Full extension with explosively controlled jump and hold landing for two seconds before next jump
60%, 70%, 80% 90% Sprint	Doubles line to doubles line and back	Focus on increasing speed on each of the four repetition

Table 6.3: National/collegiate junior warm-up.

FLEXIBILITY EXERCISES

CALF STRETCH

Major Muscles:
Gastrocnemius, Soleus
Level of Exercise: Beginner,
Intermediate, Advanced,
Professional
Coaching Cues: Lean forward with body while pushing backward with heel to increase stretch.

Figure 6.1: Calf stretch.

GLUTE STRETCH

Major Muscles: Gluteus Maximus,
Gluteus Medius, Gluteus Minimus
Level of Exercise: Beginner,
Intermediate, Advanced,
Professional
Coaching Cues: Relax head and neck and pull on opposite hamstring group to increase stretch.

Figure 6.2: Glute stretch.

STANDING HAMSTRING STRETCH

Major Muscles: Hamstring group (Bicep
Femoris, Semitendinosus, Semimembranosus),
Popliteus
Level of Exercise: Beginner, Intermediate,
Advanced, Professional
Coaching Cues: Slight knee bend and anterior pelvic tilt to increase the active stretch on the hamstring.

Figure 6.3: Standing hamstring stretch.

STANDING HIP FLEXOR STRETCH

Major Muscles: Psoas, Illiacus, Quadricep Group (Rectus Femoris, Vastus Intermedius, Vastus Medialis, Vastus Lateralis)

Level of Exercise: Beginner, Intermediate, Advanced, Professional

Coaching Cues: Muscle being stretched is positioned as the back leg and have the athlete focus on pushing the hip in the anterior direction.

Figure 6.4: Standing hip flexor stretch.

SINGLE LEG LOWER BODY STRETCH

Major Muscles: Quadratus Lumborum, Multifidus

Level of Exercise: Beginner, Intermediate, Advanced, Professional

Coaching Cues: Relax head and neck and pull bent leg towards chest.

Figure 6.5: Single leg lower body stretch.

TWO LEG LOWER BODY STRETCH

Major Muscles: Quadratus Lumborum, Multifidus

Level of Exercise: Beginner, Intermediate, Advanced, Professional

Coaching Cues: Relax head and neck and pull both legs towards chest.

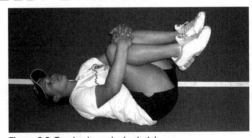

Figure 6.6: Two leg lower body stretch.

SCORPION STRETCH

Major Muscles: Psoas, Illiacus, Obliques, Tensor Fasciae Latae
Level of Exercise: Beginner, Intermediate, Advanced, Professional
Coaching Cues: Slowly attempt to touch toe to opposite elbow.

Figure 6.7: Scorpion stretch.

SHOULDER STRETCH

Major Muscles: Posterior Deltoid, Supraspinatus, Infraspinatus, Teres Minor, Latissimus Dorsi
Level of Exercise: Beginner, Intermediate, Advanced, Professional
Coaching Cues: Relax head and neck and slowly stretch arm across the body.

Figure 6.8: Shoulder stretch.

POSTERIOR SHOULDER STRETCH

Major Muscles: Posterior and Medial Deltoid, Infraspinatus, Teres Minor
Level of Exercise: Advanced, Professional
Coaching Cues: Relax head and neck and gently place top of hand on lower back. With other hand gently apply an active stretch behind the elbow gently increasing the stretch.

Figure 6.9: Posterior shoulder stretch.

SIT AND REACH

Major Muscles: Hamstring group
(Bicep Femoris, Semitendinosus,
Semimembranosus), Quadratus
Lumborum, Multifidus, Popliteus
Level of Exercise: Beginner,
Intermediate, Advanced, Professional
Coaching Cues: Slowly reach arms
toward the toes to the point of stretch.

Figure 6.10: Sit and reach.

GROIN STRETCH

Major Muscles: Adductor Muscles (Longus and
Brevis), Pectineus and Gracilis
Level of Exercise: Beginner, Intermediate,
Advanced, Professional
Coaching Cues: While seated place heels
together and slowly pull heels towards the body.
For an advanced stretch slowly push elbows
down gently on inside of legs.

Figure 6.11: Groin stretch.

PEC STRETCH

Major Muscles: Pectoralis Major, Pectoralis Minor,
Subclavius
Level of Exercise: Beginner, Intermediate, Advanced,
Professional
Coaching Cues: Place arm against fence (or wall) and
slowly turn away from fence while maintaining origi-
nal arm position.

Figure 6.12: Pec stretch.

TRICEP STRETCH

Major Muscles: Tricep Brachii and Anconeus

Level of Exercise: Beginner, Intermediate, Advanced, Professional

Coaching Cues: Reach hand behind the head by bending elbow attempting to reach down the center of the back.

Figure 6.13: Tricep stretch.

1-LEG WALKING OPPOSITE

Major Muscles: Hamstring group (Bicep Femoris, Semitendinosus, Semimembranosus), Quadratus Lumborum, Multifidus, Gluteals, Popliteus

Level of Exercise: Intermediate, Advanced, Professional

Figure 6.14: 1-Leg walking opposite.

Coaching Cues: As the athlete lowers their body they need to keep lower back and head straight. The body should look like a "T".

WALKING QUAD STRETCH

Major Muscles: Quadricep Group (Rectus Femoris, Vastus Medialis, Vastus Lateralis, Vastus Intermedius)

Level of Exercise: Intermediate, Advanced, Professional

Coaching Cues: The athlete needs to focus on maintain good upperbody position and pushing up on the opposite toe and holding at the top for two seconds.

Figure 6.15: Walking quad stretch.

A-Skip

Although A-skip is not considered a basic flexibility exercise, the benefit of using the A-skip during the warm-up is to help improve an athlete's muscle firing pattern and motor-coordination.

Major Muscles: Majority of lower body muscles special emphasis on hip flexors

Level of Exercise: Intermediate, Advanced, Professional

Coaching Cues: Focus on maintaining tall body position and solid ground contact.

Figure 6.16: A-skip.

Gambetta Lunge

Major Muscles: Majority of lower body muscles

Level of Exercise: Intermediate, Advanced, Professional

Coaching Cues: Extend legs out as far as comfortable on a 45°-60° angle in front of the body. The hands are walked out following the feet while the athlete focuses on keeping his/her glutes low to the ground.

Figure 6.17: Gambetta lunge.

HAMSTRING MARCH

Major Muscles:
Hamstring group (Bicep Femoris, Semitendinosus, Semimembranosus), Popliteus

Level of Exercise:
Intermediate, Advanced, Professional

Coaching Cues: Extend one leg out straight as high as possible under control while keeping head, shoulders and back as straight as possible.

Figure 6.18: Hamstring march.

HEEL WALK

Major Muscles: Anterior Tibialis, Peroneus Longus,

Level of Exercise: Intermediate, Advanced, Professional

Coaching Cues: Extend walk on the heels while pointing toes to the sky.

Figure 6.19: Heel walk.

TOE WALK

Major Muscles: Gastrocnemius, Soleus, Tibialis Posterior, Plantaris

Level of Exercise: Beginner, Intermediate, Advanced, Professional

Coaching Cues: Slowly walk on your toes and holding the top position for 1-2 seconds.

Figure 6.20: Toe walk.

HAMSTRING HANDWALK ("INCHWORM")

Major Muscles:
Hamstring group (Bicep
Femoris,
Semitendinosus,
Semimembranosus),
Gastrocnemius, Soleus
Level of Exercise:
Advanced, Professional
Coaching Cues: Start

Figure 6.21: Hamstring handwalk ("inchworm").

with hands out in front of the body and slowly walk the feet up to the hands while attempting to keep legs as straight as possible (without locking the knees).

KNEE-TO-CHEST WALK

Major Muscles: Quadratus
Lumborum, Multifidus
Level of Exercise: Intermediate,
Advanced, Professional
Coaching Cues: After taking a step
forward slowly pull knee up to chest
and hold position between 1-2 sec-
onds.

Figure 6.22: Knee-to-chest walk.

LATERAL LUNGE

Major Muscles: Adductor Longus, Adductor Brevis,
Pectineus, Adductor Magnus, Gracilis
Level of Exercise: Intermediate, Advanced,
Professional
Coaching Cues: After taking a large lateral step
slowly push hip out over the outstretched leg while
maintain a solid upper body position.

Figure 6.23: Lateral lunge.

WALKING LUNGE

Major Muscles: Majority of lower body muscles

Level of Exercise: Intermediate, Advanced, Professional

Coaching Cues: Perform a standard lunge focused on maintaining solid core position and increasing hip flexor ROM on each step.

Figure 6.24: Walking lunge.

LUNGE WITH ROTATION

Major Muscles: Majority of lower body muscles

Level of Exercise: Advanced, Professional

Coaching Cues: Perform a standard lunge focused on maintaining solid core position and increasing hip flexor ROM on each step. While lowering into strong lunge position slowly rotate at the waist to increase rotational ROM.

Figure 6.25: Lunge with rotation.

TIME SUGGESTIONS FOR FLEXIBILITY IN DAILY PROGRAMS

	COMPETITIVE USTA LEAGUE PLAYER (2.5-5.0)	JUNIOR PLAYER	NATIONAL/ INTERNATIONAL JUNIOR OR COLLEGIATE PLAYER	PROFESSIONAL LEVEL
DYNAMIC WARM-UP	6-10min	10min	15min	25min
TRAINING	60-120min	120min	190min	190min
POST TRAINING FLEXIBILITY	5-15min	15min	25min	45min
NIGHT FLEXIBILITY	5-15min	20min	45min	45min

Table 6.4: Daily flexibility guidelines.

HURDLE MOBILITY EXERCISES

Adding variety to an athlete's flexibility program is important for many reasons; but when it comes to flexibility training most athletes find this the most tedious and monotonous portion of training for competitive tennis. Adding hurdle training to a program is a great training tool to improve ROM while providing variety to the program. Hurdle training involves the athlete walking or skipping over hurdles in a controlled manner which improves hip flexor ROM. The importance of hip flexor ROM can not be underestimated due the fact that tennis movements require athletes to be in a low crouched position which actually causes the muscles that flex the hip to shorten, which reduces ROM. Therefore, specific emphasis on improving hip flexor ROM is important and hurdle drills are a great method to accomplish this. The following hurdle mobility table provides a list of different hurdle mobility exercises that would be appropriate for tennis athletes. These exercises can be performed either before or after training and on recovery days (Table 6.5).

Hurdle Mobility	Height	Distance		Reps
Hurdles Walkover (continuous lead leg)	30inch	rail-to-rail	MIN 6 HURDLES	x2
Hurdles Walkover (alternate lead leg)	30inch	rail-to-rail		x2
Hurdle Walkover Skip (continuous lead leg)	30inch	spacing 1 foot		x2
Hurdle Walkover Skip (alternate lead leg)	30inch	spacing 1 foot		x2
Knee-to Armpit Walk (hurdles)	33inch	spacing 1 foot		x2
Knee-to-Armpit Skip (hurdles)	33inch	spacing 1 foot		x2
On Fence				
Knee-to-Chest & out the back	x10			x1
Dog and out the back	x10			x1

Table 6.5: Hurdle mobility exercises.

Chapter 7

Resistance Training & Tennis Performance

- Adaptations to Resistance Training
- Muscle Fiber Types
- Types of Muscular Contractions
- Needs Analysis
- Training Variables
- Motions of Resistance Exercises
- Methods of Training
- Daily Program Design
- Training Goals

Introduction

In recent years resistance training for tennis players has become more common. In the past resistance training may have been avoided by tennis players and coaches for a variety of reasons, including a fear of getting too muscular, decreasing flexibility, and limited time between on-court practice or tournaments. If a resistance training program is planned properly, these problems can be avoided. Significant increases in muscle mass will not be a goal of resistance training programs specifically designed for tennis. When resistance training is performed properly through a sport-specific range of motion combined with a proper flexibility program, there will be no decrease in flexibility, and if performed correctly, should actually increase functional flexibility. Resistance training for elite players can be diffi-cult to plan because they can play in tournaments nearly every week. The concept of periodization is therefore an important component for integrating resistance training into an overall program for maximizing performance and allowing recovery for major tournaments. Periodization will be discussed further in Chapter 15.

With the increased power and speed in today's game, resistance training is a vital component to compete at an elite level. Today, tennis players are bigger, stronger, more powerful, and faster than before, and they are hitting the ball hard-er than ever before. There are two major functions of a resistance training program for tennis players. The first function is to improve maximal force and power outputs. Because of the pace of today's game, maximal power is critical to success. The sec-ond function of resistance training is to decrease the risk of injuries. There is no real off-season in tennis, and many players will play too many tournaments with too lit-tle rest and experience injuries as a result. A well-planned resistance training pro-gram designed to decrease injury risk is also critical to the success of a tennis player.

ADAPTATIONS TO RESISTANCE TRAINING

In response to a resistance training program, various adaptations to the body will occur. Resistance training enhances both absolute and relative muscular strength (6). Absolute muscular strength refers to the maximal strength an individual can develop regardless of their body weight. Relative muscular strength is dependent on a person's body weight. It is calculated by dividing a person's absolute muscular strength by his/her body weight. Males generally have a greater absolute muscular strength than females due to their increased muscle mass. When relative muscular strength is considered, there is little difference between males and females (2).

Increased muscular strength is one of the main benefits of resistance training. These increases are generally due to both neural factors and muscle hypertrophy. The greatest strength increases are seen in the early weeks of training and are pri-marily due to neural factors (24). These can be divided into intermuscular and intra-muscular adaptations. Intramuscular adaptations include the increasing of both the number of motor units that can be recruited at once and the activation rate of those motor units (6). These two factors combine to produce greater force than can be accomplished without resistance training.

Intermuscular adaptations refer to the improved coordination of muscle firing patterns. As exercise technique improves, muscles will work more efficiently and less energy is required to perform the exercise and the resistance can be increased (13). Increased force production and coordination are the main reasons for the initial strength increases seen in previously untrained individuals. These neural factors are what contribute to an athlete's increase in strength over the first 5-8 weeks of training without having any noticeable changes in muscle size.

Another factor related to increased muscular strength as a result of resistance training is hypertrophy (23, 31). Hypertrophy is the enlargement of the diameter of the individual muscle fiber. Muscle hypertrophy does not become apparent until weeks 5-8 of training (27). Hypertrophy is caused by progressive overload, proper muscle recruitment, and adequate energy intake (9). Another theory for the increased cross-sectional area seen in muscle fibers with resistance training is hyperplasia. Hyperplasia refers to the splitting of the muscle into additional muscle fibers. Scientific evidence suggests this likely does not occur in humans (22).

The force a muscle is capable of producing is strongly related to its cross-sectional area. Muscles with a larger cross-sectional area are able to produce greater force. When muscles are properly loaded they adapt to this stress by synthesizing more protein, specifically actin and myosin. Actin and myosin are referred to as "contractile proteins" as they are the structures within muscle that attach and develop tension during muscle contraction. This increase in contractile proteins causes the increases in cross-sectional area in muscle tissue. Greatest gains in hypertrophy are seen most with intensities between 60 and 80 percent of the maximum amount of weight which can be lifted one time (1RM) and a higher volume of training (19).

Another adaptation to resistance training is increased bone density (26). Increased bone density will reduce the risk of injury due to a fracture. Adaptation occurs by increasing mineralization in the area of stress. Multi-joint weight bearing exercises such as squats and lunges are most beneficial in improving bone mineral density (26).

Other adaptations to resistance training are dependent on the type of training which takes place. High-intensity resistance training can promote significant increases in muscle glycogen, creatine phosphate, ATP (energy), and glycolytic enzymes stores (16). These changes will increase the ability of the muscle to repeatedly produce power over a period of time. Low-intensity, high-volume training may improve a muscle's endurance capacity (16). Muscular endurance is important for tennis players to prepare them for long matches.

MUSCLE FIBER TYPES

Three main fiber types have been identified and studied in humans. These fibers are Type I, Type IIa, and Type IIx. Type I fibers, also referred to as slow oxidative, have a slow contraction time and are highly resistant to fatigue. They are used predominantly in low intensity, long duration activities which require oxidative pathways to produce ATP. They produce low amounts of force and velocity and are most often found in muscles which provide posture and support. Due to their aerobic nature these fibers have many mitochondria and are rich in myoglobin, which produces their red color.

Type IIa fibers, or fast-oxidative, are intermediate fibers with moderate resistance to fatigue and contraction time. Type IIx fibers, or fast-glycolytic fibers, contract very quickly and fatigue very rapidly. They are very powerful and are used predominantly in activities which require a short burst of energy over a very short period of time. Fast-twitch muscle fibers typically increase in cross-sectional area more than slow-twitch fibers as a result of resistance training (1, 23). As the speed of the game has increased, power output from the fast twitch muscle fibers has become an important factor in improving performance. In addition to increasing the size of the fast twitch muscle fibers, nervous system adaptations occur with ballistic training that facilitate the recruitment of fast twitch muscle fibers.

TYPES OF MUSCULAR CONTRACTIONS

There are various types of contractions which are seen in human movement. Isotonic contractions involve a constant resistance throughout the movement. Isotonic resistance training is dynamic requiring active joint movement as well as shortening and lengthening of the muscle fibers. During isotonic resistance training two types of muscle actions occur—concentric and eccentric. Concentric actions occur when muscle fibers contract and shorten. An example of a concentric muscle action is the "upward" portion of a biceps curl. When the weight is raised upward, the biceps are shortening and a concentric action occurs. Eccentric actions occur when the muscle fibers lengthen. An example of an eccentric action can be seen in the downward motion of a biceps curl. As the weight is lowered the muscles lengthen and an eccentric action occurs. Isotonic resistance training is used most often by tennis players as it is more specific to the sport compared to other types of training. Except for gripping the tennis racquet, muscle actions in tennis involve dynamic movement with a fixed resistance.

Isometric strength training, on the other hand, involves maximal force exerted against an immovable object. There is no joint movement and the muscle fibers do not shorten or lengthen. Trying to move an object which is too heavy to move is an example of an isometric contraction. Isometric strength training is used very rarely by tennis players as it is not specific to the sport.

Isokinetic training generally involves specialized equipment that varies the resistance. Isokinetic training requires a constant velocity of movement with a variable resistance. Through a range of motion, isokinetic equipment attempts to keep the speed of joint movement constant by varying the resistance. This form of training requires specialized equipment and is not practical for most tennis players. Additionally, an isokinetic muscle action is not specific to the sport.

NEEDS ANALYSIS

The first step in designing a resistance training program is to perform a needs analysis of the activity and the athlete. In order to maximize performance the program must be specific to both the sport and the athlete. The major muscle groups used, the types of movements, the speed of movements, and the common sites of injury should all be taken into consideration. The athlete's physical strengths, weaknesses, and injury history should all be considered in a needs analysis (30).

An analysis of the muscle groups used in tennis should consider all the strokes and movement patterns.

MUSCLE GROUPS USED

FOREHAND

Push-off: Soleus, Gastrocnemius, Quadriceps, Gluteals
Trunk Rotation: Obliques, Spinal Erectors
Forehand Swing: Anterior Deltoid, Pectorals, Shoulder Internal Rotators, Biceps, Serratus Anterior

Figure 7.1: Forehand muscles in action.

BACKHAND

Push-off: Soleus, Gastrocnemius, Quadriceps, Gluteals
Trunk Rotation: Obliques, Spinal Erectors
Backhand Swing: Rhomboids, Middle Trapezius, Posterior Deltoid, Middle Deltoid, Shoulder External Rotators, Triceps, Serratus Anterior
Nondominant Arm (2-handed Backhand Only): Pectorals, Anterior Deltoid, Shoulder Internal Rotators (29).

Figure 7.2: Backhand muscles in action.

MOVEMENTS USED

Tennis requires many lunging movements and a large amount of torso rotation. It is important to note that tennis is a ground-based sport. Force is generated against the ground by the lower body. This force is transferred to the trunk and eventually the upper extremity. Increasing the force with which the player can "push" into the ground will increase the force of a hit tennis ball.

MOVEMENT SPEEDS

As the resistance a muscle has to overcome increases, the velocity of movement decreases (Figure 7.3). Likewise, as resistance decreases the velocity of movement will increase. Tennis is played at the high-velocity, low-resistance end of this continuum. Hitting a serve, running to hit a wide forehand, and lunging for a volley all require explosive, high-velocity movements with a relatively light resistance. Therefore a majority of the training should take place on this end of the force/velocity continuum.

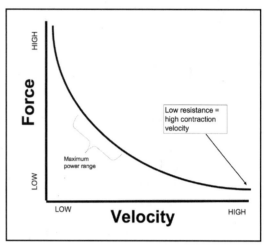

Figure 7.3: Force-velocity curve. Tennis is played at high velocity and low resistance.

TRAINING VARIABLES
VOLUME

The total volume of training can be determined by multiplying the number of sets by the number of reps by the weight lifted.

Total volume = sets x reps x weight

A repetition is a single execution of the exercise from beginning to end. A set is a group of repetitions which are followed by a rest period. Total volume of a training program has a strong influence on many of the effects of a resistance training program. The number of repetitions should be determined by the goals of the training session. Total volume of training is heavily dependent on the number of sets performed. Should a player do single or multiple sets? In terms of improving athletic performance, training with multiple sets will likely provide superior results to training with one set (28, 32). Single sets may be appropriate for beginners or for advanced athletes during a maintenance phase. Programs which use a high volume typically have a greater influence on body composition and endurance.

INTENSITY

Intensity in a resistance training program refers to the amount of weight that is lifted. There is an inverse relationship between intensity and the number of repetitions performed. A common measure of intensity is the percentage of the individual's one repetition maximum (1RM). A 1RM is simply the maximum amount of weight an athlete can lift one time. A 1RM load will require maximal recruitment of available motor units. As resistance decreases below the 1RM load, fewer motor units are required to perform the exercise. For maximum strength development higher percentages of 1RM should be used, and for development of muscular endurance lower percentages of 1RM should be used.

FREQUENCY

Frequency refers to how often resistance training sessions occur. The frequency a person should train depends on the goals of training as well as the experience of the athlete. Training sessions must occur frequently enough to produce physiological changes, but provide enough rest to allow complete recovery and decrease the risk of overtraining. Sessions that use multiple-joint exercises, heavy loads, and large muscle groups may require greater recovery time prior to the next session. If proper recovery time between training sessions is not given, tissue repair and energy repletion will not take place. A general recommendation is to train similar muscle groups two to three times per week. Tournament schedules have a large impact on the frequency of training. During a tournament the frequency of training may need to be reduced or completely eliminated, particularly if the tournament is perceived as important.

CHOICE OF EXERCISE

Prior to choosing exercises a needs analysis on the sport must be performed. According to the principle of specificity, the more similar a resistance training exercise is to tennis performance the greater the probability of transfer to the court (5, 32). There are numerous exercises that can be used to target similar muscle groups or movement patterns. These exercises may be interchangeable in a resistance training program in order to get variety and prevent boredom. The exercises still must meet the specific goals of the exercise session. When choosing an exercise, the specificity of the exercise to the sport, the goal of the training session, and the ability of the participant, should all be considered.

Options for varying exercises include changing the mode, the angle of the exercise, and utilizing both single-limb and double-limb movements. When choosing exercises the relationship between agonists and antagonists should be taken into consideration. The agonists are the prime movers of a movement and the antagonists are the opposing muscle group. Resistance training and sports-specific movements will cause significant adaptations to increase performance in the agonist muscle groups. However, as the agonist muscles become stronger, the antagonist muscles may become increasingly susceptible to injury. Therefore, both agonist and antagonist muscle groups should be trained to prevent muscle imbalances, and to minimize the risk of injury. This concept is particularly important for tennis players because of the predominant use of the muscles in the chest and front of the shoulder. Training the antagonist muscles in the upper back and shoulder is critical to avoid injury.

TEMPO

Tempo refers to the speed the weight is moved both in the concentric and eccentric portions of the lift. The tempo of an exercise will vary based on the specific goals of the activity. Tempo can be regulated by measuring the time under the load. The time under load can be divided into four parts—the concentric and eccentric actions and the pauses between these contractions. When prescribing training programs the desired time under load is generally given in the order of eccentric action, pause, concentric action, pause. An example of a time under load prescription is 3, 1, 2, 1. This would require the lifter to perform the eccentric action over a count of 3 seconds, pause one second, then perform the concentric action over a period of two seconds, then pause for another second, and repeat the cycle for the prescribed number of reps. Intentionally slow movement velocities have been shown to be less effective at increasing work, power output, volume (21, 25), and increasing the rate of strength gains (14) when compared to moderate and fast movement speeds. Resistance training for the purpose of developing pure strength will usually have a moderate tempo since it is not dependent on time. Training for power, which by definition is measured per unit of time, will use a faster tempo to mimic more sports-specific activities. Because tennis requires explosive powerful movements, much of the training will be performed at a faster tempo.

REST

Rest is the amount of time allowed between sets. The amount of rest between sets is dependent on the goals of that session. In strength and power training, the rest period is longer so that ATP can be replenished. Following exhaustive anaerobic exercise it takes approximately three minutes for the ATP stores in the muscle to be 100% replenished (13). It is generally recommended that for maximal strength or power training, there be two to three minutes of rest between sets. If proper rest is not given, the muscles may not be sufficiently recovered and the exercise will not be as productive. When muscular endurance is the goal of the training session, less rest is required. Rest periods of a minute or less are often prescribed for this type of training.

EXERCISE ORDER

Exercise order is the sequence of exercises performed in a training session. The sequence can have a significant affect on fatigue and performance during a training session (12). It is generally recommended that multi-joint exercises which use large muscle groups be performed early in the training session when fatigue is minimal (18). For example, squats should be performed prior to leg curls. It is also recommended that exercises which require explosive power be performed prior to exercises which are aimed at muscular hypertrophy (20). Olympic lifts and plyometric exercises which require power should always be performed early in the training session.

MOTIONS OF RESISTANCE EXERCISES

Resistance training exercises can be classified by the movement pattern that occurs during the exercise. The major movement patterns are the press, pull, squat, lunge, flexion/extension, adduction/abduction, and rotation. Examples of each motion are given in Table 7.1. Developing a resistance training program requires the understanding of these motion patterns so that the program is effective and balanced. In order to provide variation these motion patterns may be combined.

Press motion: Bench press, Overhead press
Pull motion: Upright row, Pull-down
Squat motion: Squats, Dead lifts
Lunge motion: Lunge, Step-up
Flexion/extension motion: Crunch, Back hyperextensions
Abduction/adduction: Hip abduction, Hip adduction
Rotation: Shoulder rotation, Rotary crunches

Table 7.1: Motions of resistance training exercises

METHODS OF TRAINING

There are various methods of training that can be used in a training program. This section will discuss many of these methods and their application to tennis.

SINGLE-JOINT VS. MULTIPLE-JOINT

During a single-joint exercise only one joint undergoes movement, while a multi-joint exercise uses multiple muscle groups and joints at the same time. A biceps curl is an example of a single-joint exercise. A lunge is an example of a multi-joint exercise because it requires movement at the hip, knee, and ankle. Multi-joint exercises require more complex neural activation and coordination, and they are also more effective at increasing muscular strength and power (17, 18). Since tennis performance requires multi-joint movements, multi-joint exercises are more specific to tennis. Single-joint exercises also have less risk of injury because of the reduced level of skill and technique required to perform the lift (18). It is doubtful that single-joint exercises will have as much impact upon performance, although they can be used if there is a specific muscular imbalance or to help prevent injury to specific muscle groups.

MULTI-PLANAR EXERCISES

Exercises can be categorized by which of three primary planes of motion they occur in. These three primary planes are the transverse, sagittal, and frontal planes. Exercises which occur in more than one plane are referred to as multi-planar exercises. Multiplanar exercises closely resemble the movements seen in tennis because the movements seldom occur in one of the primary planes. An example of a multiplanar movement is a cable lift where an athlete lifts a weight from low to high moving it across their body at the same time.

FREE WEIGHTS

Free weight exercises use a free-standing load and require the athlete to stabilize the weight while moving it through a movement pattern. Additional

Figure 7.4: Free weights.

muscle activation is required to stabilize the weight. The resistance of the free weight is constant, so the load that is lifted is limited by the weakest point in the range of motion. Because of the freedom of movement allowed by free weights, they can be used to mimic tennis specific movements. Dumbbells and barbells are both examples of free weights. An example of a tennis specific movement with free weights is a dumbbell lunge.

MACHINES

Machines provide a resistance training alternative to free weights. Many machines do not require that the weight be stabilized which tends to decrease the requirement for synergistic support and stabilization. Machines may be more appropriate for beginners who may be intimidated by free weights or unable to balance the load. Machines are also able

Figure 7.5: Machines.

to isolate specific muscles or muscle groups and are easier to learn. Because of this, machines can also be used to rehabilitate injuries and improve muscular imbalances.

BODY WEIGHT

Using the athletes own body weight can be an effective form of resistance training. The ability to control your own body weight is critical for success in tennis. Exercises such as push-ups, pull-ups, and body-weight lunges all use body weight as the form of resistance.

Figure 7.6: Body weight.

ELASTIC TUBING

Elastic tubing can be used as a form of resistance training. As the tubing is stretched, the resistance increases. This is not compatible with the human strength curve. Tennis players often use elastic tubing to perform prehabilitation exercises for the shoulder. Because of its small size and light weight, elastic tubing is easy to transport wherever you go. Since tennis players are often traveling this is an easy option for resistance training.

Figure 7.7: Elastic Tubing.

STANDARD TRAINING VS FUNCTIONAL TRAINING

Functional training has become a popular method of training in recent years. Functional training emphasizes training movement patterns as opposed to muscle groups. Because tennis and almost all other sports are played in a standing position with no outside support, functional training emphasizes movements performed in a standing position without outside support such as with machines. Because sports are not played with single joints working in isolation, functional training also emphasizes multi-joint movements. Balance and proprioception are also an important part of functional training. There is a continuing debate regarding the benefits of functional training and the balance between functional training and isolated training.

DAILY PROGRAM DESIGN

There are multiple methods of structuring daily program design for tennis players. The choice of program depends on the ability level of the athlete as well as the stage of the periodized cycle.

FULL BODY ROUTINE

In this program the athlete trains all major muscle groups in one day. This program is most often used with novice weightlifters or individuals with time constraints. During in-season phases of training, this will often be used because of the lack of time available for off-court training. This program should have one day of rest between each session and should be repeated no more than four times a week. In each session the total number of exercises performed should rarely exceed ten. Because of the limited training days and exercises available, the program must be both efficient and effective. The focus is on training major muscle groups, with few isolated single joint exercises included.

UPPER BODY/LOWER BODY SPLIT ROUTINE

This program is usually used with more experienced lifters. It separates the body into two training days. On the first day the upper body is trained, and on the second day the lower body is trained. Core training may be structured as part of one training session or performed as a separate training session. Each session should not exceed ten exercises. Following the two training days is a rest day and then the cycle can be repeated again. This program allows for greater number of training days because of the ability to train on consecutive days. Extra rest days can be added as necessary to fit the goals of training and the tournament schedule. This program is most often used in the offseason or between tournaments when the athlete is trying to increase the number of training sessions.

TRAINING GOALS

Resistance training can be used to improve multiple aspects of athletic performance. By manipulating different training variables, resistance training can be used to improve muscular strength, power, and endurance.

STRENGTH

General strength is important for tennis players to reduce injury risk and provide a base for power training. In order to improve strength, resistance training should use loads that represent approximately 60 to 80 percent of the 1RM. Rest periods can vary but should typically be 2-3 minutes in duration for primary exercises. The tempo for strength training should be submaximal. This tempo requires the recruitment of stabilizing muscle groups to control the weight. A submaximal tempo also provides variety from the maximal velocity power training which is necessary for tennis.

HYPERTROPHY

If the goal of the athlete is muscular hypertrophy, loads should be in the range of approximately 60 to 80 percent of the IRM. It is important that maximal effort is given in every set. In order for complete ATP recovery rest periods should generally be in the range of 2-3 minutes. Athletes who are focusing on muscle hypertrophy typically use multiples sets, and 6 to 12 repetitions (7). Hypertrophy training also uses up to four to six exercises for one muscle group in the same training session. Maximal hypertrophy is typically not a goal of most tennis players because they do not want to become too muscular and lose flexibility. However, for some players who lack muscle mass, some degree of muscle hypertrophy may be advantageous.

POWER

Power can be defined as the amount of work done per unit of time.

$$Power = \frac{Work}{Time} \quad or \quad \frac{Force \; x \; Distance}{Time}$$

Therefore muscular power is a function of both strength and speed of movement. If two people lift the same weight but one lifts in a slow controlled manner and the other lifts it very quickly, the second person produces more power. Training for power improves the contributions of the neuromuscular system in several ways. Power training improves the rate at which force can be applied (10), increases muscular strength at both slow and fast contraction velocities (15), as well as improves coordination and movement efficiency (35). Each of these neural changes will lead to improved power on the tennis court. A significant strength base is necessary prior to performing the exercises involved in power development for maximal adaptation to occur.

When training for power, athletes should progress to sport-specific loads and velocities. Since tennis players must accelerate a light load extremely fast, training should move to this end of the force velocity curve. Research has shown that the use of light to moderate loads at high velocities increases force output at higher velocities (11). The optimal load for maximal power output has been shown to be between 30-60% of 1-RM depending on the choice of exercise (34, 3, 4). Rest between sets should be between 2-3 minutes to allow complete recovery between sets.

It has been suggested that simultaneously training for strength with heavy loads and power with light loads will provide the optimal increases in power output by increasing both the force and time components of the power equation (30).

Olympic Lifts/Modified Olympic Lifts. Olympic lifts and their variations are a common method of training for power improvement. The Olympic lifts are the clean and jerk and the snatch. There are numerous other lifts which are derived from these two lifts. Olympic lifts have been shown to produce the highest power outputs of any strength training exercise when performed correctly (8). These lifts are performed in a standing position and are a total body exercise requiring explo-

Figure 7.8: Olympic lift is similar to the ready position.

sive movement and coordination. In addition, because the position of the body when performing an Olympic lift is similar to the ready position on the tennis court (Figure 7.8) they transfer well to sports performance. When performing Olympic lifts, speed of movement should be emphasized over the weight lifted. A disadvantage of Olympic lifting is that they require a lot of teaching and time to learn. If they are performed incorrectly they can lead to injury. When learning Olympic lifts, start with light weight and focus on correct technique.

Plyometrics. Another common training method to develop power is plyometric training. Plyometric exercises begin with a rapid stretching of the muscle in an eccentric contraction. This is immediately followed by a rapid concentric contraction. The time between the eccentric contraction and the concentric contraction is called the ammoritization phase. The goal of plyometric training is to shorten the ammoritization phase, thus increasing the power output. Rapidly combining eccentric and concentric actions increases the muscular force and power output during the concentric phase (33).

Lower-body plyometrics include various jumping and bounding drills for the purpose of improving lower-body power and explosiveness. Upper-body plyometrics include various medicine ball throwing exercises designed to improve upper body power and explosiveness.

MUSCULAR ENDURANCE

Muscular endurance can be defined as the ability to repeatedly contract a muscle or muscle group over a short period of time. Because tennis matches can last several hours, muscular endurance is important so that players will be able to maintain power outputs late in the match. In order to improve muscular endurance, higher repetitions should be used along with low-to-moderate-intensity loads, generally below 60 percent of the 1RM (30). Short rest periods of 30 to 45 seconds should be used to simulate match conditions.

Circuit Training. Circuit training is a common method used to train muscular endurance. Circuit training uses stations which are completed one exercise after another. At each station there is an exercise to be performed for a specified number of repetitions or for a prescribed time period. Resistance training can be used at each station or some stations can use various conditioning exercises such as short sprints. Following each station there is a brief timed rest period. Circuits can range from 6-12 stations. Following the completion of a circuit there is a longer rest period. It is recommended that the rest periods follow tennis-specific guidelines. Therefore rest between stations would be less than 25 seconds and the rest between circuits would be 90 seconds to simulate the change of ends. The total number of circuits performed during a training session may vary from two to six depending on the training objective.

There are several advantages to performing circuit training. Due to the constant variation, circuit training provides a unique workout which may prevent boredom and overtraining. Because of the fast pace of the workout, circuit training is a highly efficient form of training. By alternating exercises and muscle groups each is given more time to rest before it is worked again. Circuit training is also very effective for training groups of players at the same time.

SUMMARY

This chapter has discussed the major issues relevant to resistance training tennis players. The following chapter will give specific exercises and program designs which can be implemented.

Chapter 7

REFERENCES

1.   Alway, S. E., W. H. Grumbt, W. J. Gonyea, and J. Stray-Gundersen. Contrasts in muscle and myofibers of elite male and female bodybuilders. J Appl Physiol. 67:24-31, 1989.

2.   Baechle, T. R. B. R. G. Weight training: steps to success. Champaign, Il: Human Kinetics, 1998, 6-10.

3.   Baker, D., S. Nance, and M. Moore. The load that maximizes the average mechanical power output during explosive bench press throws in highly trained athletes. J Strength Cond Res. 15:20-24, 2001.

4.   Baker, D., S. Nance, and M. Moore. The load that maximizes the average mechanical power output during jump squats in power-trained athletes. J Strength Cond Res. 15:92-97, 2001.

5.   Behm, D. G. Neuromuscular implications and applications of resistance training. J Strength Cond Res. 9:264-274, 1995.

6.   Cissik, J. M. The basics of strength training. New York: The McGraw-Hill Companies, Inc., 2001, 17-21.

7.   Fleck, S. J., Kraemer, W.J. Designing Resistance Training Programs. 2nd ed. Champaign, IL: Human Kinetics, 2004

8.   Garhammer, J. A Review of Power Output Studies of Olympic and Powerlifting: Methodology, Performance Prediction, and Evaluation Tests. The Journal of Strength and Conditioning Research. 7:76-89, 1993.

9.   Graham, J. F. Resistance exercise techniques and spotting. In: Conditioning for Strength and Human Performance. T. J. Chandler and L. E. Brown (Eds.) Baltimore: Lippincott, Williams, and Wilkins, 2008, pp. 182-236.

10.   Hakkinen, K. and P. V. Komi. Changes in electrical and mechanical behavior of leg extensor muscles during heavy resistance strength training. Scand J Sports Sci. 7:55-64, 1985.

11.   Hakkinen, K. and P. V. Komi. The effect of explosive type strength training on electromyographic and force production characteristics of leg extensor muscles during concentric and various stretch-shortening cycle exercises. Scand J Sports Sci. 7:65-76, 1985.

12.   Hakkinen, K., P. V. Komi, and M. Alen. Effect of explosive type strength training on isometric force- and relaxation-time, electromyographic and muscle fibre characteristics of leg extensor muscles. Acta Physiol Scand. 125:587-600, 1985.

13.   Harris, R. T. and G. Dudley. Neuromuscular anatomy and adaptations to conditioning. In: Essentials of Strength Training and Conditioning. T. R. Baechle and R. Earle (Eds.) Champaign, IL: Human Kinetics, 2000, pp. 19-20.

14. Hay, J. G., J. G. Andrews, and C. L. Vaughan. Effects of lifting rate on elbow torques exerted during arm curl exercises. Med Sci Sports Exerc. 15:63-71, 1983.

15. Kaneko, M., T. Fuchimoto, H. Toji, and K. Suei. Training effect of different loads on the force-velocity relationship and mechanical power output in human muscle. Scand J Sports Sci. 5:50-55, 1983.

16. Kraemer, W. Physiological adaptations to anaerobic and aerobic endurance training programs. In: In Essentials of Strength Training and Conditioning. T. a. E. Baechle, RW, (Ed.): Human Kinetics, 2000, p. 156.

17. Kraemer, W. J., K. Adams, E. Cafarelli, G. A. Dudley, C. Dooly, M. S. Feigenbaum, S. J. Fleck, B. Franklin, A. C. Fry, J. R. Hoffman, R. U. Newton, J. Potteiger, M. H. Stone, N. A. Ratamess, and T. Triplett-McBride. American College of Sports Medicine position stand. Progression models in resistance training for healthy adults. Med Sci Sports Exerc. 34:364-380, 2002.

18. Kraemer W.J., A. K., Cafarelli E, et al. American College of Sports Medicine position stand. Progression models in resistance training for healthy adults. Med Sci Sports Exerc. 34:364-380, 2002.

19. Kraemer, W. J. and N. A. Ratamess. Endocrine responses and adaptations to strength and power training. In: Strength and Power in Sport. P. V. Komi (Ed.) Malden: Blackwell Science, 2003, pp. 361-386.

20. Kraemer, W. J. and N. A. Ratamess. Fundamentals of resistance training: progression and exercise prescription. Med Sci Sports Exerc. 36:674-688, 2004.

21. Lachance, P. F. and T. Hortobagyi. Influence of cadence on muscular performance during push-up and pull-up exercises. J Strength Cond Res. 8:76-79, 1994.

22. MacDougall, J. D., D. G. Sale, S. E. Alway, and J. R. Sutton. Muscle fiber number in biceps brachii in bodybuilders and control subjects. Journal of Applied Physiology. 57:1399-1403, 1984.

23. McCall, G. E., W. C. Byrnes, A. Dickinson, P. M. Pattany, and S. J. Fleck. Muscle fiber hypertrophy, hyperplasia, and capillary density in college men after resistance training. J Appl Physiol. 81:2004-2012, 1996.

24. Moritani, T. and H. A. deVries. Neural factors versus hypertrophy in the time course of muscle strength gain. Am J Phys Med. 58:115-130, 1979.

25. Morrissey, M. C., E. A. Harman, P. N. Frykman, and K. H. Han. Early phase differential effects of slow and fast barbell squat training. Am J Sports Med. 26:221-230, 1998.

26. Nutter, J. Physical activity increases bone density. NSCA Journal. 8:67 - 69, 1986.

27. Phillips, S. M. Short-term training: when do repeated bouts of resistance exercise become training? Can J Appl Physiol. 25:185-193, 2000.

28.   Rhea, M. R., B. A. Alvar, S. D. Ball, and L. N. Burnett. Three sets of weight training superior to 1 set with equal intensity for eliciting strength. J Strength Cond Res. 16:525-529, 2002.

29.   Roetert, P. and T.S. Ellenbecker.   Complete Conditioning for Tennis. Champaign, IL: Human Kinetics, 1998, pp.63-64.

30.   Spiering, B. A., Kraemer W. J. Resistance exercise prescription. In: Conditioning for Strength and Human Performance. T. J. Chandler and L. E. Brown (Eds.) Baltimore: Lippincott, Williams, and Wilkins, 2008, pp. 273-291.

31.   Staron, R. S., D. L. Karapondo, W. J. Kraemer, A. C. Fry, S. E. Gordon, J. E. Falkel, F. C. Hagerman, and R. S. Hikida. Skeletal muscle adaptations during early phase of heavy-resistance training in men and women. J Appl Physiol. 76:1247-1255, 1994.

32.   Stone, M. H., Plisk, S.S., Stone, M.E., Schilling, B.K. O'Bryant H.S. and. Pierce, K.C. Athletic performance development: Volume load- 1 set versus multiple sets, training velocity and training variation. Strength Cond:22-31, 1998.

33.   Walshe, A. D., G. J. Wilson, and G. J. Ettema. Stretch-shorten cycle compared with isometric preload: contributions to enhanced muscular performance. Journal of Applied Physiology. 84:97-106, 1998.

34.   Wilson, G. J., R. U. Newton, A. J. Murphy, and B. J. Humphries. The optimal training load for the development of dynamic athletic performance. Med Sci Sports Exerc. 25:1279-1286, 1993.

35.   Young, W. A., A. Jenner, and K. Griffiths. Acute enhancement of power performance from heavy squat loads. J Strength Cond Res. 12:82-84, 1998.

CHAPTER 8

RESISTANCE TRAINING PROGRAMS FOR TENNIS

- PYLOMETRIC EXERCISES
- MEDICINE BALL EXERCISES
- OLYMPIC EXERCISES
- MACHINES
- FREE WEIGHTS
- RESISTANCE BAND EXERCISES
- CORE EXERCISES
- SAMPLE TRAINING PROGRAMS

INTRODUCTION

This chapter provides a list of resistance exercises and related exercises, that can be used by tennis players to optimize strength and power. Exercises presented in this chapter range from strength to power to prehabilitation. Sample resistance training programs are also presented at the end of the chapter.

PLYOMETRIC EXERCISES

STANDING LONG JUMP

Level of Exercise:
Intermediate
Coaching Cues:
Squat down and jump up and forward in an explosive manner. The goal is to jump the farthest distance forward.

Figure 8.1: Standing Long Jump.

SQUAT JUMP

Level of Exercise: Intermediate
Coaching Cues: Squat down and jump up in an explosive manner. The goal is to jump as high as possible.

Figure 8.2: Squat jump.

BARRIER JUMP

Level of Exercise: Intermediate to Advanced. The level of this exercise can be altered by the height of the barrier.
Coaching Cues: Jumps side to side over the barrier to the starting position. Focus on jumping off the ground quickly, clearing the barrier, and changing directions rapidly.
Variations: This drill can also be done by jumping side to side and front to back.

Figure 8.3: Barrier jump.

LUNGE JUMP

Level of Exercise: Advanced

Coaching Cues: Perform a stationary lunge and then jump up in the air as high as possible from the lunge position. While in the air, switch legs and land in a lunge position on the opposite leg. Jumps are continued with alternating legs on each jump.

Figure 8.4: Lunge jump.

MEDICINE BALL EXERCISES
CHEST PASS

Level of Exercise: Intermediate

Coaching Cues: Throw the medicine ball with a two-handed chest pass. Extend both arms as quickly and forcefully as possible.

Variations: This exercise can be done by throwing the ball forward with one arm and using the other arm to hold and balance the ball.

Figure 8.5: Chest pass.

OVERHEAD TOSS

Level of Exercise: Intermediate
Coaching Cues: Take the medicine ball back behind the head with both hands. Throw the ball forward as far as possible using the entire body to generate force.

Figure 8.6: Overhead toss.

FOREHAND AND BACKHAND THROWS

Level of Exercise: Intermediate
Coaching Cues: Throw the medicine ball from the side with two hands simulating a two handed forehand or backhand. Generate force using legs and core. Do not throw the ball with just your arms.
Variations: Medicine ball throws can be done from an open or closed stance.

Figure 8.7: Forehand and backhand throws.

UNDERHAND TOSS

Level of Exercise: Intermediate
Coaching Cues: Beginning in a ready position, hold a medicine ball, squat down, and brings the medicine ball down between the legs. Forcefully push up with your legs and throw the ball up as high as possible using an underhand throw.
Variations: The ball can also be thrown as far forward as possible.

Figure 8.8: Underhand toss.

PUSH PRESS

Level of Exercise: Intermediate

Coaching Cues: Squat down holding the medicine ball at chest level. Forcefully push up with your legs and extend your arms, releasing the ball. The goal is to throw the ball as high in the air as possible.

Figure 8.9: Push press.

OLYMPIC EXERCISES

Prior to performing Olympic exercises it is important to consult with a certified professional who has experience teaching the Olympic lifts.

CLEAN

Major Muscles: Gluteus maximus, hamstrings quadriceps, soleus, gastrocnemius, trapezius, and deltoids.

Level of Exercise: Advanced

Coaching Cues: Squat down and grip the bar slightly wider than shoulder width. Keep the back arched tightly and arms straight. Pull the bar up off the floor by extending the hips and knees. As the bar passes the knees raise the shoulders quickly while keeping the barbell close to the thighs. Continue extending the hips, knees, and ankles explosively so that the feet come off the floor. Shrug the shoulders and pull the barbell upward with the arms, allowing the elbows to flex to the sides. Aggressively pull the body under the bar by rotating the elbows around the bar. Catch the bar on the shoulders while moving into a half squat position.

Figure 8.10: Clean.

SNATCH

Major Muscles: Gluteus maximus, hamstrings, quadriceps, soleus, gastrocnemius, upper trapezius, deltoids, and triceps.

Level of Exercise: Advanced

Coaching Cues: Squat down and grip the bar slightly wider than shoulder width. Keep the back arched tightly and arms straight. Pull the bar up off the floor by extending the hips, knees, and ankles. As the bar passes the knees raise the shoulders quickly while keeping the barbell close to the thighs. Continue extending the hips, knees, and ankles explosively so that the feet come off the floor. Shrug the shoulders and pull the barbell upward

Figure 8.11: Snatch.

while keeping the arms straight. Aggressively pull the body under the bar by rotating the elbows around and under the bar. Catch the bar at arms length while moving into a half squat position.

MACHINES
CHEST PRESS

Major Muscles: Pectoralis Major, Triceps
Level of Exercise: Beginner
Coaching Cues: Keep your head and back flat against the machine and extend the arms.

Figure 8.12: Chest press.

SEATED ROW

Major Muscle: Latissimus Dorsi
Level of Exercise: Beginner
Coaching Cues: Keep chest against pad on machine. Pull back with arms until the elbows are behind the back and the hands are almost to the chest.

Figure 8.13: Seated row.

OVERHEAD PRESS

Major Muscle: Anterior Deltoid
Level of Exercise: Beginner
Coaching Cues: Press arms upward until they are fully extended. Return weight to the shoulder.

Figure 8.14: Overhead press.

LAT PULLS

Major Muscle: Latissimus Dorsi
Level of Exercise: Beginner
Coaching Cues: While sitting up straight, keep your back flat and pull your arms down towards your chest.

Figure 8.15: Lat pulls.

LEG CURLS

Major Muscle:
Hamstrings
Level of Exercise:
Beginner
Coaching Cues: Keep
your back flat against
machine. Bend at the
knees and pull your legs
back toward the
machine.

Figure 8.16: Leg curls.

LEG EXTENSION

Major Muscle:
Quadriceps
Level of Exercise:
Beginner
Coaching Cues: Keep
your back flat against
machine. The knee
should be lined up with
the pivot point of the
machine. Extend the
knees until the legs are
straight.

Figure 8.17: Leg extension.

LEG PRESS

Major Muscle: Quadriceps
Level of Exercise: Beginner
Coaching Cues:
Push away from the
platform by extend-
ing the knees and
hips, but do not lock
the knees at full
extension. Keep
knees and toes point-

Figure 8.18: Leg press.

ed straight ahead. The heels should not rise off the platform.

FREE WEIGHTS

Free weight exercises use an external resistance and move it through a specified path of motion. External resistance can be dumbbells, medicine balls, barbells, resistance bands, and other nonconventional forms of resistance. The exercises presented can be done with the type of resistance desired.

BENCH PRESS

Major Muscles: Pectoralis Major, Triceps
Level of Exercise: Intermediate
Coaching Cues: Lie flat on a bench and begin with the arms extended. Lower weight to chest and then extend the arms back out until they are straight. A spotter should be used for this exercise.
Variation: This exercise can be done on an incline or a decline bench to change the angle.

Figure 8.19: Bench press.

OVERHEAD PRESS

Major Muscle: Anterior Deltoid
Level of Exercise: Intermediate
Coaching Cues: Press arms upward until they are fully extended. Return weight to the shoulder.

Figure 8.20: Overhead press.

BENT ROW

Major Muscle:
Latissimus Dorsi
Level of Exercise:
Intermediate
Coaching Cues:
Kneel over bench
with one arm and leg
to the side. Begin

Figure 8.21: Bent row.

with arm extended and pull up towards the chest. Do not rotate the body to get
the weight up.

UPRIGHT ROW

Major Muscle: Lateral Deltoid, Upper
Trapezius
Level of Exercise: Intermediate
Coaching Cues: Begin with arms
extended and pull weight upwards
with the elbows leading. Raise arms
until they are parallel to the ground.

Figure 8.22: Upright row.

DUMBBELL FLY

Major Muscle:
Pectoralis Major
**Level of
Exercise:**
Intermediate
**Coaching
Cues:** Begin by
laying down on
a bench with
arms extended
above the chest

Figure 8.23: Dumbbell fly.

with the arms slightly bent. Lower arms to sides until arms are parallel to the
ground. Bring arms back together in a hugging motion.

PULL OVER

Major Muscle: Latissimus Dorsi
Level of Exercise: Intermediate
Coaching Cues: Begin with arms extended above chest with the arms slightly bent. Lower arms over head until the arms are parallel to the rest of the body.

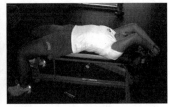

Figure 8.24: Pull over.

CABLE ROW

Major Muscle: Latissimus Dorsi
Level of Exercise: Intermediate
Coaching Cues: Stand upright with knees slightly bent and hold onto handles. Pull arms back towards chest and focus on

Figure 8.25: Cable row.

squeezing the shoulder blades together as the movement occurs.

FRONT SHOULDER RAISE

Major Muscle: Anterior Deltoid
Level of Exercise: Beginner
Coaching Cues: Begin with arms extended at side. Raise arms in front of body until they are parallel to the floor.

Figure 8.26: Front shoulder raise.

SIDE SHOULDER RAISE

Major Muscle: Medial Deltoids

Level of Exercise: Beginner

Coaching Cues: Begin with arms extended at side. Raise arms to the side of body until they are parallel to the floor.

Figure 8.27: Side shoulder raise.

STEP UP

Major Muscle: Quadriceps

Level of Exercise: Intermediate

Coaching Cues: Begin with one leg on bench and one leg on the ground. Extend the leg on the bench and step up so that both legs are now on the bench. Make sure the torso remains upright during the exercise.

Variations: Step ups can also be done to the side of the box.

Figure 8.28: Step up.

ROMANIAN DEAD LIFT (RDL)

Major Muscle: Hamstrings

Level of Exercise: Intermediate

Coaching Cues: With knees slightly bent, lower weight to the feet by bending at the hips and waist. Lift the weight by extending hips and waist until standing upright with shoulders back.

Figure 8.29: Romanian Dead Lift.

SQUATS

Major Muscles: Quadriceps, Hip Extensors

Level of Exercise: Intermediate

Coaching Cues: Bend knees until thighs are parallel to floor. To ascend, extend knees and hips until legs are straight. Keep head forward, back straight and feet flat on the floor.

Figure 8.30: Squats.

LUNGES

Major Muscle: Quadriceps

Level of Exercise: Intermediate

Coaching Cues: Step forward with one leg. Lower your body by flexing knee and hip of front leg until the knee of the rear leg is almost touching the ground. Return to the starting position by pushing off the ground and extending the hip and knee of the forward leg. Make sure the torso stays upright during the exercise.

Figure 8.31: Lunges.

Variations: Lunges can be performed in various directions to add variety. They can be done to the side, backward, or by crossing over.

SQUAT PRESS

Major Muscles: Quadriceps, Anterior Deltoid

Level of Exercise: Advanced

Coaching Cues: Begin by holding weight just above the shoulders. Perform a squat as described above. During the ascent phase extend the arms completely as in the overhead press.

Figure 8.32: Squat press.

SQUAT PULL

Major Muscles: Quadriceps, Latissimus Dorsi

Level of Exercise: Advanced

Coaching Cues: Begin in a standing position holding onto handles. Perform a squat as described above. During the ascent phase pull the handles towards the chest as in the standing cable row.

Figure 8.33: Squat pull.

BACK HYPEREXTENSION

Major Muscle:
Hamstrings
Level of Exercise:
Intermediate
Coaching Cues: Lower body by bending at the hips and waist as if trying to touch your toes. To return to the starting position, raise upper body until hip and waist are fully extended.

Figure 8.34: Back hyperextension.

RESISTANCE BAND EXERCISES

EXTERNAL ROTATION

Major Muscles: Rotator Cuff
Level of Exercise: Beginner
Coaching Cues: Keep elbow at your side and externally rotate the shoulder. Do not twist during the movement.
Variations: This exercise can be done at various arm angles such as 90 and 45 degrees of glenohumeral abduction.

Figure 8.35: External rotation.

CORE EXERCISES
BENCH SIT-UP

Major Muscle: Rectus Abdominis

Level of Exercise: Beginner

Coaching Cues: Weight

Figure 8.36: Bench sit-up.

can be added by holding it at the chest for added difficulty.

V-UP

Major muscle: Rectus Abdominis

Level of Exercise: Intermediate

Coaching Cues: Begin lying flat on back and raise straight legs and torso at the same time. Bring the hands toward the feet while keeping the knees straight throughout movement.

Figure 8.37: V-up.

HIP CROSSOVER

Major Muscle: Obliques

Level of Exercise: Intermediate

Coaching Cues: Lie supine on floor with arms extended out to sides and legs raised upward with knees slightly bent. Lower legs to one side until the side of the thigh is touching the floor. Raise legs back to starting position and lower legs to opposite side.

Figure 8.38: Hip crossover.

Variations: A medicine ball or physioball can be held between legs for increased difficulty.

BICYCLE CRUNCH

Major Muscle: Obliques
Level of Exercise: Intermediate
Coaching Cues: Lie supine on floor with knees and hips bent and hands held behind the head. Raise upper body off the ground by flexing and twisting at the waist to one side. Return until the back of the shoulders return to the ground.

Figure 8.39: Bicycle crunch.

SAMPLE TRAINING PROGRAMS

Sample Circuit Training Endurance Session*		
	Sets	Reps
Bench Press	1	15
Jogging	1	45 sec
Squats	1	15
Jump Roap	1	45 sec
Bent Rows	1	15
Stationary Bike	1	45 sec
RDL	1	15
Stair Stepper	1	45 sec
DB Fly	1	15
Jogging	1	45 sec
Crunches	1	20
Jump Rope	1	45 sec
Upright Row	1	15
Stationary Bike	1	45 sec
Bicycle Crunches	1	20
Stair Stepper	1	45 sec
*The circuit can be repeated for as many sets as desired.		

Table 8.1: Circuit training endurance session.

BEGINNER RESISTANCE TRAINING PROGRAM 2 DAY A WEEK PROGRAM					
	Day 1			Day 2	
	Sets	Reps		Sets	Reps
Chest Press	2	12	Chest Press	2	12
Seated Rows	2	12	Seated Rows	2	12
Overhead Press	2	12	Front Shoulder Raise	2	12
Lat Pulls	2	12	Side Shoulder Raise	2	12
Leg Extension	2	12	Leg Press	2	12
Leg Curls	2	12	Body Weight Lunges	2	12
Crunches	2	20	Bench Sit-Up	2	20
Leg Lifts	2	20	Bicycles	2	20

Table 8.2: Beginner resistance training program.

ADVANCED RESISTANCE TRAINING PROGRAM 4 DAY A WEEK PROGRAM					
	Day 1			Day 2	
	Sets	Reps		Sets	Reps
Cleans	3	5	MB Chest Pass	2	12
DB Bench Press	2	10	MB Overhead Toss	2	12
Bent Rows	2	10	MB Underhand Toss	2	12
Overhead Press	2	10	Squat Jump	2	8
Pullovers	2	10	Front Lunges	2	10
Front Shoulder Raise	2	12	Squats	2	10
Side Shoulder Raise	2	12	Back Hyperextension	2	15
Shoulder Ext Rotation	2	15	V-Up	2	15
90 Ext Rotation	2	15	Hip Crossover	2	15
45 Ext Rotation	2	15	Bench Sit Up	2	15

ADVANCED RESISTANCE TRAINING PROGRAM 4 DAY A WEEK PROGRAM (cont.)					
	Day 3			Day 4	
	Sets	Reps		Sets	Reps
Snatch	3	5	MB Forehand Toss	2	12
Bench Press	2	10	MB Backhand Toss	2	12
Cable Rows	2	10	MB Push Press	2	12
DB Fly	2	10	Barrier Jump	2	8
Upright Row	2	10	RDL	2	10
Front Shoulder Raise	2	12	Step Ups	2	10
Side Shoulder Raise	2	12	Back Hyperextension	2	15
Shoulder Ext Rotation	2	15	V-Up	2	15
90 Ext Rotation	2	15	Hip Crossover	2	15
45 Ext Rotation	2	15	Bench Sit Up	2	15

Table 8.3: Advanced resistance training program.

133

SAMPLE COMPLEX TRAINING POWER SESSION		
	Sets	Reps
Bench Press	2	8
MB Chest Pass	2	8
Pullover	2	8
MB Overhead Toss	2	8
Squat Pull	2	8
MB Underhand Toss	2	8
Squat Press	2	8
MB Push Press	2	8
Lunge	2	8
Lunge Jump	2	8

Table 8.4: Complex training power session.

NATIONALLY RANKED COMPETITIVE JUNIOR AGED 15-18 3 DAY A WEEK PROGRAM		
DAY 1 - Hypertrophy Focused		
	Sets	Reps
Cleans	3	4
DB Squats	3	12
Lunges	4	15
RDL	4	12
DB Bench Press	4	12
One-Arm DB Row	4	12
Side Shoulder Raises	3	10
90 Ext. Rotation Shoulder	3	15
45 Ext. Rotation Shoulder	3	15
Core (5 minutes)		
DAY 2 - Strength Focused		
Cleans	3	4
Squats	4	6
Back Hyperextensions	4	6
Step-ups	3	12
Bench Press	5	4
Lat Pulls	4	4
Front Shoulder Raises	3	10
90 Ext. rotation Shoulder	3	15
45 Ext. Rotation Shoulder	3	15
Core (5 minutes)		
DAY 3 - Power Focused		
MB Chest Pass	5	4
MB Overhead Throws	5	4
Squat Jumps	6	2
Squat Pulls	4	6
DB Bench Press	4	3
Squat Press	4	10
Overhead Press	3	10
90 Ext. Rotation Shoulder	3	15
45 Ext. Rotation Shoulder	3	15
Core (5 minutes)		

Table 8.5: Nationally ranked competitive junior.

USTA LEAGUE 2.5 - 4.5 ADULT 3 DAY A WEEK PROGRAM		
DAY 1		
	Sets	Reps
DB Squats	3	12
Lunges	3	12
Leg Curl	3	12
Bench Press	3	12
Seated Row	3	12
Side Shoulder Raises	3	12
90 Ext. Rotation Shoulder	3	10
45 Ext. Rotation Shoulder	3	15
Core (5 minutes)		
DAY 2		
Step Ups	2	15
Leg Extension	2	15
Back Hyperextensions	3	10
DB Flies	3	15
Pullovers	3	15
Upright row	3	12
Front Shoulder Raises	3	10
90 Ext. Rotation Shoulder	3	15
45 Ext. Rotation Shoulder	3	15
Core (5 minutes)		
DAY 3		
Leg Press	3	12
Bench Press	3	12
Lunge Jump	2	6
Squat Pulls	3	10
DB Bench Press	4	10
One-Arm DB Row	4	10
Overhead Press	3	10
90 Ext. Rotation Shoulder	3	15
45 Ext. Rotation Shoulder	3	15
Core (5 minutes)		

Table 8.6: USTA League

Chapter 9

Cardiorespiratory Endurance & Tennis Performance

- Cardiorespiratory Fitness Defined
- Adaptations to Cardiovascular Training
- Tennis Specificity & Cardiorespiratory Training
- Potential Pitfalls of Cardiorespiratory Endurance Training for Tennis

Introduction

There is an ongoing debate about the aerobic nature of tennis. It is obvious the sport of tennis contains both aerobic and anaerobic components. This is sometimes misinterpreted by the coach or athlete as meaning the tennis player should run long, slow distances for training.

Previous research has suggested that tennis is an aerobic sport due to the length of matches which can last from 2-5 hours (9) with relatively moderate mean heart rate values found during play (1). Because of this, many coaches have recommended long distance runs of thirty minutes or more or long interval runs of 1-2 minutes. This training is often performed 3-5 times per week. Using heart rate ranges as a measure of energy system contribution can be misleading. Heart rate ranges during a match are rather wide due to the continual stop/start movements involved in tennis; therefore, mean measures do not accurately represent the explosive nature of the sport. It would be remiss to suggest that tennis is predominantly an aerobic sport. It might be better to classify the sport as an anaerobic-predominant activity requiring high levels of aerobic conditioning to avoid fatigue and aid in recovery between points.

CARDIORESPIRATORY FITNESS DEFINED

Cardiorespiratory fitness is the ability of the heart and lungs to transport oxygen to working muscles to aid in energy production. VO_2max is often used as an indicator of cardiorespiratory fitness. VO_2max is defined as the maximum amount of oxygen an athlete can uptake, or utilize, to make ATP. There is a linear relationship between VO_2 and heart rate. As heart rate increases with exercise, VO_2 will also increase at the same rate. Because of this linear relationship, the volume of oxygen being utilized to produce energy at any point in time may be estimated using heart rate at a steady work rate. With training, the efficiency of ATP production improves, and movement economy (running economy in runners) improves so the athlete is more efficient at using the ATP produced. In the sport of tennis, the work rate is not steady, and therefore heart rates are continually going up and down.

If we were able to get an average heart rate throughout a point, or throughout a match, we would find that the tennis player with higher cardiorespiratory fitness would likely have the lower average heart rate. From this average heart rate, we could estimate the average oxygen consumption during the point or during the match. While this would not be as accurate as during a "steady state" activity, the general idea is the same. Improving cardiorespiratory fitness to a point can positively influence the ability of the athlete to perform physical work. In tennis, the methods used to produce increases in cardiorespiratory fitness become very important. As we will discuss below, long slow distance training is counterproductive to training the tennis player for the short explosive bursts of activity needed for tennis.

ADAPTATIONS TO CARDIOVASCULAR TRAINING

Training for aerobic endurance enhancement will result in a number of cardiovascular adaptations. The adaptations that occur are specific to the method of training.

VO₂

Traditional long, slow endurance training will produce increases in VO_2max. Increases in VO_2max are attributed to increases in cardiac output as well as an improved extraction capability within skeletal muscle. During exercise, VO_2 is increased above resting levels to meet the higher energy demands of the exercising muscle. As intensity of exercise increases, VO_2 will also increase.

HEART RATE

As exercise intensity increases, heart rate also increases in a linear fashion until it reaches a plateau. Endurance training will cause a decrease in resting heart rate and a decrease in heart rate at any given submaximal VO_2 (11). The decrease in heart rate during submaximal exercise is a result of both improved cardiac output through increases in stroke volume (amount of blood pumped per beat) and more efficient exercise movement. Maximal heart rate is unaffected by endurance training. By improving movement economy, the tennis player can perform more work per volume of oxygen consumed. Because of the adaptations to the heart (increased stroke volume, decreased heart rate at a given work load) and the adaptations related to improved movement economy, the tennis player will be able to work at higher workloads for longer periods of time.

STROKE VOLUME

Stroke volume is the amount of blood ejected from the left ventricle in one heart beat. During exercise, stroke volume increases as the intensity of exercise increases. Resting stroke volume and maximal stroke volume are improved by endurance training because the increased ventricular filling, or preload, seen during endurance exercise enlarges the ventricular chamber. The increase of the preload is believed to be due to the expanded plasma volume seen in endurance training (3).

CARDIAC OUTPUT

Cardiac output is the amount of blood pumped from the heart in one minute. It is a function of heart rate and stroke volume. At rest cardiac output is approximately 5 L, but during maximal endurance exercise cardiac output may increase to 20 L, and may reach 40 L in endurance trained male athletes (7). Since maximal heart rate is unaffected by training, the increase in cardiac output is primarily a result of improved stroke volume. With all things being equal, the tennis player with a greater cardiac output will be able to perform at a higher level for a longer period of time. Tennis players should consider the most effective training methods for improving cardiac output and stroke volume, but not those that have a negative effect on speed and power output.

RESPIRATORY ADAPTATIONS TO TRAINING

In general, the respiratory system does not limit the amount of oxygen provided to the exercising muscles. Respiratory capacity does not appear to be significantly affected by endurance training. Therefore, breathing heavier and trying to get more oxygen in, will not improve tennis performance, since the amount of oxygen available is not a limiting factor.

BLOOD VOLUME ADAPTATIONS TO TRAINING

Hypervolemia is an increase in blood volume. Endurance training has been shown to cause hypervolemia, which occurs in the first 2–4 weeks of training. Hypervolemia is thought to be the result of plasma volume expansion and an increase in the number of red blood cells (13).

TENNIS SPECIFICITY & CARDIORESPIRATORY TRAINING

While aerobic fitness is necessary for tennis, the amount of traditional long, slow aerobic exercise that is necessary is not clear. Tennis requires both aerobic and anaerobic metabolic pathways for a continuous supply of energy throughout the match. Anaerobic pathways are used to supply energy during points and allow for the quick explosive movements required. Aerobic pathways are used to supply energy between points so that the player can recover and perform again in 25 seconds. The efficiency of both of these energy systems is necessary for optimal tennis performance.

According to the principle of specificity, training should be as specific to the sport as possible in order to get maximum results. Watching a tennis match will demonstrate that tennis requires repeated quick explosive movements followed by a rest period. While long distance runs and long intervals will improve aerobic capabilities, it is not specific to the physiological demands of the sport of tennis. Using short interval sprints which match the work/rest intervals and the movement patterns of tennis is a more sport specific way to aerobically train tennis players. This method of training will still require the aerobic system to be used during the recovery periods and will use aerobic metabolism in the same manner it is used during actual tennis play.

WORK/REST INTERVALS

Analyzing the length of the points and rest periods during matches yields relevant work/rest intervals that can be used for training. Several studies have examined the work/rest intervals in tennis matches. For high level play, work/rest ratios have been found to range from 1:2 to 1:5 (9). Total amount of match play has been shown to be 20 to 30 percent of the total match time (1, 8).

The length of points can vary greatly depending on factors such as surface, playing style, and level of play. A review of studies examining the length of points in tennis matches found the average point length ranged from 3 to 15 seconds depending on the surface (9). The average point length in all of these reviewed studies was 8 seconds.

This study also found a downward trend in the average point length in the last 20 years (9). One study which compared the 1988 men's US Open final (4) to the 2003 men's US Open final found that the average point length decreased by over 50% in that 15 year period. This should come as no surprise as racquet technology, an increase in resistance training, and increasing athleticism in tennis players has increased the power in tennis dramatically. This study also found that the time between points also decreased by approximately 50%. Even though the length of points has decreased, the actual work to rest ratios did not change significantly in the last 15 years. Additionally, 90% of the points were less than ten seconds (10).

Style of play has also been shown to affect the length of points. Attacking players play shorter points than players who prefer to play from the baseline (2). A player's style of play should be taken into consideration when a designing conditioning program. Strength and conditioning coaches should perform a work/rest analysis for each player in order to design individualized conditioning programs. This evaluation should include multiple analyses using opponents with various styles and on different surfaces.

Based on available information, interval training for elite tennis players should include a majority of the time spent in work intervals of 3-15 seconds. Rest periods should also match the rest intervals seen in match play. There should be two to five seconds of rest for every second of work, making the ratios 1:2 to 1:5 (10). The work and rest periods can be adjusted within these ranges according to the individual player's style and the competitive surface being utilized. It is also recommended that following a series of 10-15 repetitions of intervals that a longer rest period of 1-2 minutes be given to simulate the rest periods during changeovers.

HEART RATE & TENNIS

Heart rate can be used to measure intensity during practice or match play. During tennis matches heart rate has been shown to increase as the match progresses, with a decrease during the changeovers (2). Heart rates were measured on a group of collegiate tennis players during 85 minutes of match play, and the mean heart rate was found to be 144.6 beats/minute, which is significantly higher than prematch heart rates (1). There is a wide range of heart rates found during a match due to the constant changing from work to rest and the variability of the length of the work period. It should be noted that the heart rate profile for a tennis match is much more similar to interval sprints than long distance running. This is further evidence for using short interval sprints instead of long distance running.

VO₂ & TENNIS

A recent review of VO_2max values in competitive high-level tennis players found that VO_2max results ranged from 44 to 69 ml/kg/min (9) with the vast majority of these tennis players having VO_2max values above 50 ml/kg/min. These values would classify tennis players as being highly aerobically trained. Based on this information it is recommended that high level competitive tennis players have VO_2max values higher than 50 ml/kg/min in order to train and compete at the desired level of play.

VO_2 increases as the match progresses with a decrease during the rest periods while changing ends (2). Aggressive attacking players had lower VO_2 values during play than baseline players (2). It can therefore be assumed that baseliners need a higher level of aerobic fitness than attacking players. Consequently, baseliners should perform slightly longer intervals over a longer time period than attacking players.

BLOOD LACTATE

Although decreases in both technical and tactical performance occur when blood lactate concentrations exceed 7-8 $mmol \cdot L^{-1}$ (12), research has shown that blood lactate levels remain relatively low during match play (1) because regular rest periods between points and games allows for sufficient recovery. The lack of accumulation of blood lactate indicates that the alactic anaerobic energy system (ATP-PC) provides a majority of ATP production during the match. The aerobic energy system is active during recovery to replace the ATP used during the previous point.

While match play does not typically produce high blood lactate, the intensity and duration of some training sessions may produce high enough levels of lactate to decrease performance during drills. Many tennis players train at a much higher practice intensity and duration than what occurs during actual match play (5). Tennis players and coaches should take into account potential lactate levels when designing drills. If technical development is the goal, it is important for the athlete to be fresh with low levels of lactate so that performance is not negatively affected. If the goal of the training session is to improve conditioning, specificity of training would suggest that a training program for tennis players should progress toward sport-specific work/rest and intensity levels as the competitive season approaches.

POTENTIAL PITFALLS OF CARDIORESPIRATORY ENDURANCE TRAINING FOR TENNIS

Cardiorespiratory training may have negative effects on other aspects of training. It is obvious that speed and power are critical to success in tennis. There is some evidence that performing aerobic training concurrently with strength training is detrimental to strength production (6). Because of the close relationship between strength and power, it is possible this will cause a decrease in power output as well. Aerobic training may cause adaptations to muscle fibers that may decrease their ability to produce force. Additionally, the slow rhythmic contractions performed in aerobic training may cause an adaptation in the nervous system which could interfere with speed and quickness.

Continuous long distance running may make the athlete slower or make it difficult to gain muscle mass if this is a desired goal of training. Excessive amounts of aerobic training could also lead to overtraining and injury. Shin splints are a common result of overtraining through long distance running. Interval training can provide the tennis specific endurance required without the potential negative effects of traditional aerobic training. By using the appropriate work/rest intervals, interval training can more closely mimic the metabolic requirements of the sport.

While traditional long slow distance aerobic training may not be appropriate in general for tennis players, there are certain athletes who might benefit from periods of traditional aerobic training. This would include athletes who lack moderate fitness levels or are over the desired playing weight. When possible this training should be done in the off-season so that more sport specific training can be done prior to tournaments.

CARDIO TRAINING VS SHORT INTERVAL TRAINING

There are several differences between long distance endurance training and short interval sprint training. Short interval training has a heart rate profile which is specific to tennis while endurance training does not. Short interval training also uses neural patterns similar to tennis play because of the rapid contractions required while long distance endurance training does not. Interval training can be performed on a court with multiple changes of directions and footwork patterns in each sprint while long distance training cannot. Both methods of training will improve aerobic

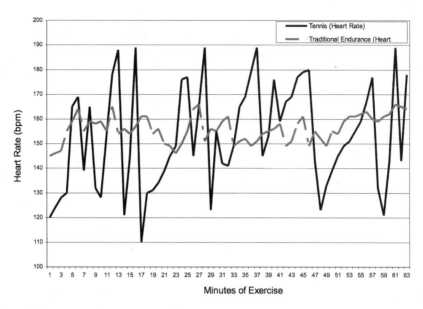

Figure 9.1: Heart rate during tennis and traditional endurance exercise.

fitness, but because of its specificity to tennis in each of these areas, short interval training is recommended over long distance endurance training for tennis players for a majority of the training cycle (Figure 9.1).

SUMMARY

Cardiorespiratory fitness is important for tennis players as can be seen by their high VO_2 values and the need for aerobic recovery between points. The training method used for cardiorespiratory fitness is important. For variety, off-season aerobic training can include longer distance runs. As the season approaches, training should move in the direction of short sport-specific intervals. Short intervals which match the demands of tennis should be used during the pre-competitive and competitive periods because of their specificity to the game and possibility that traditional aerobic training may decrease power outputs. The following chapter will provide sample conditioning drills which can be performed in tennis specific intervals for optimal carryover to the court.

REFERENCES

1. Bergeron, M. F., C. M. Maresh, W. J. Kraemer, A. Abraham, B. Conroy, and C. Gabaree. Tennis: a physiological profile during match play. Int J Sport Med. 12:474-479, 1991.

2. Bernardi, M., G. De Vito, M. E. Falvo, S. Marino, and F. Montellanico. Cardiorespiratory adjustment in middle-level tennis players: are long term cardiovascular adjustments possible? In: Science and Racket Sports II. A. Lees, I. Maynard, M. Hughes, and T. Reilly (Eds.) London, UK: E & FN Spon, 1998, pp. 20-26.

3. Bonow, R. O. Left ventricular response to exercise. In: Cardiovascular Response to Exercise. F. GF (Ed.) Mount Kisco, NY: Futura Publishing Co, Inc., 1994, pp. 31-48.

4. Chandler, T. J. Work/rest intervals in world class tennis. Tennis Pro. 3:4, 1991.

5. Davey, P. R., R. D. Thorpe, and C. Williams. Fatigue decreases skilled tennis performance. J Sport Sci. 20:311-318, 2002.

6. Häkkinen, K., M. Alen, W. J. Kraemer, E. Gorostiaga, M. Izquierdo, H. Rusko, J. Mikkola, A. Häkkinen, H. Valkeinen, E. Kaarakainen, S. Romu, V. Erola, J. Ahtiainen, and L. Paavolainen. Neuromuscular adaptations during concurrent strength and endurance training versus strength training. European Journal of Applied Physiology. 89:42-52, 2003.

7. Hoffman, J. R. The Cardiorespiratory System. In: Conditioning for Strength and Human Performance. T. J. Chandler and L. E. Brown (Eds.) Baltimore, 2008, pp. 20-39.

8. König, D., M. Huonker, A. Schmid, M. Halle, A. Berg, and J. Keul. Cardiovascular, metabolic, and hormonal parameters in professional tennis players. Med Sci Sport Exercise. 33:654-658, 2001.

9. Kovacs, M. S. Applied physiology of tennis performance. British Journal of Sports Medicine. 40:381-386, 2006.

10. Kovacs, M. S., E. Strecker, W. B. Chandler, J. W. Smith, and D. D. Pascoe. Time analysis of work/rest intervals in men's collegiate tennis. In National Strength and Conditioning Conference. Minneapolis, MN, p. e364, 2004.

11. MacDougall, J. D. Blood pressure responses to resistive, static, and dynamic exercise. In: Cardiovascular Response to Exercise. F. GF (Ed.) Mount Kisco, NY: Futura Publishing Co, Inc., 1994, pp. 155-174.

12. McCarthy-Davey, P. R. Fatigue, carbohydrate supplementation and skilled tennis performance. In: Tennis Science and Technology. S. Haake and A. O. Coe (Eds.) Oxford: Blackwell, 2000, pp. 333-340.

13.   Toner, M. M., EL Glickman, WD McArdle. Cardiovascular adjustments to exercise distributed between the upper and lower body. Med Sci Sport Exercise. 22:773-778, 1990.

Chapter 10

Cardiorespiratory Fitness Programs for Tennis

- Junior Programs
- National Junior Programs
- Adult League Player

Introduction

This chapter provides information on cardiorespiratory conditioning programs for tennis and how to implement this into a complete program. The following is a list of sample conditioning programs which can be implemented. Many of the agility drills presented in Chapter 12 can be used as conditioning drills by extending the work period and lowering the rest period. Other exercises which can be used for conditioning drills are track sprints, jumping rope, and riding a stationary bike. Remember to take into account the science behind endurance training as outlined in the previous chapter when designing and implementing your programs. Proper work/rest ratios should always be used when designing conditioning programs.

JUNIOR PROGRAMS

TENNIS SPECIFIC ENDURANCE SESSION NATIONAL JUNIOR/COLLEGE LEVEL			
Dynamic Warm-Up Routine			
	Time	Intensity	
Jump Rope			
2 feet	180sec	Slow	
2 feet	60sec	Medium	
Left leg	30sec	Fast	
Right leg	30sec	Fast	
Alt. Leg	60sec	Fast	
Doubles	30sec	Fast	
	Reps	Sets	Work : Rest
MK Drill	1	1	1 : 1
This drill involves the athlete starting on the	2	1	1 : 2
doubles line and running to the other	3	1	1 : 2
doubles line and back.	4	1	1 : 3
	5	1	1 : 3
	6	1	1 : 4
	5	1	1 : 3
(one of the best on-court endurance drills)	4	1	1 : 3
	3	1	1 : 3
	2	1	1 : 2

Table 10.1: Tennis specific endurance session.

ENDURANCE MOVEMENT TRAINING YOUNG JUNIOR PLAYER			
DYNAMIC WARM-UP ROUTINE	(Doubles line to Doubles line)		
TENNIS SPECIFIC ENDURANCE ON COURT PROGRAM	Reps	Sets	Work : Rest
D-line to T-line Drill	3	1	1 : 3
D-line to T-line Drill- Shuffling	3	3	1 : 3
Short X Drill	4	1	1 : 2
Long Spider Drill	3	1	1 : 4
Slalom Drill	4	1	1 : 3

Table 10.2: Endurance movement training (young junior player).

GYM CIRCUIT TRAINING PROGRAM			
DYNAMIC WARM-UP ROUTINE			
	Reps	Sets	Work : Rest
Bike			
45 seconds	1	1	1 : 2
30 seconds	2	1	1 : 2
15 seconds	4	1	1 : 3
Elliptical			
45 seconds	1	1	1 : 2
30 seconds	2	1	1 : 2
15 seconds	4	1	1 : 3
Stair Stepper			
45 seconds	1	1	1 : 2
30 seconds	2	1	1 : 2
15 seconds	4	1	1 : 3
Treadmill			
45 seconds	1	1	1 : 2
30 seconds	2	1	1 : 2
15 seconds	4	1	1 : 3

Table 10.3: Gym circuit training program.

NATIONAL JUNIOR PROGRAMS

ENDURANCE MOVEMENT TRAINING NATIONAL JUNIOR/COLLEGE LEVEL			
DYNAMIC WARM-UP ROUTINE	(Doubles line to Doubles line)		
TENNIS SPECIFIC ENDURANCE ON COURT PROGRAM	Reps	Sets	Work : Rest
Slalom Cone Run	4	1	1 : 3
Short X Drill	5	1	1 : 2
Long X Drill	4	1	1 : 2
Spider Drill	5	1	1 : 3

Table 10.4: Endurance movement training (national junior/college level).

TRACK ENDURANCE MOVEMENT TRAINING NATIONAL JUNIOR/COLLEGE LEVEL			
DYNAMIC WARM-UP ROUTINE	(Doubles line to Doubles line)		
TENNIS SPECIFIC ENDURANCE OFF COURT PROGRAM (off-season)	Reps	Sets	Work : Rest
10m	10	1	1 : 2
20m	10	1	1 : 2
50m	5	1	1 : 2
100m	5	1	1 : 3
200m	5	1	1 : 4
300m	4	1	1 : 4
(track program)			

Table 10.5: Track endurance movement training.

ADULT PROGRAMS

TENNIS-SPECIFIC ENDURANCE ADULT LEAGUE PLAYER			
DYNAMIC WARM-UP ROUTINE			
OFF COURT PROGRAM			
Bike Sprints	Reps	Sets	Work : Rest
10 Seconds	6	1	1 : 2
20 Seconds	3	1	1 : 2
30 Seconds	2	1	1 : 2
Track Sprints			
20m	5	1	1 : 2
50m	4	1	1 : 3
100m	3	1	1 : 3
200m	2	1	1 : 4

Table 10.6: Tennis specific endurance program off-court (adult league player).

TENNIS-SPECIFIC ENDURANCE ADULT LEAGUE PLAYER			
DYNAMIC WARM-UP ROUTINE	(Doubles line to Doubles line)		
ON COURT PROGRAM	Reps	Sets	Work : Rest
D-line to T-line Drill	5	1	1 : 3
Short X Drill	4	1	1 : 3
Spider Drill	2	1	1 : 4

Table 10.7: Tennis specific endurance program on-court (adult league player).

CHAPTER 11

SPEED, QUICKNESS & AGILITY

- BASIC SCIENCE BEHIND THE HOW AND WHY OF SPEED
- WHAT HAPPENS AFTER THE FIRST STEP INTO THE GROUND
- PHASES OF EACH STEP DURING TENNIS MOVEMENT

INTRODUCTION

What separates the good players from the very good and the very good from the best? Many responses could answer this question, but too often a limiting factor is an athlete's speed. It is all too common to see a talented competitor hit a very clean ball but be handicapped by poor movement and be unable to capitalize on a well-struck shot or a well-thought-out strategy.

All the top tennis players have a common trait—exceptional movement. Having great movement starts with the first few steps. First-step speed is paramount in most sports, but due to the limited confines of a tennis court (27 feet wide and 39 feet from baseline to the net), a difference of as little as a 1/10 of a second improvement in speed can alter a defensive position into an offensive position. Training for court-specific speed is very different than speed training for other sports. In sports

Chapter 11

Factors that influence first step speed for tennis

- Proper starting position
- Low center of gravity
- Lower body mechanics
- Upper body mechanics
- Core strength
- Maximal strength
- Power
- Reaction time
- Anticipation

such as football and soccer the field is so vast that if the player's first-step speed is questionable, it may be hidden by a strong acceleration phase (the first 40 yards) and in some longer situations (> 40 yards) maximum speed technique becomes an important factor. In tennis, due to limited court size, a slow first-step cannot be hidden behind good acceleration or maximum speed. It is imperative for athletes to focus consistently on developing first step speed in all directions. Most competitive players will spend hours training stroke mechanics and strategy, but very few spend appropriate time on movement training.

BASIC SCIENCE BEHIND THE HOW & WHY OF SPEED
REACTION TIME

Reaction time (RT) is defined as the time from the stimulus (typically the opponent making contact with the ball) until the production of muscle force. RT is broken into two separate parts—"premotor" and "motor" time. Premotor time is defined as the time from the stimulus until the first sign of electromyography (EMG) activity in the muscle. Motor time is defined as the time from the first change in EMG activity in the muscle until the production of visible force (limb movement) by the muscle (1). Having great RT is a major advantage in tennis play. It allows the athlete to move sooner, be in better position sooner, and have better court position. Reaction time training needs to be an important part of every tennis athlete's program, and it can be developed in conjunction with other speed, agility, and quickness drills as well during on-court hitting sessions.

Although no scientific study has been performed specifically on tennis players' reaction time, some interesting studies have been performed on track sprinters which can be applied to tennis players. Top class male sprinters usually have reaction times of < 0.15 seconds (2, 3). The goal for high level tennis players is reduce RT below 0.2 seconds. Females have slightly slower reaction times than men (4); therefore, it is not always appropriate to compare male and female tennis players when it comes to reaction time training.

EMG studies that monitor muscle contraction in explosive speed movements have shown that leg extensor muscles (hamstrings and glutes) are contracting before any visible movement occurs. Therefore, to help improve first-step quickness and improved RT, training needs to focus on developing power in the major muscles involved (gluteals, hamstrings, and gastroc-soleus complex). As a result every good training program needs to include power exercises such as plyometrics and strength focused movements that will develop these muscles and quicken the first step.

PROPRIOCEPTORS

Proprioceptors are sensory receptors located within joints, muscles, and tendons. They provide the central nervous system with the information needed to maintain muscle tone and perform coordinated movements (5). The two major propriocep-tors involved in speed movements are the muscle spindles and the golgi tendon organs (GTOs). The muscle spindles provide information to the nervous system regarding the muscle's length and rate of change to the length. The muscle spindles are responsible for the phenomenon of rapidly stretching skeletal muscles resulting in a reflex contraction known as the stretch reflex (6). The GTO's are located in the tendons near the muscle and tendon junction. GTO's are responsible for sensing tension in the muscle and are thought to provide a protective mechanism against excessive tension (5).

The ability to train and improve the function of the proprioceptors contributes to improved speed performance by allowing the athlete to push the muscle and ten-dons further than would be accomplished without appropriate training. The stretch reflex is also thought to enhance the stiffness of the tendo-muscular system (7). This stiffness can affect the use of the stretch-shortening cycle by more efficiently stor-ing and using elastic energy. The benefit gained by utilizing the stored elastic ener-gy is a major reason why plyometric training has become such a widely used train-ing routine. Plyometric training develops the body's ability to use this stored elastic energy for productive acceleration, whether it be vertical (jumping) or horizontal (running). This stiffness is important because the length of the musculature changes rapidly during speed movements. During explosive movement, the muscles are exposed to large forces, causing tension within the muscles. The roles of both the muscle spindles and the GTOs are to prevent damage and injury to the muscle. If these inhibitory factors can be limited (to a safe degree) the muscles can work at a greater length and under greater tension. This would lead to better speed perform-ance (5).

WHAT SHOULD THE ARMS BE DOING DURING TENNIS MOVEMENTS?

The arm movement and upper body position are important in any speed move-ment, as they counterbalance the angular momentum produced by the hip rotation at the first movements. This counterbalancing effect aids in the production of force during movement, especially during the critical first few steps (see figure 11.1). Without the ability for the arms to counterbalance the large hip rotations, athletes would have difficulty maintaining balance, and this would cause inefficient movement. Training the arms to work in a productive and cohesive manner is vital when training for speed.

During the first few steps on the court, the arms work in opposition to the legs, with the left arm (via shoulder flexion) and right leg (via hip flexion) coming forward

as the right arm (via shoulder extension) and left leg (via hip extension) go backwards (and vice versa). The arm swing is initiated and controlled from the shoulder girdle. The trapezius should be relaxed, and the relative elbow angles of both arms should be maintained at approximately a 90-degree angle throughout each arm swing. Although running with a tennis racquet is slightly different, it should only change upper body technique over the last few steps before ball contact. The first few steps in explosive movement (i.e., to track down a drop shot) should be technically very similar to a wide receiver at the line of scrimmage or a track sprinter working from a standing start.

Figure 11.1: Counter-balancing of arms and legs.

WHAT HAPPENS WHEN AN ATHLETE RESPONDS TO AN OPPONENT'S SHOT?

Once the tennis player has reacted to the stimulus (opponent making contact with the ball), the athlete begins movement as quickly and powerfully as possible. Four important mechanical principles must be considered with respect to performing the initial movement from a stationary "ready position." These include Newton's three laws of motion and the kinetic concept of impulse.

NEWTON'S 1ST LAW: INERTIA

An object will remain in a state of rest or move in a straight line with constant velocity if there are no forces (outside/unbalanced) acting upon the object.

Initiating Movement

Going from the ready position to loading the back leg for push off is an example of this principle (Figure 11.2).

Figure 11.2: The athlete is loading the back leg (right leg) and is using this leg in a similar manner to the way

a sprinter uses a starting block. It allows the athlete to push hard into the ground and utilize the ground reaction forces which helps the athlete break inertia and start to accelerate.

NEWTON'S 2ND LAW: ACCELERATION

The acceleration of an object is directly proportional to the net force acting on the object, is in the direction of the net force, and is inversely proportional to the mass of the object (Figure 11.3).

$$Force = Mass \ X \ Acceleration$$
$$Acceleration = Force/Mass$$

NEWTON'S 3RD LAW: ACTION-REACTION

Whenever one object exerts a force on a second object, the second object exerts an equal and opposite force on the first (Figure 11.4).

• The force of the athlete pushing hard into the ground and the reactionary force of the ground pushing equal force in the opposite direction leads to the athlete's movement. The angle that the athlete pushes his/her foot into the ground is important depending on which direction of movement is desired.

Figure 11.3: First step from ready position and outlining 2nd law.

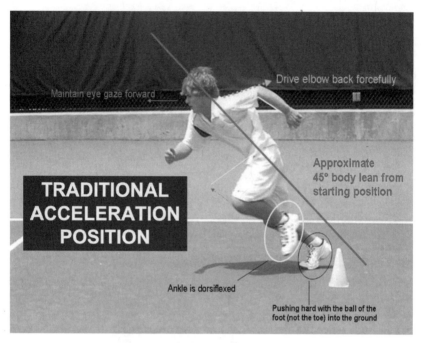

TRADITIONAL ACCELERATION POSITION

Maintain eye gaze forward

Drive elbow back forcefully

Approximate 45° body lean from starting position

Ankle is dorsiflexed

Pushing hard with the ball of the foot (not the toe) into the ground

Figure 11.4: Pushing hard into the ground and the ground equally pushing back leads to movement.

IMPULSE-MOMENTUM THEOREM

Impulse (J) = Force x Time

The impulse-momentum relationship is probably the most important component in the movement from a stationary start.

Force = Mass x Acceleration

Acceleration = (Velocity$_{final}$ – Velocity$_{initial}$) / Time

Therefore,

Force = Mass x (Velocity$_{final}$ – Velocity$_{initial}$) / Time

Or,

Force = (Mass x Velocity$_{final}$ – Mass x Velocity$_{initial}$)/Time

Hence,

Force X Time = (Mass X Velocity$_{final}$) – (Mass X Velocity$_{initial}$)

This equation states that the impulse (J) is equal to the change in momentum (an objects momentum is equal to its mass times its velocity) that it produces. When a tennis player is in the stationary "ready position," his initial velocity is zero and his mass remains constant. Therefore, the athlete's horizontal displacement (forward movement) divided by the time (velocity) is directly proportional to the magnitude of the impulse exerted to the ground and the consequent reaction. An effective way to improve acceleration is to produce a large force into the ground, with a very small amount of time actually spent on the ground. Impulse represents the average amount of force serving to propel the athlete and the time over which this force acts.

Studies measuring impulse rates of world class sprinters show that they produce horizontal and vertical impulses that are about 30% greater than state or regional level athletes (4, 8, 9). Therefore developing impulse (increasing force into the ground while reducing time spent on the ground) is one of the major differences separating top class speed athletes. The forces imparted to propel an athlete forward are a combination of horizontal and vertical forces, and both need to be trained to improve a tennis player's movement. This is one reason plyometric training and other horizontal and vertical power training techniques have become popular over the last decade—these types of movements develop force while limiting time spent on the ground.

Neuromuscular (physiological)	Biomechanical	Psychological
Firing Rate	Foot shape	Intrinsic Motivation
Motor Unit Recruitment	Muscle Insertion on Bone	Extrinsic Motivation
Muscle Spindles	Force Production	Arousal Level
Golgi Tendon Organs	Joint Mobility	Discipline
Neural Fatigue	Mechanics (Efficient Angles)	Pain Threshold
Reaction Time		Concentration
Fiber Type		Consistency
Muscle Size		
Muscle Elasticity		

Table 11.1: Components involved in developing good speed (reprinted with permission (10)).

WHAT HAPPENS AFTER THE FIRST STEP INTO THE GROUND
ACCELERATION

After breaking inertia and exploding from the ready position, the athlete must increase acceleration (increasing the rate of forward displacement per unit time). This acceleration is achieved by increasing stride length and stride frequency per unit of time. Scientists have found that mean ground contact times for the first step in elite male sprint athletes have ranged between 0.160 seconds - 0.194 seconds (3, 8, 11) and similar for the second ground contact. These ground contact times accounted for 82% and 76% of total stride time (ground contact time and flight time (11)) for the first two strides, respectively. Although this research was performed in track sprinters, the same general patterns are seen in tennis players with a large amount of total stride time being spent pushing into the ground over the first couple of steps.

Flight time for the first two steps from a stationary starting position ranged between 0.03 seconds and 0.08 seconds (11). The interesting thing to note about acceleration is that most world class track sprinters accelerate slower than other athletes (2). Yet they increase speed later in the race and are able to maintain top-end speed longer than other athletes. Therefore, using the 100 meter sprint as a test for tennis speed should be avoided as it is not specific to tennis movement and is actually a better measure of how well the athlete can run at top-end speed (maximum velocity) and how little the athlete will decelerate towards the end of the 100 meter sprint. Therefore when testing speed for tennis the distances should be no more than 20 meters, which is the maximum distance that an individual would ever run in one shot on a tennis court.

In every speed sport the majority of acceleration takes place within the first 25 meters, as tennis players never cover more than this distance in any one shot, a tennis player's movement is always in this acceleration phase (Figure 11.5). However, many coaches and trainers do not take this information into account when devising speed and agility programs. It is not uncommon for coaches and athletes to train for maximum speed and even speed maintenance in training sessions. It is common to see well-meaning coaches have tennis athletes run 100 and 200 meter sprints as a method to train for improvement in speed and acceleration. This violates the principle of specificity. If the goal is to train for tennis movement no single linear or lateral sprint should cover distances more than that occurring during play. Therefore, when designing speed programs the distances should be below 20 meters and involve linear, lateral, and multi-directional explosive movements.

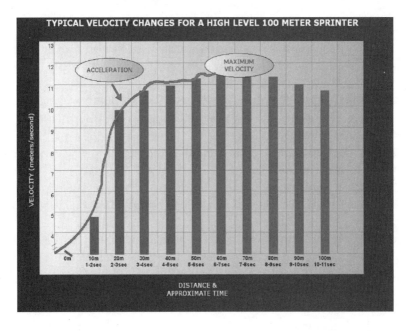

Figure 11.5: Time and distance between acceleration and maximum velocity for 100 meter sprinter.

Using Shin & Trunk Angles to Improve Speed in Training

Shin angle is an important marker of body position during acceleration. The coach should monitor an athlete's shin angle to judge if he/she is using proper acceleration technique. The angle between the anterior shaft of the tibia (shin bone) and the ground starts at a very small angle. This small angle allows for low center of gravity as well as the ability to push backwards (into the ground) which consequently aids in forward propulsion.

Trunk angle from the horizontal is another important aspect of quick movement. It is important that the athlete has a trunk angle between 45°-10° when accelerating.

Phases of Each Step During Tennis Movement

During each stride, an athlete travels through phases. These phases have been broken down into six separate, yet interrelated components (12), and the quality of each phase is determined by the preceding phase. Listed below is a sample of one cycle. This cycle is repeated continuously in tennis movement.

Phases of Each Sprint Cycle

1. *Residual phase*–The moment the right toe leaves the ground until the right thigh comes forward, via hip flexion.
2. *Recovery phase (a.k.a. "swing phase")*–The moment the right thigh comes forward (via hip flexion) until the right thigh stops ("blocking").
3. *Transition phase*–From the moment the right thigh stops (end of recovery phase) until the right thigh starts accelerating towards the ground, via hip extension.
4. *Ground preparation*–From the end of the transition phase (point of first acceleration of the right leg toward ground) until the right foot touches the ground.
5. *Ground phase* (divided into two separate phases):
   a. *Frontside ground phase*–From the instance the foot touches the ground until the body's center of mass is over the ground contact point of the front foot. This can also be described as the ground braking phase.
   b. *Backside ground phase*–From the midstance of support over the front foot (end of frontside ground phase) until the foot leaves the ground into the next residual phase, and the cycle continues. This can also be known as the ground propulsion phase.

Tennis-Specific Lateral & Multi-directional Movements

As tennis is a reactive and dynamic sport, the athlete must respond to the opponent's shot. The athlete must be able to move in all directions in an environment that causes him/her to be off-balance and out of position. One of the major differences separating the top professional players from college players and college players from club players is how well they hit the ball while being out-of-position. Apart from how well they hit the out-of-position tennis stroke, even more impressive is how well they can recover back to a ready-position and be in good position to react to the opponent's next shot. One research study that tested the relation between acceleration, maximum velocity, and agility suggested that these three variables are individual, and each specific quality is independent of the other (13). Therefore, training linear speed will not improve multi-directional or change of direction movements. Thus it is important to train tennis players in the specific movement patterns that are encountered during match play. If the goal is to improve an athlete's agility, training linear speed will not result in an improvement. Therefore, specificity of training needs to be at the forefront of your program design.

When working with junior tennis players it is vitally important that between the ages of 5-12 agility should be a major focus of the training program. This time period is when the greatest agility improvements will be seen (14) and it is important to stress these movements at this age to help train the neuromuscular system to the stop-start movements and to develop the strength requirements in the joints, ligaments, and tendons.

Movement Techniques On Court

Some of the techniques listed below are appropriate at different times throughout a point depending on the where in the court the ball is as well as where in the court you and your opponent are.

Open Hip First Step

This movement is usually used for balls which are close to the athlete (usually within 8 feet). The benefit of this movement (Figure 11.6) is it allows the athlete to set–up for an open stance forehand or backhand with very little effort. It also allows the athlete to impart more hip and lower body rotation into the stroke, theoretically allowing greater racquet head speed and greater spin and power into the shot. However, for many juniors and club players this movement pattern can lead to "lazy" footwork and poor set-up for the tennis stroke, causing the athlete to get to the ball late and make poor contact causing a poor stroke.

Figure 11.6: Open hip first step.

CLOSED HIP FIRST STEP

This movement takes a fraction of a second longer to initiate than the open hip movement, but it can produce more force into the ground and subsequent acceleration (Figure 11.7). Therefore, it is more appropriate for movements of less than 5 feet. It is also preferable for movements in a forward direction. The forward direction may be straight ahead or on a diagonal.

Figure 11.7: Closed hip first step.

THE GREAT DEBATE: SHUFFLE VS CROSS-OVER LATERAL MOVEMENTS

Like most controversies, both sides have valid arguments. The shuffle is a quicker more powerful movement and is better for shorter distances. This would typically occur if the ball is within a 3-5 feet diameter of the player. The shuffle is also more suited to hard court surfaces because the force applied into the ground in the shuffle is greater and, therefore, the reactive force of the ground into the body and subsequent powerful movement is greater. On a slower clay court, the reactive forces are less because some of the energy is lost because the extra time that the athlete spends on the ground. The sinking into the court on a clay (or grass) surface reduces foot and toe power returned from hard quick ground contacts.

The cross-over requires slightly less energy, yet it does produce less force into the ground. The benefits of less energy expended versus slower movements (over a short distance) must be weighed by the athlete. Most athletes growing up on clay courts use the cross-over method, whereas athletes who grow up playing on hardcourts typically prefer the shuffle. However, both movements need to be trained and are required during different movements on-court.

RECOVERY MOVEMENT

Recovering from tennis strokes and being ready for the next shot is a part of tennis that is vital to overall success, yet is rarely a focus of training. Having a good understanding of basic muscle recruitment and how best to transfer body weight is important in helping to determine the most productive technique to aid in recovery. Open stance and closed stance stroke technique requires the athlete to recover in a vastly different manner (Figure 11.8).

Open stance technique (for a right-handed player) causes a loading of the right hip and leg to a great degree and large rotational torques are seen through the hip lower back, core region, and legs. After contact the athlete will need to transfer weight to the left side of the

Figure 11.8: Recovery movement.

body to regain dynamic balance, and this will allow for the athlete to then take off using the left leg as the stabilizing pillar. The first step after recovery needs to be forcefully executed into the ground to allow for a quick turn-around and movement to the next stroke.

SUMMARY

The following chart is designed to assist coaches in the training of linear acceleration. It summarizes how the optimum aspects of linear sprint running changes as an athlete increases velocity and can be used as an aid in developing the straight ahead speed of tennis athletes (10).

STRIDE LENGTH short→medium→medium/long 1.30m→1.47m (during acceleration)	Initially, short strides increase to moderate to longer strides throughout the acceleration stage.
TOTAL STRIDE TIME relatively constant throughout the race range from 0.21 seconds to 0.26 seconds	Total stride time is the combination of ground contact time and flight time (time in air). Total stride time is relatively constant; however, the percentage of time spent during ground contact and flight time is vastly different during the different stages of the race.
GROUND CONTACT TIME long→short→shorter and maintain 0.22 seconds→0.11 seconds→0.09 seconds	The amount of time the foot is in contact with ground. Ground contact time moves from long ground contacts at the beginning of acceleration (as a mechanism to generate force into the ground) to very short ground contacts as velocity increases.
FLIGHT TIME short→longer→longest 0.03 seconds→0.08 seconds→0.119 seconds	The time during each stride spent in the air. Flight time is short during the first few strides of acceleration, but becomes longer as velocity increases.
SHIN ANGLE TO GROUND small→medium→medium and maintain	The angle between the anterior shaft of the tibia and the ground starts at a very small angle. As stride length increases and body position changes (more upright) as velocity increases.
VELOCITY slow→fast→fastest?fast (0 m/s→7 m/s →10 m/s→12 m/s)	Slow at the onset of the race and increases rapidly over the first 20 meters. Velocity increases more gradually for the next 30-40 meters until maximum velocity is reached, between 50-70 meters. Once maximum velocity is reached it can only be maintained for approximately 10-20 meters.
STRIDE FREQUENCY	Slow stride frequency at the beginning of the race increases rapidly as velocity increases.
HEEL HEIGHT FROM THE GROUND	This is directly related to the height of knee lift throughout each stride. At the beginning of acceleration, the heel height and knee height are rather low. As the athlete increases their velocity the heel and knee height increase throughout the acceleration period.

Table 11.2: Coaching speed chart adapted with permission (10).

REFERENCES

1.   Schmidt R.A., Lee T.D. Motor Control and Learning: A Behavioral Emphasis. 3rd ed. Champaign, IL: Human Kinetics; 1999.

2.   Gambetta V., Winckler G. Sport Specific Speed: The 3S System. Sarasota, FL: Gambetta Sports Training Systems; 2001.

3.   Mero A., Komi P.V. Reaction time and electromyographic activity during a sprint start. Eur J Appl Physiol 1990;61:73-80.

4.   Mero A., Komi P.V., Gregor R.J. Biomechanics of sprint running. Sports Medicine. 1992;13(6):376-392.

5.   Harris R.T., Dudley G. Neuromuscular anatomy and adaptations to conditioning. In: Baechle T.R., Earle R., editors. Essentials of Strength Training and Conditioning. Champaign, IL: Human Kinetics; 2000. p. 19-20.

6.   Powers S.K., Howley E.T. Exercise Physiology: Theory and application to fitness and performance, fourth edition. New York, NY: McGraw-Hill; 2001.

7.   Nichols T.R., Houk J.C. Improvement in linearity and regulation of stiffness that results from actions of the stretch reflex. J Neurophiosiology 1976;39:119-142.

8.   Mero A. Force-time characteristics and running velocity of male sprinters during the acceleration phase of sprinting. Res Q Exerc Sport 1988;59(2):94-98.

9.   Mero A., Luhtanen P., Komi P.V. A biomechanical study of the sprint start. Scandinavian Journal of Sport Sciences 1983;5(1):20-28.

10.   Kovacs M. Understanding speed- The science behind the 100 meter sprint. Birmingham, AL: Metis Publishing; 2005.

11.   Atwater A. Kinematic analysis of sprinting. Track and Field Quarterly Review 1982:12-16.

12.   Seagrave L. Speed Mechanics Seminar. In; 2001; Bradenton, Florida; 2001.

13.   Little T., Williams A.G. Specificity of acceleration, maximal speed and agility in professional soccer players. J Strength Cond Res 2005;19(1):76-78.

14.   Moreau X., Perrotte N., Quetin P. Speed and agility. In: Reid M., Quinn A., Crespo M., editors. ITF strength and conditioning for tennis. London, UK: ITF; 2003. p. 149-163.

CHAPTER 12

SPEED, QUICKNESS, & AGILITY DRILLS

- CONE & LINE DRILLS
- STAIR DRILLS
- RESISTANCE RUNNING
- WALL DRILLS
- RESISTANCE MOVEMENT TRAINING WITH RACQUET
- SAMPLE PROGRAMS

INTRODUCTION

This chapter provides information to help plan and implement speed, quickness, and agility exercises and programs for athletes. The goal of the following information is to provide an extensive list of exercises and methodologies so that coaches and trainers can apply appropriate exercises and program designs depending on the level and specific goals of the athletes. Remember to take into account the science behind speed and agility training as outlined in the previous chapter when designing and implementing your programs.

CONE & LINE DRILLS
SLALOM CONE RUN

Energy System Focus:
ATP, ATP-PC

Level of Exercise:
Beginner, Intermediate, Advanced, Professional

Coaching Cues: Maintain acceleration position and explode to each cone and focus on low hard cutting movements.

- Great exercise to develop deceleration and reacceleration (stop start movements).
- Cue the athlete to push hard on the outside leg and drive hard to reaccelerate.
- Work-to-Rest ratio for this drill should be between 1:20-25 for speed focused development or 1:5 for speed/endurance training.

Figure 12.1: Slalom cone run.

SHORT X DRILL

Energy System Focus: ATP, ATP-PC, Glycolysis

Level of Exercise: Beginner, Intermediate, Advanced, Professional

Coaching Cues: Start explosively from the ready position and focus on maintaining eye contact towards the net at all times.

Variations: This exercise as shown is called the short X drill and it can be taken out to the full size of a singles court which is called the long X drill. The long X drill is more focused on longer sprints and has a greater percentage of energy coming from glycolysis instead of ATP-PC. Therefore, this needs to be taken into account in the program design.

Figure 12.2: Short X drill.

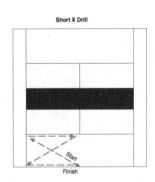

SPIDER DRILL

Energy System Focus: ATP, ATP-PC, Glycolysis

Level of Exercise: Beginner, Intermediate, Advanced, Professional

Coaching Cues: Start explosively from the ready position and run to each cone (starting on the right and going counterclockwise) and back to the center T.

Variations: This exercise as shown is called the Spider and is one of the most well-known agility drills for tennis players. The Long Spider uses similar movements but the cones are setup at the net instead of on the service line. This requires greater contribution from the glycolytic energy system.

Female	Excellent	Good	Average	Needs Improvement
Adult	<17.30	17.30-18.00	18.00-18.30	>18.30
Junior	<17.10	17.10-17.16	17.16-17.34	>17.34
Male	Excellent	Good	Average	Needs Improvement
Adult	<15.00	15.00-15.30	15.30-16.00	>16.00
Junior	<14.6	14.60-15.00	15.00-15.40	>15.40
Data collected by the USTA 1				

Table 12.1: Time goals for spider drill.

Figure 12.3: Spider drill.

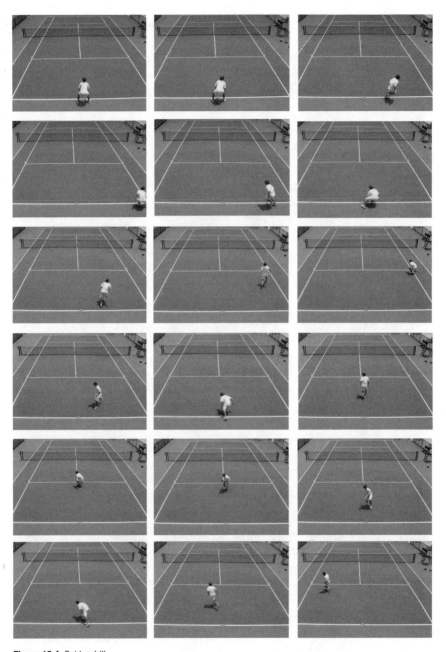

Figure 12.4: Spider drill.

SLOW GAMBETTA WHEEL DRILL

Energy System Focus: ATP, ATP-PC, Glycolysis

Level of Exercise: Beginner, Intermediate, Advanced, Professional

Coaching Cues: This drill is designed to work on correct stance and posture. It is performed with the athlete sprinting fast to each cone but then stopping and holding position for a count of three and then exploding out of the stance back to the middle. Repeat for all the cones.

Figure 12.5: Slow Gambetta wheel drill.

Variations: This exercise should also be performed at full speed without any pauses at the cones. The goal for the Fast Gambetta Wheel Drill is to work on explosive turns while maintaining low solid body position.

Also, to add difficulty, it is possible to add a tennis ball or a reaction ball to add another stimulus which will work on the athlete's ability to perform speed movements while also maintaining focus on an object.

ALLEY JUMPS

Energy System Focus: ATP, ATP-PC

Level of Exercise: Intermediate, Advanced, Professional

Coaching Cues: Explode from doubles sideline to single sideline.

Variations: Alley jumps can be performed in many different variations:

- Speed-focused: Explode as fast as possible from side to side while minimizing time spent on the ground.
  - < 10 seconds for speed-focused training.
  - > 10 seconds for speed/endurance-focused training.

Figure 12.6: Alley jumps.

- Power-focused: Explode as fast as possible while jumping in a forward position form doubles line to singles line from the baseline to the net and vice-versa. Minimize the time spent on the ground but jump as far as possible on each jump.
- Stabilizing Strength: Jump as high as possible from doubles line to singles line and then stick the landing and hold on one-leg for 2 seconds. This variation works the stabilizing muscles around the hip, knee and ankle.

D-LINE TO T-LINE DRILL

Energy System Focus: ATP, ATP-PC, Glycolysis

Level of Exercise: Beginner, Intermediate, Advanced, Professional

Coaching Cues: Start half-way between doubles line and middle (T) line and run as fast as possible touching each line with the hand. Work on acceleration and deceleration over the short distances.

Variations:

- 15 second drill – run as fast as possible repeating movements from D-line to T-line and count how many times the lines can be touched. Record this number to evaluate over the course of weeks and months. This time frame focuses on speed/endurance.

Figure 12.7: D-Line to T-Line drill.

BALL DROPS

Energy System Focus: ATP, ATP-PC, Glycolysis

Level of Exercise: Beginner, Intermediate, Advanced, Professional

Coaching Cues: Focus on first step speed and keeping hips low and head/eyes straight.

Variations:

- 5 feet or 10 feet from athlete single arm ball drop (beginner).
- 5 feet or 10 feet from athlete and double arm ball drop (intermediate).
- 5 feet or 10 feet form athlete and double arm ball drop with 2nd ball thrown once first ball has been tracked down.

Figure 12.8: Ball drops.

SHADOW TRAINING

Energy System Focus: ATP, ATP-PC, Glycolysis

Level of Exercise: Beginner, Intermediate, Advanced, Professional

Coaching Cues: Two athletes face each other and one person is offense and other is defense. The offense person moves linearly and laterally for 15 seconds and the defensive person has to mimic the movements in real time.

Variations:

- Increase or decrease time 5 sec-25 sec.
- Increase or decrease distance covered from 5-20feet.

Figure 12.9: Shadow training.

AGILITY WITH MEDICINE BALL THROW

Energy System Focus: ATP, ATP-PC, Glycolysis (if drill lasts more than 10 seconds)

Level of Exercise: Beginner, Intermediate, Advanced, Professional (One change of direction with one

Figure 12.10: Agility with medicine ball throw.

MB for a beginner up to 10 changes of direction with 10 MB for professional level).

Coaching Cues: Start explosively and push hard into the ground on the turns making sure to keep body position low to the ground.

Variations: This exercise can be performed using many variations. The example shown is designed to combine standard cone drill exercises with explosive MB throws to simulate forehand or backhand strokes. The goal is to develop explosive speed as well as trunk rotational power.

5-10-5 TENNIS VARIATION

Energy System Focus: ATP, ATP-PC

Level of Exercise: Beginner, Intermediate, Advanced, Professional

Coaching Cues: Start in athletic position and explode to the right and focus on staying low

Figure 12.11: 5-10-5 tennis variation.

and pushing hard into the turns and exploding hard out from the turns.

STAIR DRILLS
TWO-FEET STAIR JUMP

Energy System Focus: ATP, ATP-PC

Level of Exercise: Intermediate, Advanced, Professional

Number of Steps: 5 for intermediate, 8-10 for Advanced, 10-12 for Professional.

Figure 12.12: Two-feet stair jump.

Coaching Cues: Jump explosively from the bottom step to the top step minimizing ground contact time on each jump.

Variations: This exercise can be performed on one leg, but it is an advanced exercise and should only be performed after the athlete has undertaken an appropriate strength training program.

STAIR SPRINT RUNNING

Energy System Focus: ATP, ATP-PC

Level of Exercise: Intermediate, Advanced, Professional

Number of Steps: 10 for Intermediate, 10-15 for Advanced, 15-20 for Professional

Coaching Cues: Sprint explosively up stairs one step at a time.

Variations: This exercise can be performed by sprinting up every second step which will stress the

Figure 12.13: Stair sprint running.

quads to a greater extent. Triple steps are even more difficult and should only be attempted after appropriate strength and speed work has been performed.

RESISTANCE RUNNING
RESISTANCE RUNNING FORWARD

Energy System Focus: ATP, ATP-PC, Glycolysis

Level of Exercise: Advanced, Professional

Coaching Cues: Only applicable for athletes that have a good base of core strength and sprinting technique before attempting to add

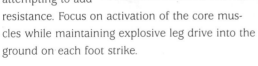

resistance. Focus on activation of the core muscles while maintaining explosive leg drive into the ground on each foot strike.

Figure 12.14: Resistance running forward.

RESISTANCE RUNNING BACKWARD

Energy System Focus: ATP, ATP-PC, Glycolysis

Level of Exercise: Advanced, Professional

Coaching Cues: Only applicable for athletes that have a good base of core strength and sprinting technique before attempting to add resistance.

Figure 12.15: Resistance running backward.

RESISTANCE RUNNING LATERAL

Energy System Focus: ATP, ATP-PC, Glycolysis

Level of Exercise: Advanced, Professional

Coaching Cues: Only applicable for athletes that have a good base of core strength and sprinting technique before attempting to add resistance. Focus on low body position while pushing laterally.

Variations: Adjusting work-to-rest ratios and resistance can focus more on stabilizing strength, power, speed, or even tennis-specific endurance.

Figure 12.16: Resistance running lateral.

WALL DRILLS
WALL DRILL POSTURE

Energy System Focus: ATP, ATP-PC

Level of Exercise: Beginner, Intermediate, Advanced, Professional

Coaching Cues: This drill is designed to work on developing strength and stability in the muscles involved in maintaining a good acceleration position.

- Total body lean at approximately 45°.
- Cue the athlete activate transversus abdominus "tummy tight" hips tall, and butt underneath the shoulders.

Variations: This position is the beginning position to teach the wall drill. After initial training it is important that you increase the body lean in each session until you reach a consistent 45° position and can hold that

Figure 12.17: Wall drill posture.

position for a full 20 seconds. For a beginner a 5 second hold will be difficult. Technique is more important than time when teaching this position.

WALL DRILL DRIVE-UP

Energy System Focus: ATP, ATP-PC

Level of Exercise: Beginner, Intermediate, Advanced, Professional

Coaching Cues: Maintain same position as Wall Drill Posture. This drill is designed to work on developing explosive power and stability strength. The goal of this movement is to develop the muscle pattern and muscle activation of the movements required to perform the residual and recovery phase of the 6 phases of each sprint cycle.

- Total body lean at approximately 45°.
- Cue the athlete to activate transversus abdominus "tummy tight", hips tall, and butt underneath the shoulders.

Figure 12.18: Wall drill drive-up.

- Explode right leg up to approximately 90 while maintaining strong core posture (repeat for left leg).
- Ankle dorsiflexion (point toe to sky).
- Do 4 reps per leg for beginner.
- Up to 10 reps per leg for advanced athlete.

181

WALL DRILL DRIVE-DOWN

Energy System Focus: ATP, ATP-PC

Level of Exercise: Intermediate, Advanced, Professional

Coaching Cues: Maintain same position as wall drill posture. This drill is designed to work on developing on explosive power and stability strength. The goal of this movement is to develop the muscle pattern and muscle activation of the movements required to perform the transition phase and ground preparation phase of the sprint cycle.

Figure 12.19: Wall drill drive-down.

- Total body lean at approximately 45°.
- Cue the athlete to activate transversus abdominus "tummy tight", hips tall, and butt underneath the shoulders.
- Explode right leg down explosively towards the ground while maintaining strong core posture (repeat for left leg).
- Ankle dorsiflexion (point toe to sky).
- When foot hits the ground jump up with opposing leg to lessen the force output on the other side of the body.
- Do 4 reps per leg for beginner.
- Up to 10 reps per leg for advanced athlete.

Variations: Once an athlete can perform the above mentioned exercises, an advanced athlete can take this movement into a Wall Run. This would be the same lower body movement mechanics as the athlete would run in an acceleration position on the wall. This is a challenging movement as the athlete needs to maintain position and perfect posture. Top level sprinters who train this on a daily basis have difficulty maintaining good acceleration running form for more than about 10 seconds. Therefore, tennis players would have a difficult time maintaining this position for more than 10 seconds.

Resistance Movement Training With Racquet
Resistance Movement Forehand

Energy System Focus: ATP, ATP-PC, Glycolysis

Level of Exercise: Advanced, Professional

Coaching Cues: Have athlete focus on stroke technique and movement footwork on each stroke while resistance increases as athlete moves further away from the resistive cord.

Variations: This can be used for multiple feeding drills with the emphasis of each drill to work on movement mechanics as well as optimum recovery mechanics.

Figure 12.20: Resistance movement forehand.

Resistance Movement Backhand

Energy System Focus: ATP, ATP-PC, Glycolysis

Level of Exercise: Advanced, Professional

Coaching Cues: Have athlete focus on stroke technique and movement footwork on each stroke while resistance increases as athlete moves further away from the resistive cord.

Variations: This can be used for multiple feeding drills with the emphasis of each drill to work on movement mechanics as well as optimum recovery mechanics.

Figure 12.21: Resistance movement backhand.

SAMPLE PROGRAMS

When implementing speed, agility, and quickness into a tennis player's program, many factors need to be considered. Refer back to Chapter 2 for what factors to take into account when designing training programs. Speed, agility, and quickness training can be performed before or after tennis training depending on the goals of the athlete and time of year. Pre-practice movement training is more important, especially in higher level competitors, because this is when they are most fresh. This means that their nervous system has not been stressed and has not fatigued. Speed training and the development of speed and agility is predominantly a neural adaptation and, as a result, requires more recovery time than other forms of training (endurance, hypertrophy, etc.) that are predominantly metabolic. Therefore, performing speed focused movement sessions before practice when the athlete is fresh allows for nervous system training resulting in the fastest and most efficient speed development. Yet, it is still important to have certain speed training sessions after practice when the body is fatigued, because late in matches the athlete needs to be familiar with moving fast even when fatigued. However, the art of coaching is to devise programs that combine before and after practice speed sessions, while allowing enough total recovery between training sessions to promote positive adaptation and improved speed and agility.

PRE-PRACTICE MOVEMENT TRAINING NATIONAL JUNIOR/COLLEGE LEVEL			
Dynamic Warm-Up Routine			
	Reps	Sets	Work : Rest
Slalom Cone Run	3	1	1 : 20
Short X Drill	4	1	1 : 20
Fast Gambetta Wheel Drill	3	1	1 : 20
	Time (sec)	Sets	Work : Rest
Resistance Running Forward	5	2	1 : 20
Resistance Running Forward	10	2	1 : 20
Resistance Running Forward	15	1	1 : 20
Resistance Running Backward	5	1	1 : 20
Resistance Running Backward	10	1	1 : 20
Resistance Running Lateral (right)	5	1	1 : 20
Resistance Running Lateral (right)	10	1	1 : 20
Resistance Running Lateral (left)	5	1	1 : 20
Resistance Running Lateral (left)	10	1	1 : 20

Table 12.2: Pre-practice movement training program for competitive junior or collegiate athlete.

PRE-PRACTICE MOVEMENT TRAINING NATIONAL JUNIOR/COLLEGE LEVEL			
Dynamic Warm-Up Routine			
	Reps	Sets	Work : Rest
D-line to T-line Drill	3	1	1 : 20
Long X Drill	2	1	1 : 20
Alley Jumps	3	1	1 : 20
	Time (sec)	Sets	Work : Rest
Resistance Movement Forehand	10	3	1 : 10
Resistance Movement Backhand	10	3	1 : 10

Table 12.3: Alternative pre-practice movement training program for competitive junior or collegiate athlete.

PRE-PRACTICE MOVEMENT TRAINING ADULT LEAGUE PLAYER			
Dynamic Warm-Up Routine			
	Reps	Sets	Work : Rest
D-line to T-line Drill	2	1	1 : 20
Short X Drill	2	1	1 : 20
Spider Drill	1	1	1 : 20

Table 12.4: Pre-practice movement training for adult league player.

45 MINUTE MOVEMENT TRAINING NATIONAL JUNIOR/COLLEGE LEVEL			
Dynamic Warm-Up Routine	(Doubles line to Doubles line)		
Toe Walk			
Heel Walk			
Side Ankle Walk			
Knee to Chest Walk			
Walking Quad Stretch			
1-leg Walking Opposite (1-leg RDL)			
Hamstring Handwalk ("Inchworm")			
Straight Leg Walk			
Walking Lunge			
Rotational Walking Lunge			
Walking lunge + Elbow into Knee Pushout			
Hip Handwalk (Spiderman crawl)			
Lateral Lunge			
Wall Drills	**Reps**	**Sets**	**Time (sec)**
Wall Drill Posture	5	2	5, 10, 15
Wall Drill Drive-Up	5	2	5
Wall Drill-Drive-Down	5	2	5
Wall Run	5	1	5
Speed, Agility, Quickness	**Reps**	**Sets**	**Work : Rest**
Slalom Cone Run	3	1	1 : 20
Short X Drill	4	1	1 : 20
Fast Gambetta Wheel Drill	3	1	1 : 20
Ball Drop Variations	10	3	1 : 20
Shadow Training	5	2	1 : 10
Resistance Running	**Time (sec)**	**Sets**	**Work : Rest**
Resistance Running Forward	5	2	1 : 20
Resistance Running Forward	10	2	1 : 20
Resistance Running Forward	15	1	1 : 20
Resistance Running Backward	5	1	1 : 20
Resistance Running Backward	10	1	1 : 20
Resistance Running Lateral (right)	5	2	1 : 20
Resistance Running Lateral (right)	10	2	1 : 20
Resistance Running Lateral (left)	5	2	1 : 20
Resistance Running Lateral (left)	10	2	1 : 20

Table 12.5: Sample 45 minute speed, agility and quickness program for a competitive junior or collegiate level tennis player.

3 DAY A WEEK FULL FITNESS PROGRAM FOR HIGH LEVEL COMPETITIVE PLAYERS			
DAY 1 - Dynamic Warm-Up			
Agility Drills (100% Effort on EAch Rep)	Reps	Work:Rest	Record Time
Short Five Corner Drill	5	1:15	
Short X Drill	5	1:15	
MB Power Drills (2-3lb MB)	Reps	Rest	
Regular Ovhd MB Throw	5	20 sec.	
Serve Stance MB Throw	5	20 sec.	
Opposite Serve Stance MB Throw	5	20 sec.	
Forehand MB Throw	5	20 sec.	
Backhand MB Throw	5	20 sec.	
MB Anaerobic Capacity	Time		
Forehand MB Throw (continuous against wall)	30 sec.		
Backhand MB Throw (continuous against wall)	30 sec.		
MB Chest Pass (continuous against wall)	30 sec.		
ESS Tennis Development		Rest	
Doubles LIne to Doubles LIne (and back)	1	1 to 3	
	2	2 to 3	
	3	3 to 3	
	4	4 to 3	
	5	5 to 3	
	5	6 to 3	
	5	7 to 3	
	4	8 to 3	
	3	9 to 3	
	2	10 to 3	
	1	11 to 3	

Table 12.6: 3 day a week speed, power and agility program for competitive players.

3 DAY A WEEK FULL FITNESS PROGRAM FOR HIGH LEVEL COMPETITIVE PLAYERS (cont.)			
DAY 2 - Dynamic Warm-Up			
Anticipation/Reaction	Time	Rest	Record Time
Back of Knee Slap Game (w/ partner) Each person slapper x2	30 sec.	120 sec.	
Mirror Drill (w/ partner)	20 sec.	90 sec.	
Plyometrics	Reps	Rest	
Alley Jumps			
Jump-Stick-Hold (2 sec)	5	45 sec.	
Jump for Height & Distance	5	45 sec.	
Jump for Speed	5	45 sec.	
Plyo Jumps			
Mini Jump + Vertical Jump	5	30 sec.	
Mini Jump + Long Jump	5	30 sec.	
MB Power/Strength	Reps	Rest	
Lunge			
MB Catch w/ explosive rotational throw each leg x2 sets	5	60 sec.	
Anaerobic Capacity	Time	Rest	
(Mimic Low Volley) Ball Catch Drill x 4 sets	20 sec.	30 sec.	
ESS Tennis Development	Courts	Work:Rest	
Suicide	1	1 to 3	
	2	1 to 3	
	3	1 to 3	
	2	1 to 3	
	1	1 to 3	
	1	1 to 3	
	1	1 to 3	

Table 12.6: continued

3 DAY A WEEK FULL FITNESS PROGRAM FOR HIGH LEVEL COMPETITIVE PLAYERS (cont.)			
DAY 3 - Dynamic Warm-Up			
Anticipation/Reaction	Time		Record Time
Hand Slap Game	2 min.		
Ball Catch off Wall (ball thrown from behind person)	3 min.		
Agility Drills	Reps	Rest	
Star Drill	4	1 to 15	
Short X Drill	4	1 to 15	
Short Five Corner Drill	4	1 to 15	
MB Power			
MB Granny Toss	10	20 sec.	
MB Reverse Granny Toss	10	20 sec.	
MB Balance/Power/Anaerobic Capacity	Time	Rest	
One Leg Catch & Overhead Throw - each leg	30 sec.	90 sec.	
MB Mini Tennis work on quick feet & proper technique.			
Plyo/Reaction Jumps	Reps	Rest	
Box Blasts (on steps) - focus on height (ea. Leg)	10	90 sec.	
Ski Jumps	10 sec.	60 sec.	
	10 sec.	60 sec.	
	10 sec.	60 sec.	
	10 sec.	60 sec.	
ESS Tennis Development	Reps	Rest	
Double Line to Doubles Line (and back)	3	1 to 2	
	3	1 to 2	
	3	1 to 2	
	4	1 to 3	
	4	1 to 3	
	5	1 to 3	
	5	1 to 3	
	5	1 to 3	
	4	1 to 3	
	4	1 to 3	

Table 12.6: continued

REFERENCES

1.   USTA. Complete Conditioning for Tennis. Champaign, IL: Human Kinetics, 1998

Chapter 13

Training Progression: Linking Training to On-court Drills

- Depth Jumps
- Medicine Ball Throws
- Fed Ball Drills
- Slalom Cone Run
- Spider Drill
- Low Volley Drill
- Jump Squats

Introduction

According to the principle of specificity, the more specific an activity is to the sport, the greater the transfer of training will be. The most specific training for any sport is the actual sport itself. Combining training with on-court tennis specific drills may produce a high degree of transfer to tennis performance. On-court drills can be used during competitive phases in which training should become more specific.

There are several ways that training drills can be brought to the court. Various movement and conditioning drills have been presented in previous chapters. Many of these movement drills can be taken onto the court and be performed with a racquet and tennis ball as a fed ball drill. Performing these drills with a racquet in hand and requiring the athlete to hit a specific shot provides an additional level of specificity to tennis play. Numerous plyometric exercises are presented in this chapter in the form of various jumps and medicine ball throws. These exercises can be combined with various strokes as well to increase the specificity to the sport.

The rest of this chapter will provide examples of drills that can be combined with tennis strokes on court to achieve a high degree of specificity.

DEPTH JUMPS WITH SPLIT STEP TO GROUNDSTROKE

Energy System Focus: ATP, ATP-PC

Level of Exercise: The level of this exercise is dependent on the height of the box. Intermediate—6-12", Advanced—12-20"

Coaching Cues: In this exercise the athlete performs a depth jump off a box and then moves towards a fed ball and performs a specified stroke. The athlete should land in a proper split step position, on the balls of their feet, with knees bent, feet shoulder width apart, and back flat. At impact the player should move quickly in the direction of the ball and perform a groundstroke.

Variations: This exercise can also be performed by jumping over a barrier and landing in a split step. This can be performed with volleys instead of groundstrokes as well.

Figure 13.1: Depth jumps with split step to groundstroke.

MEDICINE BALL THROWS TO GROUNDSTROKES

Energy System Focus: ATP, ATP-PC

Level of Exercise: Intermediate to Advanced

Coaching Cues: In this drill alternate between the medicine ball groundstroke throws presented in Chapter 8 and hitting groundstrokes. Perform a set of 5-10 medicine ball throws followed by a set of 5-10 groundstrokes. When throwing the medicine ball, mimic a forehand or backhand groundstroke using two hands.

MEDICINE BALL OVERHEAD THROWS (SERVING) TO VOLLEYS

Energy System Focus: ATP, ATP-PC

Level of Exercise: Intermediate to Advanced

Coaching Cues: In this drill alternate between medicine-ball-serving overhead throws (as shown in chapter 8) into a volley position with the medicine ball. Perform a set of MB overhead throws and 2-4 MB volleys followed by an actual serve followed by 2-4 volleys.

FED BALL DRILLS USING TENNIS-SPECIFIC WORK/REST INTERVALS

Energy System Focus: ATP, ATP-PC, Glycolysis

Level of Exercise: All Levels

Coaching Cues: In this drill the coach feeds balls to the player moving him around the court simulating point play. Make sure to use appropriate work/rest intervals and appropriate rest between sets to simulate the breaks on the changeovers.

Example:

Number of Shots Hit	Rest Period (sec)
8	20
5	15
12	25
10	20
6	15
4	15
9	20
14	25
8	20
12	25
3	15
10	20
90 Second Rest Period for Changeover	
Then repeat program for as may sets as desired	

MEDICINE BALL POINTS

Energy System Focus: ATP, ATP-PC, Glycolysis

Level of Exercise: Intermediate to Advanced

Coaching Cues: Medicine balls can be used to simulate points. Players play in the service boxes and toss the ball with simulated forehands and backhands depending upon which side the ball comes. Players may keep score as they would in a tennis match. Players should mimic groundstrokes with their throws and use footwork identical to the footwork used during actual point play. The size and weight of medicine balls should be determined by the age, strength and level of player. For most juniors a medicine ball that weighs less than 3 kg is appropriate.

Figure 13.2: Medicine ball points.

SLALOM CONE RUN WITH GROUNDSTROKES

This drill is the same as the slalom cone run presented in Chapter 12, with the athlete hitting strokes at each of the cones.

Energy System Focus: ATP, ATP-PC

Level of Exercise: All Levels

Coaching Cues: Focus on accelerating to each cone and adjusting to the ball at the cone with small steps. Then change directions quickly and move to the next cone.

SPIDER DRILL WITH GROUNDSTROKES

This drill is the same as the spider drill presented in Chapter 12 with the athlete hitting strokes at each of the five spots on the court.

Energy System Focus: ATP, ATP-PC, Glycolysis

Level of Exercise: All Levels

Coaching Cues: Accelerate to each ball quickly and recover back to the starting position quickly after each stroke.

LOW VOLLEY DRILL

Energy System Focus: ATP, ATP-PC, Glycolysis

Level of Exercise: All Levels

Coaching Cues: This drill requires the coach to feed the player low volleys. The player starts in the middle of the service box and moves forward to hit a low volley. The player then recovers back to the middle and performs a split step as the coach feeds the next ball. The drill is repeated for 10-30 seconds. The player works on moving quickly to the ball and getting down low to each volley.

JUMP SQUATS TO SERVES

Energy System Focus: ATP, ATP-PC

Level of Exercise: Intermediate to Advanced

Coaching Cues: In this drill alternate between performing jump squats which are presented in Chapter 8 and hitting serves. Perform a set of 5-10 jump squats followed by a set of 5-10 serves. When hitting serves, have the athletes focus on using their legs and pushing up to the ball.

Variations: Overheads can be substituted for serves as the player works on moving back quickly and jumping up to hit a deep lob.

CHAPTER 14

PHYSICAL TESTING FOR TENNIS PERFORMANCE

- TEST SELECTION
- ANTHROPOMETRIC TESTING
- BODY FAT MEASURES
- BIA (BIOELECTRICAL IMPEDANCE)
- SPEED & AGILITY
- POWER

INTRODUCTION

Developing and implementing tennis workouts require knowledge of the athlete's strengths and weaknesses. Depending on the level of player, this assessment process could be as simple as a few sprints and some sit-ups to as complex as laboratory testing for maximal oxygen consumption, maximal power output, and even a full biochemical blood analysis. This chapter outlines many tests tennis players of different levels can use.

REASONS FOR TESTING

- Determine strengths and areas for improvement.
- Determines baseline levels against which improvement goals can be set.
- Motivate athletes to improve.

- Keep athletes accountable and progressing in the correct direction.
- Talent identification and analysis of the athlete's potential. Some players are just not as talented (physically, mentally, emotionally, tactically, or technically) and should be trained with this in mind.

GOAL SETTING

Defining and setting appropriate goals are a prerequisite to success. However, just setting goals is not enough. Goal getting techniques must also be employed. Ask the following questions when setting goals for tennis athletes.

- Does the athlete have the base genetic capabilities (muscle fiber type, body shape, aerobic capabilities, height, etc.) to compete successfully at the desired goal level. Being realistic about potential is important and asking advice from experienced coaches may be helpful in identifying an athlete's talent and potential.
- What are the athlete's time commitments? Designing goals and programs based on unrealistic time commitments will only result in failure to achieve those goals.
- What is the athlete's motivation? Is it external (such as parents and coaches desire for success), or does it come from the athlete's desire to get better and improve?

TEST SELECTION

There are hundreds, actually thousands, of possible ways to test for tennis players. When selecting tests, it is advisable to choose measures that will focus on specific aspects that will be a close marker to actual match performance. Knowing a tennis player's maximum bench press might be helpful for establishing the athlete's general strength and for assessing his/her motivation for surpassing such benchmarks, but it has very little correlation with match performance, and coaches should not confuse traditional tests for strength, flexibility, or aerobic capacity with tests that may be more specific to tennis performance.

Areas that need to be taken into account when selecting tennis-specific tests are:
- Training age (how many years has the athlete been training competitively)
- Chronological age
- Level of competition
- Gender
- Time available for testing and training
- Space and equipment available
- Purpose of specific tests

In designing and implementing tennis-specific testing programs it is helpful to be aware of the most common types of injuries, muscle weaknesses, and flexibility problems that typically arise from competitive tennis play. The following are some of these problems (26):

Shoulder
- Poor scapular stability.
- Loss and/or limited range of motion in internal rotation and elevation of dominant shoulder.
- Muscle strength imbalances: weak scapular stabilizers, tight internal shoulder rotator muscles (subscapularis, teres major, lattisimus dorsi, pectoralis major, deltoid (anterior).

Pelvic Girdle and Lumbar Spine
- Poor pelvic (core) stability.
- Weak stabilizers (transversus abdominis and multifidus).
- Weak gluteus medius (which helps to stabilize pelvis).
- Tight muscles which insert into pelvis (illiacus, psoas, rectus femoris, hamstrings, piriformis, illiotibial band).

Patellofemoral (knee pain)—Poor tracking of patella can be caused by:
- Tight illiotibial band.
- Weak and poor timing of vastus medialis oblique (VMO).
- Weak and poor timing of gluteus medius.
- Foot and leg alignment.
- Tight rectus femoris.
- Tight illiopsoas.

Elbow/Wrist
- Elbow/wrist problems commonly result of shoulder area problems.
- Tight wrist flexors and extensors.
- Reduced flexibility of wrist, elbow, and radio-ulna joints.
- Poor muscular endurance of muscles surrounding wrist and elbow.

Ankle and Foot
- Ligament instability.
- Weakness in muscles surrounding ankle and foot (especially peroneals).
- Tightness in gastroc-soleus complex.
- Gait pattern problems which might need remedy via orthotics.

Table 14.1: Typical tennis related problems.

ANTHROPOMETRIC TESTING

Because tennis requires fast explosive movements over a long period of time, athletes need to have enough muscle mass to help with explosive movements while maintaining low body fat. Excess body fat will actually limit an athlete's speed and aerobic ability because he will utilize more energy for the same amount of work compared to lower body fat individuals.

BODY FAT MEASURES

Body fat percentages of most tennis players are lower than the regular population but are typically not as low as some athletes in high strength and power sports such as track sprinting and gymnastics. Most competitive tennis players have body fat percentages between 7-13% (4, 5, 12, 22) for males and 17-26% (4) for females. On the following pages some methods to determine an athlete's body composition are outlined.

BMI (BODY MASS INDEX)

BMI, or body mass index, is a simple calculation that is used in healthcare for sedentary populations to determine where a person ranks on a scale ranging from underweight to severely obese. The method is simple to calculate and requires only the measurement of height and weight.

BMI CALCULATION

$$= WEIGHT/HEIGHT^2 \quad \text{(kg of body weight/ height (m)}^2\text{)}$$

Example: James is a tennis player who weighs 180 lbs and is 6 ft tall. Measuring his BMI is a simple two step process:

> **Step 1:** Convert the weight and height into metric (kg and meters)
> 180 lbs / 2.2 = **81.8 kg**
> 6 ft = 72 in
> 72 in x 0.0254 = **1.83 m**
> **Step 2:** Compute metric numbers in BMI formula
> 81.8 kg/1.83 m^2

$$BMI = 24.42$$

Although BMI measures are used extensively as health, wellness, and obesity measures, it is a measure that has little relevance to tennis athletes because all competitive tennis players must be in at least moderate physical condition just to be able to compete. The BMI measure will put nearly every competitive tennis player in the normal range, and even if on the occasion they might not be, it does not tell the coach, trainer, or scientist much about the relevant fitness level for tennis-specific performance.

BMI values are continually being refined, but for general purposes the normative ranges are:

Normal = 18.5-24.9

Overweight = 25-29.9

Obese > 30

GIRTH MEASURES

Girth measurements are designed to help the coach and athlete keep track of anthropometric changes throughout training cycles. Girth measurements are obtained by simply using a tape measure to measure the width around certain limbs of the body. Any portion of the body can be measured, but the coach has to distinguish between collecting data for the sake of data collection or actually being helpful in the training of the athlete? Girth measurements are important to track changes in different body parts and should be used especially in young athletes who are growing. Girth measures can help showcase any body parts that might be lagging in development.

SKINFOLDS

This is arguably the most recognized method of assessing body composition and for determining body fat. The skinfold technique is a manual application involving the pinching of fat mass away from the bone and muscle at different sites on the body and measuring the diameter of the pinch (Figure 14.1 and Table 14.2). The values are entered into a formula that calculates body fat and fat free mass. Although this is the most widely used method of body fat analysis, incorrect results can occur if the test is not performed by a person who is trained and experienced in skinfold measures.

Although many sites can be used to measure skinfold thickness, it is recommended that the 3- or 7-site method be implemented for the most time efficient, yet reliable, and valid results. The American College of Sports Medicine guidelines for skinfold measures are as follows(1):

Procedures:

- All measures should be made on the right side of the body.
- Caliper should be placed 1 cm away from the thumb and finger.
- Pinch needs to be maintained while reading the caliper.
- Wait between 1-2 seconds (and no longer) before reading the caliper.
- Take duplicate measures and retest if measurements are not within 2 mm.

	FOLD TYPE	DESCRIPTION
TRICEP	Vertical	On the posterior midline of the upper arm, halfway between the acromion and olecranon processes, with the arm held freely to the side of the body.
BICEPS	Vertical	Anterior aspect of the arm over the belly of the biceps muscle, 1cm above the level used to measure the triceps site.
SUBSCAPULAR	Diagonal	Diagonal fold (at a 45° angle); 1 to 2 cm below the inferior angle of the scapula.
SUPRAILIAC	Diagonal	In line with the natural angle of the iliac crest taken in the anterior axillary line immediately superior to iliac crest.
MID-ABDOMINAL	Vertical	2 cm to the right side of the umbilicus (belly button).
FRONT-THIGH	Vertical	Anterior midline of the thigh, midway between the proximal border of the patella and the inguinal crease (hip).
MEDIAL CALF	Vertical	At the maximum circumference of the calf on the midline of its medial border.
CHEST/ PECTORAL	Diagonal	1/2 the distance between the anterior axillary line and the nipple (men) or one-third of the distance between the anterior axillary line and the nipple (women).
MIDAXILLARY	Vertical	On the midaxillary line at the level of the xiphoid process of the sternum (breast bone).

Table 14.2: Standard skinfold measurement positions.

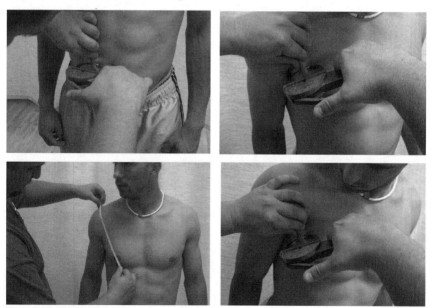

Figure 14.1: Photos of skinfolds.

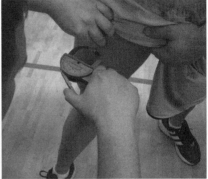

Figure 14.1 cont.: Photos of skinfolds.

Men

- 7-site (chest, midaxillary, triceps, subscapular, mid-abdominal, suprailiac, front-thigh)

  Body Density = 1.112 – 0.00043499 (Sum of 7 skinfolds)
  + 0.00000055 (sum of 7 skinfolds)^2 – 0.00028826(Age)

- 3-site formula (chest, mid-abdominal, front-thigh)

  Body Density = 1.10938 – 0.00082649 (Sum of 3 skinfolds)
  + 0.0000016 (sum of 3 skinfolds)^2 – 0.0002574 (Age)

Women

- 7-site (chest, midaxillary, triceps, subscapular, mid-abdominal, suprailiac, front-thigh)

  Body Density = 1.097 – 0.00046971 (Sum of 7 skinfolds)
  + 0.00000056 (sum of 7 skinfolds)^2 – 0.00012828(Age)

- 3-site formula (triceps, suprailiac, thigh)

  Body Density = 1.099421 – 0.0009929 (Sum of 3 skinfolds)
  + 0.0000023 (sum of 3 skinfolds)^2 – 0.0001392 (Age)

The above formulas provide the 3-site and 7-site skinfold measures. Both measures are valid and reliable, and if you are working one-on-one with athletes, the 7-site method is recommended. If you have time constraints or are testing numerous athletes in a group, the 3-site method is still a good measure. The skinfold measures need to be added and put into the above formula. These formulas provide a final body density of the individual. Once this body density is determined, this number needs to be put through the Siri formula which is listed below:

Siri formula (27) Percent Fat = [(495/body density)-450]*100

Now you have an athlete's body fat percentage. It is easy to put these formulas into a spreadsheet program so all you have to do is measure the athlete's skinfolds and input the sum of skinfolds and age into the spreadsheet formulas. However, it is recommended that you be trained in the correct methods to measure skinfold or request the services of a trained and experienced tester. Most universities with a sports science department will be able to perform this test successfully, or you can search out experienced strength and conditioning coaches or certified personal trainers who can measure skinfold accurately.

BIA (BIOELECTRICAL IMPEDANCE)

BIA measures body composition by sending a low, safe electrical current through the body. The current passes freely through the fluids contained in muscle tissue, but encounters difficulty/resistance when it passes through fat tissue. This resistance of the fat tissue to the current is termed "bioelectrical impedance." BIA machines are typically part of traditional weight scales or can be a hand-held device. Using a person's height and weight, the machine can then compute the body fat percentage. BIA measures are rather accurate if some pre-testing guidelines are followed.

BIA PRE-TESTING GUIDELINES
- No eating or drinking within 4 hours of the test.
- No exercise within 12 hours of the test.
- Athlete urinates within 30 minute of the test.
- No alcohol within 48 hours of test.
- No diuretics within 7 days of the test.

HYDROSTATIC UNDERWATER WEIGHING

Hydrostatic weighing, based on Archimedes' Principle, has typically been regarded as the "gold standard" for body composition assessment. However, the equipment required is expensive and cumbersome and is not practical for most coaches and athletes. Because body fat is less dense than water, it increases one's buoyancy, while the fat-free mass, which has a density greater than water, makes one sink.

After correcting for residual volume (RV)—the amount of air remaining in the lungs following maximal expiration, which increases buoyancy and decreases the underwater weight—the fat percentage can be calculated based on the underwater weight. The largest source of error in underwater weighing is thought to be the determination of residual volume.

BOD POD

Bod Pod also known as air displacement plethysmography (ADP), requires the athlete to enter a container and the device measures the resultant displacement of air. Since it is based on the same whole-body measurement principle as hydrostatic weighing, the Bod Pod first measures the subject's mass and volume. From these measurements, whole-body density is determined. Using this data, body fat and lean mass can then be calculated.

CARDIORESPIRATORY ENDURANCE

The typical measure of an individual's cardiorespiratory endurance (also sometimes called aerobic capacity) is the volume of oxygen consumed per minute (VO_2). Although an athlete's maximum VO_2 (VO_2max) is different depending on the competitor's age and playing standard, competitive tennis players range between 44-69 $ml \cdot kg^{-1} \cdot min^{-1}$ (3, 5, 6, 10, 11, 16, 17, 22, 28, 29). These VO_2max values would classify tennis players as being highly anaerobically trained (19). It is interesting to note that players who were considered aggressive, attacking players had lower VO_2 values during play than baseline players (6). For example, players with similar playing styles to Pat Rafter or Martina Navratilova will have lower VO_2 values during play compared to players whose style is similar to Rafael Nadal or Jim Courier. Individual's VO_2max values can change rather substantially during time off or when training is reduced. These reductions may range between 4-14% with reduced training (22, 24). Therefore, consistent monitoring of maximal oxygen consumption is appropriate to help ascertain training intensity and improvement. Many tests are available to measure an athlete's VO_2. Some methods measure VO_2max directly using laboratory equipment, whereas other methods use field tests and an estimate is then calculated. The vast majority of coaches and athletes do not have access to laboratory equipment, but field tests do an adequate job of estimating an athlete's oxygen consumption. Lab tests can be obtained for high level competitive tennis players at a select few private facilities, but most universities with a sports science or exercise science department will have the equipment and should be contacted to see if they will be able to measure an athlete's VO_2.

SHUTTLE TEST

This test is an accurate measure of aerobic power (7), and it is somewhat similar to tennis movements as it has continual stop, start movements over distances not much larger than a tennis court (20 m). Another benefit of this test is that is can be performed on large groups simultaneously.

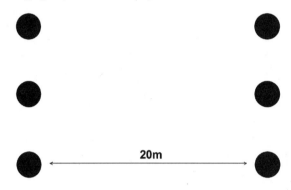

Figure 14.2: Shuttle test.

The equipment required is a space at least 20 m long and a copy of the CD.

- This test involves continuous running between two lines 20 m apart in time to recorded beeps. For this reason the test is also often called the "beep" or "bleep" test. The time between recorded beeps decreases each minute (level). There are several versions of the test, but one commonly used version has an initial running velocity of 8.5 km/hr, which increases by 0.5 km/hr each minute.
- The athlete's score is the level and number of shuttles reached just before he/she was unable to keep up with the tape recording. This score can be converted to a VO_2max equivalent score.
- Equipment needed: Flat, non-slip surface, marking cones, 20 m measuring tape, pre-recorded CD and the chart to compare the results with estimated VO_2max values.
- There are published VO_2max score equivalents for each level reached. The correlation to actual VO_2max scores are high.

SPEED & AGILITY

Tennis has often been described as a game of continual emergencies because with every shot the opponent hits, a ball can have a different velocity, a different type and rate of spin, and can be placed in many different parts of the court (20). This complexity requires tennis athletes to have fast reaction times and explosive "first-step" speed. Tennis players need to be exceptional movers in a linear, lateral, and multi-directional movements. Training, and therefore testing, needs to focus on all types of movement. In a practical research study that tested the relationship between acceleration, maximum velocity, and agility, it was found that these three variables are individual and each specific quality is independent of the other (23), it is therefore important to train tennis players in the specific movement patterns that are encountered during match play. If specificity principles are used to design training programs, it is imperative that specificity is applied during testing as well. Make sure that linear, lateral, and multi-directional speed and agility exercises are tested for the tennis athlete.

AGILITY & SPEED TEST
SPIDER TEST
- 12"x18' rectangle behind center of baseline, place a ball on each corner where baseline and singles sidelines meet, singles sideline and service line meet, and on the T. Retrieve each ball counterclockwise and put in the rectangle (Figure 12.4, pg 171).

Other possible tests that measure speed and agility for tennis are: (See descriptions in Chapter 11 of some of the exercises that can also be used as exercises for testing):
- 5-10-5
- Short X Drill (Figure 12.2, pg 169)
- Long X Drill
- 5 m, 10 m, 20 m timed linear sprint

STRENGTH
There are hundreds of exercises that can be used to measure an athlete's strength. The most important thing is how specific and relevant the testing exercises are to tennis performance. Although having good strength levels in traditional exercises such as the squat and bench press are important, being able to bench press 200 kg or squat 300 kg is great for a football player, but it is not an important statistic for a tennis. Testing for strength should include all major muscles involved in tennis play, both in the upper and lower body. Some typical exercises that are good strength tests are:
- Sit-ups
- Push-ups
- Squats

- Pull-ups
- Bench Press
- RDL (Romanian Deadlift) (Figure 14.5)
- Grip Strength

GRIP STRENGTH

Figure 14.3: Romanian deadlift.

Solid contact between the racquet and the ball is required for optimum stroke execution, and this is influenced by grip strength. A firm wrist is necessary to prevent the racquet head from straying from its intended path under the influence of high angular speeds and torques (2). Maximal grip strength of 600 N has been reported in elite level tennis players, as well as greater grip endurance compared to nontennis players (21). It has also been found that grip strength and grip endurance was not well correlated. Therefore, grip strength and grip endurance should be tested separately and trained accordingly (21).

The shoulder region is highly involved in all tennis strokes, and it has been shown that shoulder internal, external, and diagonal peak torques contribute substantially to serve velocity (25). Therefore, it is not surprising that the shoulder region has been a major focus of tennis-related performance and injury prevention/rehabilitation research. Eccentric muscular contractions play a role in functional activities, but in the tennis shoulder, specifically the rotator cuff, the infraspinatus and teres minor are of major importance during the follow-through of the groundstrokes, but more specifically in the service motion (8). These two muscles undergo high decelerative eccentric muscle contractions to preserve healthy joint movement (13). Adequate strength and ROM in the rotator cuff muscles are essential in preventing overhead overuse injuries as they are vital in stabilizing and movement throughout the extreme ROM experienced during tennis strokes—specifically the service motion (2, 18).

The speed of the serve or throwing motion depends partly on a rapid and forceful concentric internal rotation in the acceleration phase of the serve (13). The eccentric phase of training may specifically affect the decelerative phase which may determine the trajectory and velocity components of performance (14).

POWER
VERTICAL JUMP

The vertical jump is one of the simplest yet most used fitness tests. Even though measuring an athlete's vertical jump does not directly measure his/her power output, the results are highly correlated with power output.

One of the problems when comparing vertical jump between different athletes is that there are many different methods of measuring a vertical jump, and this can lead to problems if trying to compare results between different people in different training environments. Although various methods are used to gauge different types of leaping ability, the standard measure of a player's vertical jump can be obtained by following the steps below.

Testing Steps:

1. Stand with your side to a wall and have someone mark off the highest point you can reach while flat-footed.
2. Cover the underside of the tip of your middle finger in chalk.
3. Move one step back from the first mark (that of your reach).
4. Without taking more than a step into it, jump off of both feet and touch the highest point possible on the wall.
5. Repeat this three times.
6. Measure the heights of your standing reach and the highest point you touched on the wall.
7. Subtract your standing reach from the height of the highest point you touched on the wall. That number is your vertical jump.

For example, if your standing reach is seven feet, and the highest point you touch on the wall is ten feet, your vertical jump will be three feet (thirty-six inches).

The vertical jump has many variations including:

- Starting from a stationary start and dipping down (countermovement) and then exploding up as high as possible.
- Starting from a stationary start and not dipping down and then jumping straight up as high as possible.
- Single leg (countermovement) jump using the same method as no.1. Do both legs and compare between legs. Usually one leg is a little better than the other.

BROAD JUMP

The broad jump measures horizontal instead of vertical jumps. The broad jump is one of the simplest, yet most useful tests for lower body explosion and power.

Testing steps:

- The player starts in ready position and jumps forward. Distance is measured from the line to where the athlete lands (measure at the heel of the athlete).

Figure 14.4: Broad jump.

MEDICINE BALL (MB) THROWS FOR POWER

The goals and purposes of the MB throws are to simulate movements that may be utilized during tennis play. Below is a list of the most commonly used MB throws for testing, and all these movements can also be used to develop power in tennis athletes. Different size medicine balls should be used depending on the

Figure 14.5: Overhead service toss.

Figure 14.6: Chest pass.

Figure 14.7: Granny toss.

type of throws and the age of the athletes. All athletes should start using the doubles line as the starting position and having a tape measure extended out to measure the medicine ball distance.

AGE	12's	12's	14's	14's	16's	16's
GROUP	Boys	Girls	Boys	Girls	Boys	Girls
Overhead (m)	6.54	6.47	9.00	7.83	10.72	9.14
Sidearm Right (m)	8.01	7.15	9.50	8.25	12.16	10.76
Sidearm Left (m)	7.31	7.24	8.90	7.88	12.43	10.24

Table 14.3: Comparative measures (meters) for three MB throws for boys and girls 12-16 years of age. (Table adapted from (26)).

FLEXIBILITY

The following flexibility tests are all good measures for tennis players. More information about the specifics of these tests can be obtained from the USTA.

   -sit and reach (right)
   -lying hamstring test
   -hip test (patrick's test)
   -Shoulder (internal/external rotation)

Figure 14.8: Sit and reach.

SUMMARY

Testing is a vital part of a competitive tennis player's annual plan. It is important to monitor the results from different tests to see if the training programs are producing the intended results. Also, consistent testing is important to determine if certain training programs are not producing appropriate results so that changes can be made. Many tests can be used, but it should be highly specific to the style of athlete, age, time constraints, and most importantly, the goals of the athlete.

References

1. ACSM. ACSM's guidelines for exercise testing and prescription. 7th Edition ed. Baltimore, MD: Lippincott, Williams & Wilkins, 2005

2. Behm, D. G. A kinesiological analysis of the tennis service. NSCA Journal. 10:4-14, 1988.

3. Bergeron, M. F., L. E. Armstrong, and C. M. Maresh. Fluid and electrolyte losses during tennis in the heat. Clin Sports Med. 14:23-32, 1995.

4. Bergeron, M. F., C. M. Maresh, L. E. Armstrong, J. F. Signorile, J. W. Castellani, R. W. Kenefick, K. E. LaGasse, and D. A. Riebe. Fluid-electrolyte balance associated with tennis match play in a hot environment. Int J Sport Nutr. 5:180-193, 1995.

5. Bergeron, M. F., C. M. Maresh, W. J. Kraemer, A. Abraham, B. Conroy, and C. Gabaree. Tennis: a physiological profile during match play. Int J Sport Med. 12:474-479, 1991.

6. Bernardi, M., G. De Vito, M. E. Falvo, S. Marino, and F. Montellanico. Cardiorespiratory adjustment in middle-level tennis players: are long term cardiovascular adjustments possible? In: Science and Racket Sports II. A. Lees, I. Maynard, M. Hughes, and T. Reilly (Eds.) London, UK: E & FN Spon, 1998, pp. 20-26.

7. Brewer, J., R. Ramsbottom, and C. Williams. Multistage Fitness Test. Canberra, Australia: Australian Coaching Council, 1988

8. Chandler, T. J. Conditioning for tennis: preventing injury and enhancing performance. In: Science and Racket Sports II. A. Lees, I. Maynard, M. Hughes, and T. Reilly (Eds.) London, UK: E&FN Spon, 1998, pp. 77-85.

9. Chandler, T. J. Exercise training for tennis. Clinics in Sports Medicine. 14:33-46, 1995.

10. Christmass, M. A., S. E. Richmond, N. T. Cable, P. G. Arthur, and P. E. Hartmann. Exercise intensity and metabolic response in singles tennis. J Sport Sci. 16:739-747, 1998.

11. Christmass, M. A., S. E. Richmond, N. T. Cable, and P. E. Hartmann. A metabolic characterization of single tennis. In: Science and Racket Sports. T. Reilly, M. Hughes, and A. Lees (Eds.): E&FN Spon, 1994, pp. 3-9.

12. Dawson, B., B. Elliott, F. Pyke, and R. Rogers. Physiological and performance responses to playing tennis in a cool environment and similar intervalized treadmill running in a hot climate. J Hum Mov Stud. 11:21-34, 1985.

13. Duda, M. Prevention and treatment of throwing arm injuries. Physician Sports Medicine. 13:181-185, 1985.

14. Ellenbecker, T. S., G. J. Davis, and M. J. Rowinski. Concentric versus eccentric isokinetic strengthening of the rotator cuff. American Journal of Sports Medicine. 16:64-69, 1988.

15.   Ellenbecker, T. S. and E. P. Roetert. An isokinetic profile of trunk rotation strength in elite tennis players. Med Sci Sports Exerc. 36:1959-1963, 2004.

16.   Ellliott, B., B. Dawson, and F. Pyke. The energetics of singles tennis. J Hum Mov Stud. 11:11-20, 1985.

17.   Faff, J., M. Ladyga, and C. Starczewska, J. Physical fitness of the top Polish male and female tennis players aged form twelve years to senior category. Biology of Sport (Warsaw). 17:179-192, 2000.

18.   Fleisig, G., R. Nicholls, B. Elliott, and R. Escamilla. Kinematics used by world class tennis players to produce high-velocity serves. Sports Biomechanics. 2:51-71, 2002.

19.   Green, J. M., T. R. Crews, A. M. Bosak, and W. W. Peveler. A comparison of respiratory compensation thresholds of anaerobic competitors, aerobic competitors and untrained subjects. European Journal of Applied Physiology. 90:608-613, 2003.

20.   Groppel, J. L. The biomechanics of tennis: An overview. International Journal of Sport Biomechanics. 2:141-155, 1986.

21.   Kibler, W. B. and T. J. Chandler. Grip strength and endurance in elite tennis players. Med Sci Sports Exerc. 21:S65, 1989.

22.   Kovacs, M. S., R. Pritchett, P. J. Wickwire, J. M. Green, and P. Bishop. Physical performance changes in NCAA division I tennis players after the unsupervised break between fall and spring semester. 2006.

23.   Little, T. and A. G. Williams. Specificity of acceleration, maximal speed and agility in professional soccer players. Journal of Strength and Conditioning Research. 19:76-78, 2005.

24.   Mujika, I. and S. Padilla. Detraining: Loss of training-induced physiology and performance adaptations. part I. Sports Medicine. 30:79-87, 2000.

25.   Perry, A. C., X. Wang, B. B. Feldman, T. Ruth, and J. F. Signorile. Can laboratory-based tennis profiles predict field tests of tennis performance? Journal of Strength and Conditioning Research. 18:136-143, 2004.

26.   Quinn, A. and M. Reid. Screening and testing. In: ITF Strength and Conditioning for Tennis. M. Reid, A. Quinn, and M. Crespo (Eds.) London, UK: International Tennis Federation, 2003.

27.   Siri, W. E. Gross composition of the body. In: Adv Biol Med Phys. J. H. Lawrence and C. A. Tobias (Eds.) New York, NY: Academic Press, 1956.

28.   Smekal, G., S. P. Von Duvillard, R. Pokan, H. Tschan, R. Baron, P. Hofmann, M. Wonisch, and N. Bachl. Changes in blood lactate and respiratory gas exchange measures in sports with discontinuous load profiles. Eur J Appl Physiol. 89:489-495, 2003.

29.   Smekal, G., S. P. Von Duvillard, C. N. Rihacek, R. Pokan, P. Hofman, R. Baron, H. Tschan, and N. Bachl. A physiological profile of tennis matchplay. Med Sci Sport Exercise. 33:999-1005, 2001.

CHAPTER 15

PERIODIZATION

- **MAJOR COMPONENTS IN PLANNING A PERIODIZED PROGRAM**
- **CYCLES**
- **7 AREAS TO PERIODIZE**
- **AGE CONCERNS**

INTRODUCTION

Periodization refers to the manipulation of training variables over specific periods of time for the purpose of promoting maximal performance at the appropriate time and decreasing the risk of overtraining (8). Periodization, although sometimes misunderstood and not always applied effectively, is not a new concept. It has been around since the ancient Greeks. Flavius Philostratus (AD 170-245), a Greek philosopher and sporting enthusiast, wrote extensively about these periodized methods used by the ancient Greek athletes (2). Periodization should not be thought of as a set model that can be applied in the same manner to all tennis players. The beauty of periodization is that it is a dynamic concept which can be individualized to each athlete's strengths and weaknesses and can be aimed at helping them perform at their highest levels when it counts the most. Organized and planned programs that have been periodized have been shown to lead to greater performance improvements than nonperiodized programs (6). These periodized programs are not just for professional players; rather, every competitive tennis player should be on some form of a periodized program.

MAJOR COMPONENTS IN PLANNING A PERIODIZED PROGRAM

Individuality – A 10-year old female tennis player is not going to respond to the same stimulus as Andy Roddick. This is where a solid understanding of physiological changes throughout development is helpful, as is a consistent testing and monitoring program to understand each athlete's individual capabilities so he/she can train accordingly. Every tennis player should be on a specific program based on his or her own strengths and weaknesses. A group program where every athlete does the same routine is not going to be the best way to optimize each individual athlete. Some athletes can handle greater physical stress and recover sooner than others. Without solid records it is difficult, if not impossible, to accurately monitor athletes and to optimize their programs.

Specificity – How close are the activities to what will be experienced during competition? The closer the athlete can experience movements, feelings, and situations that will be experienced during competition, the better prepared the athlete will be. Also, a periodized program allows for certain periods throughout the year to focus on more general areas and other times that will focus on more specific areas to tennis performance. A balance is needed between good general physiological development (i.e., increased muscle mass and decreased 10 m sprint times) as well as tennis-specific movement patterns (i.e., medicine ball service throw or movement in the volley and overhead drill).

It is important for the coach or trainer who works with tennis athletes to understand the physiological, biomechanical, and psychological reasons behind each exercise as well as how different exercises can positively or negatively influence other exercises in the program. A good example of how many coaches do not apply the rule of specificity is seen when training for tennis endurance. Many coaches still have athletes run at a slow continuous pace for 30-45 minutes in a hope of building aerobic endurance. This slow, continuous exercise will build aerobic endurance, but it will not simulate the typical movements and work to rest ratios seen during tennis play. Therefore, this type of training does not result in a strong carryover to on-court performance and could actually hinder speed development due to the development of slow twitch (IIa) muscle fibers.

Adaptation – The number one goal of any training program is to create positive adaptations. Increasing muscle mass, decreasing fat mass, increasing ball velocity, and decreasing the time it takes to recover from hard-fought matches are all positive adaptations to training. While attempting to speed adaptation time, many athletes train and perform in a state of overload. This overload is positive adaptation for a short period of time, but many athletes are in this state for too long, and it graduates into a state known as overtraining. Overtraining results in negative consequences and reduced performance. This overtraining can cause problems such as reduced performance, poor sleep, increased injury, slower recovery, minor colds and if training is not reduced can lead to longer term problems such as chronic fatigue (3). A major purpose of periodized programs is to avoid this overtraining problem by cycling work volumes, intensities and sufficient rest periods (5).

Recovery – Recovery or regeneration is sometimes a forgotten part of training. To make continual improvements, adequate recovery is required to allow the body to adjust to the increases in workload and to help avoid long-term fatigue and chronic injuries (5). Recovery is an area that has received more research focus in the last decade, yet it is an area that could provide the biggest area for performance improvement in the future. Understanding work-to-rest ratios, hormonal changes, endocrine function, blood chemistry, and circadian rhythms can influence the individual differences in how tennis athletes recover from exercise.

Recovery techniques:
- Slow jogging
- Stretching
- Ice baths
- Hot and cold shower/bath
- Massage
- Electrical stimulation (relaxation)
- Meditation
- Sauna/steam baths

Periodization involves the manipulation of volume and intensity of training through specific periods or seasons of the year. A periodized program can be as short as one week or as long as an athlete's entire career. As would be expected, the short-term planning focuses on much more detail, including reps, sets, and rest periods, whereas the long-term planning is more focused on the overall purpose of certain periods in a long-term plan.

As we will see later in this chapter, periodized program can be created for the seven major aspects involved in optimizing tennis performance:

- Technical
- Tactical
- Physical
- Psychological
- Nutrition
- Recovery
- Academics/Work/Family

All seven aspects should be designed to work together in a well-rounded program to help create the optimum outcome for each area by manipulating the frequency, intensity, volume, recovery, and time of year.

Needs Analysis

Before a structured periodized program can be put together, a needs analysis is performed to determine the most beneficial type of training for the athlete. The needs analysis involves testing for strengths and weaknesses in as many aspects of the performance as feasible. The amount of testing and the time spent on the periodized program is dependent somewhat on the level of player. A high-level national or international junior player will have a much more detailed periodized program than a 3.5 league doubles player. However, both these players would benefit greatly from having a structured, well-thought-out program. Another important aspect of the needs analysis is to determine the major times of the year the player wants to be competing at his or her highest level. For a college player it might be at the conference tournament, while a professional player might point to the four grand slam tournaments. Areas to be tested in a needs analysis are:

- Speed
- Agility
- Power
- Strength
- Flexibility
- Aerobic endurance (tennis specific)
- Technique
- Anticipation/reaction time
- Tactical proficiency
- Recovery capabilities
- Time constraints (school, work, family, other interests)

CYCLES

The periodized conditioning program is divided into cycles. In most cases the term **macrocycle** is used to describe a yearly general plan. For junior and professional tennis players, using macrocycle to describe a yearly plan is the most appropriate; in some circumstances it may be appropriate to have two macrocycles in one calendar year. However, for the majority of instances it is just as effective to follow the calendar year for a macrocycle.

Each macrocycle contains a period of months (typically a season) called a **mesocycle.** A macrocycle could contain anywhere from 2-10 mesocycles, depending on the focus of the periodized program. Here is an example of mesocycles on the professional circuit: first mesocycle—hardcourts (Jan-April), second mesocycle—claycourts (April-June), third mesocycle—grasscourts (June-July), fourth mesocycle—US hardcourts (July-September), fifth mesocycle—Indoor (September-November), sixth mesocycle—off-season/preseason (November-December). Each mesocycle can be of different durations. The above mesocycles would be different for a clay court specialist who would prefer to play a larger part of his or her schedule on the clay courts, from March to August.

A **microcycle** is the term used to describe planning for several days. This is typically a 7-day calendar week; however, it is not uncommon to have 10- 14- or 21-day microcycles. Each cycle has a specific training goal, and the training variables are manipulated in order to achieve that goal. The following are some common training phases that can be employed when designing a periodized program.

THE GENERAL PREPARATORY PHASE

The General Preparatory Phase (GPP) is usually an introductory phase of training, either for a beginning athlete or an athlete who has taken some time away from training and needs to build back a base level of training. The GPP typically uses parameters of training that are characteristic of the strength endurance format of training—low-intensity/high-volume resistance training. The GPP has less emphasis on the development of speed, agility, and power and more emphasis on developing an overall solid base of tennis-specific aerobic endurance and strength training to prepare the body/mind for the tennis-specific training that will follow in later phases. From a technical and tactical standpoint this phase is used to correct any major flaws in a player's game, such as grips, game plans, and/or stroke mechanics. Depending on the needs, it may be coupled with interval training or other forms of training to initiate the individual to the training program. This type of phase may be employed with the novice or may be used as a reintroduction to a long-term training program for a high-performance athlete. It represents a reasonable method of introducing or reintroducing resistance training to an athlete. This phase usually will last 5-8 weeks. In the collegiate environment this is typically the first month or two of the fall season and is designed to acclimate the athletes back to heavy training and the volume and intensity are manipulated to accomplish this.

The following are situations where the GPP might be most appropriate for training:

- Athlete needs to lose 2 kg to be faster on the court.
- Athlete needs a grip change on the forehand.
- Athlete needs to start a structured strength training program to help increase ball velocity.
- Athlete needs to implement strength training to aid in preventing injuries to problem areas (shoulder, wrist, lower back and ankles).

The traditional periodization models would suggest that the athlete train in a general sense, not focusing on tennis-specific movements. However, these days with no true off-season, the GPP needs to incorporate more tennis related movements while still building a great general overall fitness base.

SPECIFIC PREPARATORY PHASE

The Specific Preparatory Phase (SPP) of training defines more specific goals with respect to the training program and the tournament schedule. Usually the intensity of the training increases, with moderate to high volumes of training. Exercises must become more goal-specific with a focusing on tennis-specific strength, speed, power, and agility training. Solidifying major changes made during the GPP is also a focus of the SPP. This phase should last between 6 and 8 weeks but may be somewhat longer or shorter as necessary. This period is not where major changes are made to a player's game. It is more appropriate for this stage to constitute the deliberate practice phase of a new skill.

PRECOMPETITION PHASE

The Precompetition Phase (PP) is marked by an increase in intensity and a decrease in the volume of resistance training. The skill component of training will increase with more matchplay-specific drills and training. Off-court work in the weight room and speed/agility movements will be more tennis- and competition-specific. The length of each phase varies due to several factors, especially the competitive schedule. The phase should be long enough for the athlete to adapt to the training program prescribed and not so long as to allow staleness.

COMPETITIVE PHASE

Unlike many sports that have rather short competitive seasons, tennis in the junior and professional ranks involves year-round competition. The collegiate tennis schedule allows for more traditional periodization plans because of the competition phase between February-May. During a competitive phase, sometimes referred to as a maintenance phase, it is important to maintain as much strength as possible. The use of moderate intensities and moderate to low volumes of training usually occur during this time.

PEAKING PHASE

The major competitions for peaking are typically evident. In a collegiate environment it would be the conference and national tournaments. In juniors (depending on the level of player) it would be the regional, state, or national tournament. In the professional ranks it would be the four grand slams and possibly Davis/Fed Cup. In USTA league play it would be the end of season regional, state, or national tournament. Prior to a major competition, the athlete who desires to peak physiologically should further decrease the volume of training to promote full rest and recovery for competition.

STAIRED PROGRESSION

Staired progression is a method of manipulating training intensity by systematically increasing intensities over a predetermined time-period. Staired progression attempts to initiate a physiological state known as supercompensation within the muscle tissue of the body. When a tennis player receives a training stimulus at the beginning of a microcycle that is higher than the previous load, fatigue will occur. If the same load is maintained over the period of this same microcycle during following training sessions, the body will begin to adapt to this new training intensity. This new level is referred to as a new ceiling of adaptation (1).

The unloading period should not return to initial levels of intensities; rather, it should be reduced to the level of intensity reached at the midpoint of the staired progression phase. Scheduling an unloading period allows for tissue regeneration and protein synthesis as well as the replenishment of energy stores that will have been depleted over the period of staired progression. This replenishment of energy stores during the unloading phase may exceed the previous levels attained before the training stimulus was initiated. The energy replenishment above the initial levels is commonly referred to as supercompensation, and it should leave the athlete in a heightened state of of training preparedness for another successive series of increasing training intensities (9).

7 AREAS TO PERIODIZE

- Technical
- Tactical
- Physical
- Psychological
- Nutrition
- Recovery
- Academics/work

1. TECHNICAL

A player's technique is at the base of all development. Without a solid foundation future development will be limited. Therefore, technical work focused on stroke development and movement mechanics needs to be at the core of all good programs. Technical work is typically at its peak during non-tournament times throughout the training cycle, where competition is removed so that the learning of the skill can be the major focus. This usually takes place during the GPP and SPP. It is very difficult to make technical corrections, especially major corrections, such as a grip change, when the stress of winning or losing is also in the equation. Therefore, the coach's role is to set up times throughout the year where technique training will be a major focus of the player's program.

The more experienced a player, the less time is focused on technique. In younger players (6-12 year old), technique training should be a major portion of the training cycle as the next 5-10 years of the athlete's tennis life will be directly building on the solid foundation. As the players get older, the technique aspect of training is reduced and hopefully only minor adjustments need to be made. As athletes age from 12-16 it is a time to solidify the technique and implement the concept of deliberate practice. Deliberate practice, unlike play, requires effort, and it does not offer the social and financial rewards of work (4). Five key areas of deliberate practice include (4):

1. Motivation to improve performance.
2. Close attention to the task.
3. Immediate informative feedback on actions.
4. Knowledge of results of performance.
5. Multiple repetition of correct actions.

Timing of technique training throughout a periodized program is essential. The athlete must not be in either a physically or psychologically fatigued state when attempting to learn a new skill (e.g., slice backhand down the line). It is important to teach new skills early in a specific period, ideally in the late stages of a recovery period or the onset of the GPP. If the coach waits until midway through the GPP, the workload (volume and intensity) in other areas (especially physical) could negatively affect the learning process of the new skill.

2. TACTICAL

Tactical training is less of a priority in younger individuals (< 12 years of age), as this time can be better spent developing physical and technical skills. However, once the athletes start competing at regional, state, national, and international tournaments, tactical proficiency is vitally important. Developing a player's strategy is one area that some coaches do not spend enough time training. It is important to determine the player's style of play and how to structure points to play into the player's strengths and hide weaknesses. It is important to know whether the player is an aggressive baseliner who likes to dominate with the forehand or is a fast, athletic, and well-trained retriever focusing on running down every ball and physically wearing out his/her opponents. Although individual strategy is not a major focus of this chapter, it is important for coaches and athletes to have a player's style and strategy instilled from a young age, and all physical and mental training should be aimed at optimizing this style of play. A serve and volley player should have a very different speed and agility program than a clay-court baseliner. The serve and volley player will focus on linear speed with explosive split step movements followed by short explosive lateral moves. These movements simulate what is experienced when an athlete moves from the baseline to the net and then attacks volleys. A claycourt baseliner will spend more time on lateral movement and recovery from strokes. Training of all components must fit with the performance goals and tactical style of the individual player.

3. PHYSICAL

The physical components of training have had the greatest amount of scientific research and practical implementation of periodization principles. The major physical components that should be periodized include linear, lateral and multi-directional speed, absolute strength, strength endurance, maximal power, power endurance, muscle hypertrophy, flexibility, and agility. The art of coaching is applying science into a cohesive program that develops all variables throughout an entire macrocycle. The problem arises when coaches try to develop too many of these variables at once. This may reduce the athlete's development by overtraining, using inappropriate volume and intensity for the different variables. Developing different performance variables requires an understanding of how these variables improve. Training for explosive speed is a predominantly neural process, meaning that the goal of training is increasing the speed of the signal from the brain to the muscle and increasing muscle firing rates. As opposed to training for speed, training for muscular endurance is predominantly a cellular process where overloading the muscle cells is the way to improve performance. Training both of these at the same time can be accomplished, but understanding the fatigue process and how these opposing processes might negatively affect each other is important.

When and where in a program to develop specific physical variables will depend on the focus of the training cycle. It is important to have a priority list for each exercise, day, week, month, and year. This list states the major and minor focus as well as the supplemental focus areas. For example, during the general preparation period the priority might be to add 3 kg of muscle mass while simultaneously develop an athlete's linear, lateral, and multidirectional speed as measured by the 20 m sprint and the Spider Agility test. To accomplish this, an understanding of how speed impacts strength and vice versa will influence how training and recovery sessions should be organized. It will be necessary to train speed when the athlete is freshest and the neuromuscular system is not fatigued. Unlike gaining muscle (which is predominantly a cellular adaptation), speed training is aimed at causing a positive adaptation to the neuromuscular system. Therefore, to gain greatest effect, the athlete needs to perform the speed exercises at the onset of practice sessions and the strength and hypertrophy focused exercises afterward when the athlete is in a more fatigued state. As tennis requires high levels of all the physical variables, it is difficult to completely focus on one area. If an athlete was to follow a traditional linear strength training periodized program, the athlete would spend 4-6 week blocks focused on one specific emphasis, such as muscle size (hypertrophy). Tennis players do not have the luxury of this form of training, and all physical variables need to be trained somewhat simultaneously. However, a program can be devised to optimize overall gains in all areas without development in one area causing a negative consequence in another area.

4. PSYCHOLOGICAL

Designing a periodized program for psychological development is an area that has not received much attention in the scientific literature. As with physical training, psychological training variables, such as visualization, relaxation training, goal setting, ritual development, and arousal training, cannot all be periodized and trained at once. Different times of the macrocycle require more focus on different areas. The age of the athlete also plays a major role in the psychological training of the athlete. Some skills such as on-court rituals (e.g., bouncing the ball three times before each serve) are easy to implement, but it is not so easy to consistently perform on every single serve, especially during high-pressure match situations. This type of routine requires continual practice and monitoring by both player and coach.

5. NUTRITION

Nutrition, like other training variables, should be periodized depending on the psychological and physical stress endured by the athlete. During times of harder physical training, energy requirements will be higher, and as a result, a structured nutrition plan should be developed to ensure adequate calories to sustain hard training and appropriate recovery (see Chapter 4 for more in-depth information). Proper nutrition can improve immune system function, increase energy, improve speed of muscle mass development, and reduce body fat. During periods of heavy training, tennis players are susceptible to colds, viruses, and respiratory infections. Periodizing calories and types of higher calorie food during periods of harder training may assist in keeping the athlete healthy as well as improving speed of recovery following hard training sessions. This quicker recovery will allow the athlete to train harder and longer allowing for quicker improvement. Also during periods of hard training, it is recommended that athletes supplement with products such as glutamine and leucine to help in protecting immune function and reduce the possible negative consequences of hard training. Nutritional periodization before and during tournaments is also important. The athlete's nutritional program must be structured to provide adequate nutrients in the days before, during, and after tournament play. Refer back to Chapter 4 to apply the nutrition principles in a periodized method.

6. RECOVERY

Recovery has just begun to be a focus of scientific investigation. Our knowledge of recovery techniques and the affect on performance is becoming clearer. Structuring recovery sessions in a periodized program is very individualized. All tennis players require proper recovery so as not to overtrain, but what is equally important is structuring recovery to speed performance improvement. Skill development such as technique cannot be developed as quickly in a fatigued state. Also, physical training cannot continually be increased with an infinite increase in performance. Monitoring an athlete's performance with objective markers is important in order to catch any performance decreases. Unless the tennis athlete has access to trained physiologists or a full service sports medicine laboratory that continually measures variables such as lactate levels, blood chemistry, and respiration values, more rudimentary measures must be taken. These include waking heart rate and subjective measures of perceived exertion, though these techniques may not catch that an athlete is overtraining until it is too late and performance has decreased and the likelihood of injury and illnesses has increased.

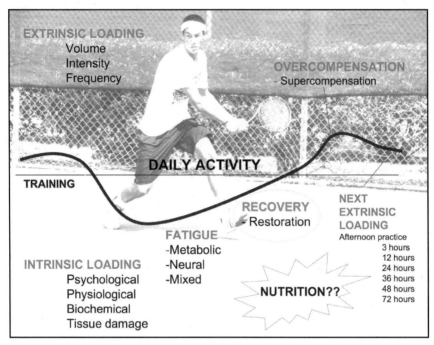

Figure 15.1: Daily recovery pattern following a training session.

7. ACADEMICS

One area that has not yet received appropriate attention is how a junior or collegiate athlete's academic responsibilities and priorities play into his or her tennis career. Exam schedule, projects, and presentations take up a lot of time and do increase an athlete's stress level. These events must be taken into account when devising programs. The challenges are vastly different for coaches who work with junior competitive players compared to collegiate coaches. When designing periodized training and competition schedules, academic landmarks such as exams, presentations, spring- break, and vacation time need to be planned into an effective program. It is important to schedule reduced training volume around exam periods or other academically time-consuming and stressful periods. To be able to get the most from the student-athletes, it is important to plan their yearly schedule with a full understanding of all the academic stressors that are likely to play a role in their development. It is more beneficial to overall development to schedule hard training weeks during light academic weeks, as the athlete will have more time and be in a less stressful mental state during these periods.

AGE CONCERNS

Age plays a major role in devising a periodized program. However, two different classifications of age must be defined. An athlete's chronological age is the birth age, whereas a player's training age is how many years an athlete has been training for tennis at a competitive level. An example would be a 16-year old male player who has been training competitively for tennis since he was 13-years old. The player's chronological age is 16 but the training age is only 3 years. As it takes at least 10 years of training before any person can be classified as expert in a skill (4, 7), such as tennis, it requires a training age of at least 10 before a tennis player can expect to be at peak abilities and performance level. Understanding this is important for determining the number of training hours per day, week, month, and year (Figure 15.2). As each individual is different, no two programs will be the same. However, basic principles should be followed when designing and implementing the program.

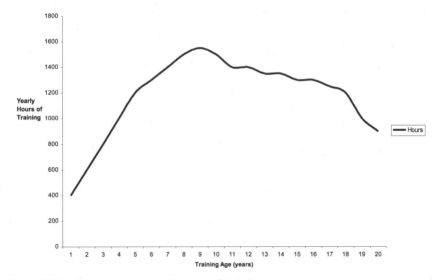

Figure 15.2: Yearly hours of training over the course of a tennis career.

THE FOCUS INDEX

The focus Index is a term that is used to describe the amount of emphasis a certain training variable has in a cycle period. Figure 15.3 shows a long term (20 year) plan with the focus index of each of the seven periodized areas. This is an example of how you can set up a long-term periodized program with certain parts focusing on specific variables.

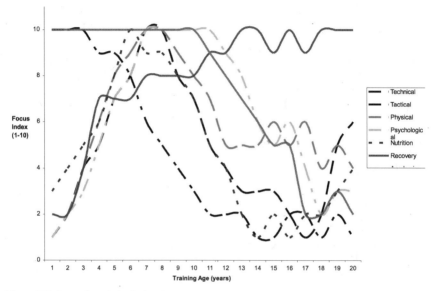

Figure 15.3: Career focus index for tennis.

This focus index describes a hypothetical plan for a young child who is attempting to become a professional tennis player. Creating a focus index as part of the periodized program is a big advantage as it provides a graphical representation of how the different training aspects influence each other and whether you are focusing on too many areas at one time. A focus index can be applied to single training session, training weeks, months, seasons, or years.

SAMPLE PERIODIZATION PLAN

CAREER LONG PERIODIZATION FOR THE TENNIS ATHLETE	
BEGINNING PHASE	This period is when the athlete is just learning the basics and is not focused on tournament play.
SKILL PHASE	The basics have been learned, and this phase is focused on developing consistency in the skills and being able to perform the skills under normal pressure situations.
COMPETITION PHASE	The skills are developed and now the athlete is ready to perform the skills under stressful tournament situations. Although tournaments are being played, the major focus should still be on development, with little emphasis on tournament results.
TOURNAMENT PHASE	This is the time for the athletes to be at their best. The years of hard practice should be paying off at this stage and results are a major focus of this phase.
PEAKING/MAINTENANCE PHASE	The first part of this stage is still focused on results and performing at a very high level. The second part of this phase is aimed at staying at a high level even though the athlete might be losing some of the physical gifts (i.e., speed, power, recovery abilities) or priorities have changed (family, etc.).

Table 15.1: Career long periodization for the tennis athlete.

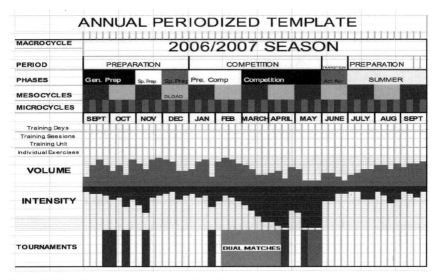

Figure 15.4: Annual sample periodized program template.

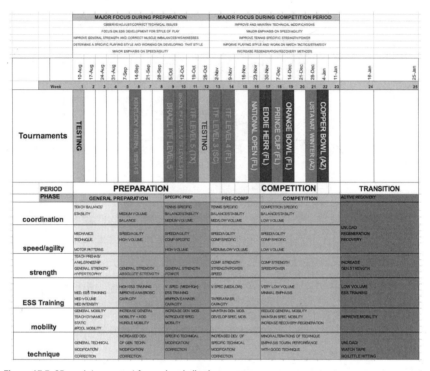

Figure 15.5: 25-week tournament focused periodized program.

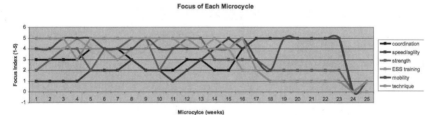

Figure 15.6: 25-Week Macrocycle for an international level junior competitor focused on the physical aspects of training

	NATIONAL OPEN (FL)	COMPETITION PERIOD		
		EDDIE HERR (FL)	PRINCE CUP (FL)	ORANGE BOWL (FL)
coordination	4	4	3	3
speed/agility	4	3	2	3
strength	2	2	1	1
ESS training	3	2	1	1
mobility	5	3	3	4
technique	3	1	1	1
MAJOR GOALS				
coordination	maintaining weight on front foot on slice bhand	rotation of hips on 2nd serve	still need to rotate more on 2nd serve	weight transfer on low balls
speed/agility	smaller steps on recovery from forehand	explosion after recovery from wide fhands	focus on split step on first volley	need to focus on arm action on linear movement
strength	add 15min a day for lower back issues	reintroduce shoulder band work 15min	maintain shoulder band work	add some calf strengthening work
ESS training	just recovery runs	pool workouts	pool workouts	pool workouts
mobility	increase flexibility time on hamstrings	maintain ROM on external shoulder	focus on loosing up tight calf	relaxation mobility work
technique	racket head above wrist on bhand volley	lengthen stroke on short fhand	keep body weight forward on deep forehand	rotate hips on aggressive x-court fhand

Figure 15.7: 4 week competition mesocycle.

REFERENCES

1. Bompa, T. O. Periodization of Strength. Don Mills, Ontario, Canada: Veritas Publishing, 1993

2. Bompa, T. O. Primer on Periodization. Olympic Coach. 16:4-7, 2004.

3. Derman, W., M. P. Schwellnus, M. I. Lambert, M. Emms, C. Sinclair-Smith, P. Kirby, and N. T.D. The 'worn-out': A clinical approach to chronic fatigue in athletes. J Sport Sci. 15:341-351, 1997.

4. Ericsson, K. A., R. T. Krampe, and C. Tesch-Romer. The role of deliberate practice in the acquisition of expert performance. Psychol Rev. 100:363-406, 1993.

5. Fry, R. W., A. R. Morton, and D. Keast. Periodisation and the prevention of overtraining. Can J Sport Sci. 17:241-248, 1992.

6. Kraemer, W. J., K. Haekkinen, N. T. Triplett McBride, A. C. Fry, L. P. Koziris, N. A. Ratamess, J. E. Bauer, J. S. Volek, T. McConnell, R. U. Newton, S. E. Gordon, D. Cummings, J. Hauth, F. Pullo, J. M. Lynch, S. A. Mazzetti, H. G. Knuttgen, and S. J. Fleck. Physiological changes with periodized resistance training in women tennis players. Med Sci Sports Exerc. 35:157-168, 2003.

7. Simon, H. A. and W. G. Chase. Skill in chess. Am Sci. 61:394-403, 1973.

8. Stone, M. H. and H. S. O'Bryant. Weight training, a scientific approach. Minneapolis, MN: Burgess, 1987

9. Zatsiorsky, V. Science and practice of strength training. Champaign, IL: Human Kinetics, 1995

Index

Index

Index

Index

ABOUT THE AUTHORS

Dr. Mark Kovacs combines extensive playing experience, which includes a top 100 ITF junior ranking, winner of a US "gold-ball," competing in many international tournaments including the US and Australian Open before attending Auburn University where he was an All-American and NCAA doubles champion. After playing professionally he pursued his graduate work performing tennis-specific research. He has combined researched scientific evidence in his coaching profession both as a high level tennis coach as well as a strength and conditioning specialist (CSCS) training hundreds of high school, collegiate, and professional athletes. He has previously been the director of a sports performance company as well as the director of education for one of the largest health and fitness certification and education companies. He is currently Assistant Professor, Exercise Science & Wellness, Jacksonville State University

Britt Chandler has a master's degree in exercise science from Auburn University and played collegiate tennis. He is certified as both a strength and conditioning specialist (CSCS) and certified personal trainer (NSCA-CPT). He also is a certified tennis coach through the USPTA. He currently works as both a tennis coach and strength conditioning specialist with some of the top juniors in the country. Britt is also the editorial assistant for the Strength and Conditioning Journal and has contributed book chapters and presentations on tennis specific research and training.

Dr. Jeff Chandler has over 20 years experience as a tennis researcher and sports science consultant, advisor, and author for many tennis organizations including the USTA, USPTA, ITF, STMS and PTR. He has over 100 scientific publications, book chapters, and presentations relating to tennis training and performance. He is currently Department Head of Health, Physical Education & Recreation at Jacksonville State University, Jacksonville, Alabama, and is the editor in chief of the Strength and Conditioning Journal published through the National Strength and Conditioning Association. Dr. Chandler is certified with distinction as both a CSCS*D, and NSCA-CPT*D. He is a Fellow in the American College of Sports Medicine (FACSM) and a Fellow in the National Strength and Conditioning Association (FNSCA).